THE
CONSPIRACY
TOURIST

Also by Dom Joly

The Dark Tourist
Scary Monsters and Super Creeps
The Downhill Hiking Club

THE CONSPIRACY TOURIST

*TRAVELS THROUGH
A STRANGE WORLD*

DOM JOLY

ROBINSON

ROBINSON

First published in Great Britain in 2023 by Robinson

1 3 5 7 9 10 8 6 4 2

A CIP catalogue record for this book
is available from the British Library.

ISBN: 978-1-47214-668-7

Typeset in Bembo by Hewer Text UK Ltd, Edinburgh
Printed and bound in Great Britain by Clays Ltd, Elcograf S.p.A.

Papers used by Constable are from well-managed
forests and other responsible sources.

Robinson
An imprint of
Little, Brown Book Group
Carmelite House
50 Victoria Embankment
London EC4Y 0DZ

An Hachette UK Company
www.hachette.co.uk

www.littlebrown.co.uk

To my lovely mum, Yvonne Joly
29 June 1929–3 January 2023

Contents

Prologue

There is no dark side of the moon really.
Matter of fact, it's all dark.
Pink Floyd

There's a man called Thomas who sits on a bench, opposite my house, at the same time every day. Thomas owns a beautiful dog called Zero who has become best buddies with my two Labradors, Truman and Fitzgerald. As a consequence of this canine friendship, I've been rather forced into making regular small talk with a stranger, something that I normally try to avoid like the plague.

Thomas, I discovered, had recently moved to Cheltenham from Lincolnshire after he had fallen off the edge of a cliff.

It was quite the story.

He'd been taking Zero for a walk along the coast when a section of cliff suddenly collapsed, sending him tumbling down towards the sea.

Thomas managed to grab on to a branch and stop his fall, just before he went over a sheer drop that would have killed him. Zero managed to shuffle down to where Thomas lay, badly injured, and stayed with him for three hours until they were spotted by a passing rambler.

This, by the way, is why you should own a dog and not a cat. A cat would have just sauntered on, completely unperturbed and moved in, and on, with one of the three other owners that all cats secretly have.

Thomas wasn't looking for sympathy. He was simply filling me in on how he'd ended up living in Cheltenham. He'd lost his house while in hospital and had now moved back to Gloucestershire, as it was where he'd grown up.

I liked Thomas. He was intelligent and well-travelled. Gradually, we started to have regular chats as our dogs chased squirrels and sniffed each other's bottoms.

This was back in 2020. The US elections were fast approaching. We never discussed politics. I just assumed that we were on the same team. Then one day, I screwed up. I made the mistake of expressing my hope that Joe Biden would win the presidency. Surely America would rid itself of the disaster that, in my view, had been Donald Trump as president.

Big mistake.

Thomas turned a vivid colour of red. He appeared almost possessed. His voice changed as he started to unload on Biden, the Democratic Party, the Libtards . . .

I had clearly disturbed a rabid conservative. This in itself was no big deal. People have different views on politics. It's good to talk, get out of our social media echo chambers.

Thomas hadn't finished, however. He segued on to ranting about George Soros, Jews and a New World Order that secretly ran everything. The COVID-19 vaccine, he told me, was a tool used by lizard leaders to control our minds. Bill Gates was apparently behind it all. As he spoke, bits of white spittle started to settle on the edges of his lips. Bill Gates, Thomas said, was facing trial in India for killing thousands of street children during unauthorised vaccine experiments . . . Dumbfounded, I made my excuses and moved on. I was in shock. How could a seemingly kind and intelligent man with a lovely dog hold views like these? He appeared to have gone over not only a physical but a metaphorical cliff.

Obviously, I'd come across similar stuff online. My social media pages were boiling cesspits of strangeness, but I'd assumed that these were just random trolls. These were not people you'd ever actually meet in real life. The needle, it seemed, had shifted. There was more and more of this 'alternative thinking' about.

Every time you got talking to somebody, you couldn't help wondering what terrible turmoil was fermenting inside their heads.

Thomas was certainly not the only person in Cheltenham, a poster-child town for conformity, to hold these views. In 2021, when walking my dogs in Pittville Park, I would keep spotting stickers placed on fences, trees, bollards. They were very amateur looking and very distinctive. They were all over the park and new ones appeared every day.

They were all on the same subject: COVID and the vaccine.

> People who haven't been sick all year
> are willing to get sick from a shot
> to feel protected from something
> that hasn't made them sick all year??

Said one.

The annual flu jab must have freaked them out. Another took the form of a dictionary definition:

anti-vaxxer
noun – informal
A person who trusts their own immune system
more than they trust pharmaceutical companies,
career politicians and the corporate media.
(See also: critical thinker)

I'd looked up the definition of critical thinker, a term often banded about by conspiracy theorists:

- Open-mindedness.
- Respecting evidence and reasoning.
- Being able to consider different perspectives and points of view: in other words, having cognitive flexibility.
- Not being stuck in one position.
- Scepticism.
- Clarity and precision.

The 'respecting evidence and reasoning' seemed to be a bit of a stretch in this case.

One day he (because I was sure it was a he) put up a sticker saying:

Wake up
The Pandemic is a hoax
The vax is a poison

That one really pissed me off.

That very day, I had a close friend in intensive care. He'd caught COVID, gone into hospital, and was now on a ventilator in a decidedly dicey situation. Thankfully, he pulled through, but it had been touch-and-go and he suffered from the after effects of long COVID for ages.

To claim that the pandemic was a hoax was the height of stupidity and, more importantly, dangerous. If somebody didn't want to take the vaccine, that was both their choice and their right. But cranks like the sticker guy and high-profile online influencers were promulgating a disparate web of ill-informed, anti-science nonsense for clicks and giggles. This had led to vulnerable people being scared off listening to informed medical advice and not having the vaccine, often with fatal results.

So, I did my bit for the rational majority. I bought some blank stickers on which I wrote:

LEAKED CIA DOCUMENTS
REVEAL THAT
PANDEMIC DENIERS
HAVE MICRO PENISES.

I would carry them in my coat pocket and, every time I saw one of his stickers, I'd stick one of mine over the top of it.

It wasn't big. It wasn't clever. But it did make me feel better.

For three months, the phantom sticker guy and I played a daily game of sticker tag in which we would cover up each other's stickers, sometimes twice a day.

Then, one day, he stopped. I never saw the stickers again. I always wondered who he was and what had happened to him. Sometimes, I wondered whether he had contracted COVID. Maybe he'd died. That would have been rough justice.

More likely he'd got a job in the GB News art department.

But how did we get here?

Most conspiracy theories used to be quite amusing. Did we land on the moon? Was there a Bigfoot? Was Elvis still alive and working in a chip shop? It was all fun and games. Then, suddenly, they weren't so funny any more.

The new theories were no longer held just by cranks and weirdos. Now, they had infected the body politic. The actual president of the United States was urging people to inject themselves with bleach and retweeting crazed theories about kidnapped kids being kept in tunnels, their organs harvested to provide moisturising products for Hollywood celebrities.

In 2023, as part of my role as an ambassador for Save the Children, I posted an appeal on Facebook for donations to the DEC appeal following the tragic earthquake in Turkey and Syria.

A man called Robert Carpenter was quick to reply.

'Hmm I wonder who caused that?' wrote Robert, adding an American flag and a puzzled emoji to imply that he suspected America to be behind the earthquake.

'You wonder who caused the earthquake?' I replied, dumbfounded.

'Tesla invented the earthquake machine over a hundred years ago and it was confiscated by the CIA and the FBI, I'm thinking they tried it out a few times,' Mr Carpenter snapped right back.

There was nowhere to go with this. How could you even reason with stuff like this? I checked the profile info. He was a British economic migrant living in Spain who was anti-vax, anti-trans and a big fan of Jeremy Clarkson. BINGO. It was a Full House.

Somebody told me to google 'HAARP'. I did.

HAARP stands for High-frequency Auroral Research Program, an ionospheric research project at the University of Alaska. HAARP was supposedly capable of unleashing earthquakes. According to one conspiracy theorist, the earthquake was a 'punitive operation by NATO or the US against Turkey as it was becoming a thorn in the neck regarding Russia'.

It was nonsense, of course.

David Malaspina, a research scientist at the Laboratory for Atmospheric and Space Physics at the University of Colorado, told Reuters that HAARP's radio waves were similar to a strong AM radio broadcast station, and that 'there is no known mechanism by which an AM radio broadcast can cause an earthquake'. He said that these kinds of radio waves penetrated less than 1 centimetre into the ground, while earthquakes were obviously much deeper. 'The 2023 earthquake in Turkey, for instance, originated seventeen kilometres below the surface of the earth.'

But if you were conspiracy disposed, then you were not going to believe him or any expert that didn't validate your theories. As Michael Gove, an actual British Cabinet minister, once famously said, 'I think the people in this country have had enough of experts.'

To me, it was this – this strange new world of 'alternative facts' – that was the truly deadly virus that faced us in the years to come. Who needed experts when we were now our own experts? Who needed facts when we could select or fabricate our own?

Nine/eleven seemed to be a significant catalyst. When people started claiming that it was all staged and that the victims were crisis actors, the groundwork was being set for snake-oil salesmen like Alex Jones, of *InfoWars* fame, to rake in the money. This, remember, was a man claiming that frogs were being turned gay by chemicals in tap water . . .

Maybe it had something to do with online interconnectivity? Every village had always had an idiot. The problem was that they could now all contact each other.

But why write a book on all this? After all, I'm not one to unquestioningly listen to authority. I have always been a contrarian who loves an argument and hates being told what to do.

I even have a rather disturbing personal connection to conspiracy theories.

In 1860 a certain Maurice Joly, a Parisian lawyer, wrote a book called *Dialogues in Hell: Conversations between Machiavelli and Montesquieu*. It was an allegorical satire of Emperor Napoleon III, a sensitive soul who had banned all direct criticism of himself.

So far, so literature.

The problem was that two-fifths of *The Protocols of the Elders of Zion*, an infamous and entirely fabricated antisemitic text, purporting to describe a Jewish plan for global domination, appeared to have been lifted verbatim from Maurice Joly's book.

The Protocols were supposed to have been taken verbatim from an international Zionist conference held at the turn of the twentieth century. The fact that Maurice Joly's book was written in 1860 clearly invalidated the whole document.

This, however, had not stopped them from being used by cynical and gullible people as an insidious antisemitic weapon.

Perhaps it was this innocent connection to a distant relative's part in this most enduring of conspiracies that made me so concerned by them.

I grew up in the Middle East. There was possibly nowhere, save in the dark recesses of the internet, where conspiracy theories were so freely promulgated. Locals were obsessed with the 'Hidden Hand', an unseen force that shaped Middle Eastern affairs. There was a constant feeling that outside forces were conspiring to do bad things to good people.

The vast majority of these conspiracy theories were totally ridiculous, but not all of them. There has been a long and well-documented history of foreign powers interfering with the internal politics of Arab nations.

And this seemed to be the problem. There were kernels of truth in most conspiracy theories. People that believed in UFOs could point you to evidence of, frankly understandable, military cover-ups. But if they had lied about those, then they must be lying about the existence of alien craft, right?

The existence of the occasional real conspiracy was camouflaged by the preponderance of insane, wacky conspiracy theories. Some conspiracy theorists even claimed that this in itself was a conspiracy: class them all as tin-foil-hat-wearing weirdos to hide the real truth.

I'd written a book, *Scary Monsters*, in which I travelled the world in search of mythical beasts such as the Yeti and Bigfoot, less as a believer and more as a curious observer. I'd also touched upon conspiracies in my book *The Dark Tourist*, when, as part of my American assassination vacation, I'd visited Dallas.

Back in 2008, as I wandered around Dealey Plaza, I came to a walkway, just below the infamous 'grassy knoll', where a veritable mini-market of conspiracy theorists had set up stalls peddling books and videos that championed their various theories. Kennedy had been killed by the Mob, the Russians, the Cubans, Marilyn Monroe, the Muppets . . .

The thing that had struck me the most, at the time, was just how impossible it was to argue with them. They had all the facts at their fingertips. They were so certain of everything.

I've never really been certain of anything in my life, except for my suspicion of people who were certain of things.

In his book *Suspicious Minds: Why We Believe Conspiracy Theories*, Rob Brotherton, a psychology professor at Goldsmiths, wrote:

> Conspiracy theories postulate a black-and-white world in which good is struggling against evil. The general public is cast as the victim of organised persecution, and the motives of the alleged conspirators often verge on pure maniacal evil. At the very least, the conspirators are said to have an almost inhuman disregard for the basic liberty and well-being of the general population. More grandiose conspiracy theories portray the conspirators as being Evil Incarnate: of having caused all the ills from which we suffer, committing abominable acts of unthinkable cruelty on a routine basis, and striving ultimately to subvert or destroy everything we hold dear.

This was probably why I found it rather difficult to get on with conspiracy theorists. Despite being a recovering goth, I was generally a glass–half-full kind of guy. I liked to see the good in most people.

I decided that I needed to get back out there. I needed to go IRL. I needed to travel through this strange new world as a wide-eyed voyager, eager to take in all the sights.

I was going more as an onlooker as opposed to a judge. There was very little point in making too many judgements. If I did, they would only be disputed by the very people I was going to meet on my travels. I would be accused of 'being part of the whole thing'. I would be called a 'shill' in the pay of the baddies.

I only wished somebody could tell me who to invoice.

There would undoubtedly be more questions than answers by the time I'd finished. But I didn't care. I wanted to travel to the edges of the flat earth. I wanted to drive across America looking for UFOs and secret tunnels. I wanted to meet QAnoners. I wanted to see if Finland really existed.

I wanted to see it all. I was off on another set of adventures. I was off to make polite conversation with Thomases all over the world.

I was a conspiracy tourist.

Finland Does Not Exist

Just because you're paranoid doesn't mean they aren't after you.
Joseph Heller

I'd decided it might be a good idea to get myself into the conspiracy mindset before diving in head first. I was going to start small and work my way up. What I really needed was a big silly theory that I could cut my conspiracy tourist teeth on. Having done a lot of reading around the subject, I found exactly what I was looking for.

I was going to try to prove that Finland existed.

It was officially the hottest day in British history. I was in Stansted Airport, in a Lebanese-themed restaurant, eating microwaved Moroccan food. As I scrolled through my social media, I kept seeing snapshots of a country in collapse. Apocalyptic fires raged in Dartford, tarmac was melting on Devon roads and a naked man was in his garden, squatting in a bin full of iced water, nursing a cocktail and hurling abuse at passers-by. It was a good day to be leaving the UK, which, like Dubai when it rains, was losing the plot.

It was a bad day, however, to be in an airport. It was packed with hordes of sweaty humanity having a collective meltdown. Stansted was my least favourite British airport at the best of times, but today it was the seventh circle of hell.

Climate change and the accompanying fear of rising global temperatures had long been dismissed by climate deniers and attention-seeking TV pundits as some sort of scientific conspiracy. What nobody ever explained was, what was in it for the scientists? Surely the occasional opportunity to be a talking head on CNN, MSNBC or the BBC was not so exciting that they would make up this doom-laden theory?

It seemed to me that climate-change deniers would simply prefer to stick their heads in the sand and hope that everything went away, as opposed to having to face up to the problem. Unfortunately for them, Camber Sands was, by all accounts, currently way too hot for that kind of behaviour.

Across the table sat my disgruntled wife, Stacey. After a long period of my travelling the world alone for work, she had put her foot down. Our kids had flown the nest and she felt it was incredibly unfair that I got to travel constantly while she stayed at home. Any attempt to defend my travels as part of my job were met with a tin ear. She had endured enough. It was, apparently, time that I took her with me.

This was weird. Part of travel writing is about being alone. Travelling alone, you get bored, meander about, get into trouble, eavesdrop, allow fate to take you where it likes. Travelling with somebody else makes for a totally different experience. But she insisted. So, under duress, I agreed and told her to get ready for a trip.

'Where are we going?' asked Stacey.

'Finland,' I replied.

'Oh ...' she said, trying hard to hide her obvious disappointment.

'Why are we going to Finland?' she continued.

'Because there is a conspiracy theory that it does not exist, and I intend to prove it does.'

'That is the dumbest thing I've ever heard. Of course it exists.'

I was 99.9 per cent sure she was right but, if I was to take a proper look at conspiracy theories, then I needed to open my mind, discard my lifetime of institutional brainwashing and embrace everything. One of the trickiest things about conspiracy theories is arguing against them. I envisioned our trip to Finland as a kind of intellectual exercise. How did you prove a negative? How could you deal logically with something so illogical?

So, what was the theory and how did it come about?

I found an article in *Vice* written in 2016 by a guy called Mack Lamoureux, which appeared to be legit. Lamoureux said that the whole theory had started with a guy called Jack.

A post on Reddit had asked people to say what was the weird-est thing that their parents ever taught them? Jack posted that, when he was eight years old, his parents had told him that Finland didn't exist.

The story that his parents told him was that, in 1918, Japan and Russia had fabricated the existence of a landmass known as Finland so that they could be the only people fishing in that area of the Baltic Sea (because . . . everybody else thought that there was land there).

It got better, and weirder. The Trans-Siberian Express was supposedly established in order to transport the fish caught in 'Finland' across Russia to Japan. If the theory was not mad enough already, it also claimed that the fish were transported to Japan under the guise of Nokia products.

As a man famous for shouting loudly into a giant Nokia phone, this rather tickled me. Nokia, it turned out, had a long history prior to the mobile phone. It had been founded in 1865 and had originally been a pulp mill, although, looking at the history of the company, its products seemed incredibly diverse. The name came from the town of Nokia, where its second pulp mill had been established.

Jack himself didn't believe the conspiracy theory but, this being the internet, a subreddit was set up by people who did believe it . . . and it blew up. These believers had new ideas. One claimed that the name Finland actually proved the theory as it alluded to the fin of a fish. They appeared to be unaware that the actual name of the country was Suomi.

The inexplicable concept of people leaving obvious clues to their conspiracies seemed to be a constant conspiracy thread in itself.

When a container ship got stuck in the Suez Canal in 2021, it had the words EVERGREEN written in large white letters on the side. After news outlets started to cover the story, the conspiracy theorists got to work. Evergreen was the name of the Taiwanese shipping company that operated the vessel. Conspiracy theorists, however, said that this was also Hillary Clinton's secret service code name (which it was). They then discovered that the stranded ship's call sign was H3RC. As these were Hillary Rodham Clinton's initials, the ship was obviously being used by Clinton to traffic children. Quite why, if Clinton was doing something so bizarre, she would want to leave these enigmatic clues to her supposed crimes, was never fully explained.

When the ship's manifest was finally revealed, the cargo consisted of electronics, machinery and parts, household goods, furniture, footwear and a 10-metre-tall plastic model of a *T. rex*, bound for an adventure golf course in Cambridge. No children were found. They were presumed to have been eaten by the *T. rex*.

Another angle to the Finland conspiracy theory was that the world 'elites' knew about the Japanese–Russian plot. They just chose to maintain the illusion of its existence as a sort of idealised liberal society that other countries could aspire to. No real country, the theory went, could be so consistently idealistic, topping global leagues for healthcare, education, literacy, sexual equality, press freedom, non-corruption.

Finnish people, according to the conspiracy theorists, believed that they lived in Finland but they actually lived in towns in Estonia, Russia and Sweden. Visitors to Finland were flown to these areas and were just told that they were in Finland.

Jack could not explain why his parents had told him this story when he was younger. Most people appeared to enjoy it for what it was – a joke or a parody of real conspiracy theories.

A hardcore minority, however, did start to believe it.

There is an internet adage called Poe's law that originates from a comment left by a man called Nathan Poe on a Christian internet forum, which states that 'it is impossible to create a parody of extreme views so obviously exaggerated that it cannot be mistaken by some readers or viewers as a sincere expression of the parodied views'.

According to Jack, 'The Finland conspiracy is a perfect case study of that. Ninety per cent of people view it as a parody but ten per cent genuinely believe it's something that needs proving or debunking.'

And so, it was decided. I was going to travel to Finland and try to debunk the theory. This was why I was sitting in Stansted with my wife. It might serve me well on my other journeys. And, who knew, maybe it was true?

I posted a tweet: 'Off to Helsinki for a couple of days. What to do?' One of the joys of having a sizeable social media presence was that I was often able to use the so-called 'wisdom of crowds' to help me on my travels. The secret was to weed out the usual suspects and to cherry pick the nuggets of wisdom.

There were not many nuggets . . .

'Go fuck yourself.' 'Ski jump.' 'Have a sauna.' 'Drink vodka.' 'Go fuck yourself.'

It was not a lot to go on. It was actually why Finland was such a perfect place to choose if you wanted to claim that somewhere didn't exist. Almost nobody had actually visited the place. Why would you, unless you were particularly keen on vodka, saunas, ski jumping or fucking yourself? We were flying Ryanair. Having paid eight pounds for a plane ticket, three hundred pounds for a seat and sixty-five pounds for the opportunity to take on a cabin bag the size of this book, it was never going to be a pleasurable experience, but hey-ho.

I actually assumed that we would be the only people travelling to a non-existent destination, but the plane was full of people pretending to be Finnish. A large percentage of them were heavily tattooed and multi-pierced. One of the few Finnish things I was familiar with was the heavy metal band Lordi, who won the 2006 Eurovision Song Contest. I had no idea why I remembered this, as I was not keen on Eurovision and never made an effort to watch it. Lordi, however, were quite memorable. They looked like the band Wizzard after an altercation with a horror special effects company. Dressed as though in some fantasy-horror movie, they were so ludicrous and over the top that they were difficult to ignore. A lot of our fellow passengers looked like they might have made it to the final rounds of the Lordi auditions.

The stewardess walked past checking seatbelts. It was time for me to start the debunking.

'Excuse me, where is this plane going to?' I asked.

She looked at me strangely.

'Helsinki.'

'In Finland?' I continued.

'Yes . . . Finland. Is that not where you are supposed to be going? May I see your boarding pass?'

'Oh yes, but I just wanted to make sure. So Finland is definitely the country we are going to land in?'

The stewardess gave me a look that indicated she thought I might be trouble.

'Can I see your boarding pass, sir?'

I showed her my boarding pass and she glanced at it before handing it back.

'Have a nice flight, sir.'

'I shall . . . it'll be my first time in FINLAND.'

I pronounced the name of the country loudly and rather sarcastically so that, if she was in on this, then she would know I was not fooled. Stacey looked at me in panic, her eyes begging me not to make a scene.

The flight was two-and-a-half hours long, which, given where Finland supposedly was on the world map, made sense, but I tried to keep an eye out for the plane making unusual turns or circling. There had been a Channel 4 show back in the day in which contestants were told that they were going to train in Russia to become astronauts. They took off and, after flying around for a couple of hours, landed back in England at a fake airbase that had been entirely converted to look as though it was in Russia. Nobody twigged. These things were possible.

I started watching a Netflix documentary on D. B. Cooper, the legendary hijacker who, in 1971, took over a plane that was flying between Portland and Seattle. Cooper claimed to have a bomb and wanted a ransom of two hundred thousand dollars. Having landed and picked up the ransom, the plane took off again with Cooper demanding to be flown to Mexico City. Cooper then opened the door of the plane and parachuted out over Washington state, never to be seen again.

People seem to love a ballsy heist and D. B. Cooper became an unlikely folk hero. His exploits sparked a series of copycat hijackings. These, in turn, led directly to commercial airlines implementing the tiresome security measures such as metal detectors and luggage searches with which we are now all too familiar.

Part of me longed for the good old days of air travel. In the 1950s, fledgling commercial airlines were hiring ex-military pilots who knew how to have a good time. One such was a friend of my father's, a certain Captain Swan. He used to have a favourite trick. The cockpit door would be left open so that passengers could see that there was no pilot as they boarded. Once all on board, the stewardess would announce that there was going to be a delay as the pilot was still somewhere in the terminal building. Captain Swan, who had been pretending to be a passenger, would then jump up, shout that he didn't have time for this and barge into the cockpit. Starting the engines, he would come over the Tannoy to the passengers.

'Good afternoon, ladies and gentlemen. I don't know about you, but I don't want to hang around here any longer than we need to. So, if you could all fasten your seatbelts, then I'm going to give this thing my best shot. After all, how hard can it be?'

The cockpit door would shut and he would then proceed to take off as the passengers screamed in fear. They were different times back then . . .

Back on my flight, as I was squeezed between a steampunk and my sharp-elbowed wife, with my legs tucked into an uncomfortable foetal position, the idea of opening a door and jumping out was worryingly tempting.

Our captain's voice came crackling over the Tannoy.

'Good evening, ladies and gentlemen, this is Captain Stubing. We are commencing our descent into Helsinki.'

But were we? Was Captain Stubing in on this conspiracy? He could land us in a random city and tell us that it was Helsinki, but how did I know for sure?

There had been a rather nice joke recently in which a prankster had written the words 'WELCOME TO LUTON' in large white letters in a field right next to Gatwick Airport. A lot of worried passengers had spotted it out of the window and presumed they had been diverted. This prank, like most things in life, was not an original one. Somebody in Australia had painted the words 'WELCOME TO PERTH' on the roof of their house, directly under the flight path of planes landing at Sydney Airport. Passengers, it seemed, were very much at an informational disadvantage.

The plane landed and, as we taxied towards our gate, I spotted a large sign on the terminal building saying 'Helsinki Airport'. A less-informed traveller might have taken this at face value, but I was more wary. This proved nothing.

9

As we entered the terminal, everything seemed to be as it should. There was a sign indicating that we were going through Finnish border control. There was what I presumed was Finnish on the advertising hoardings. But how did I know this was Finnish? It could have been gibberish . . . or Swedish . . . or Klingon. I opened Google Translate and typed in a slogan, which it identified as being Finnish and urged me to sample a particular brand of vodka. This all seemed legit but, if I was a conspiracy theorist, I would not be swayed by this either. The set dressing at the airport, big corporations like Google . . . they were all in on it.

I scanned the people lining up in front of me at the passport queue. Had they all been duped into thinking they were in Finland? Were they all actors, paid for by whoever was responsible for maintaining this massive lie? If it was fake, then it was an expensive one. Who was financing it? Bill Gates was normally blamed. It would make sense if Russia was still behind it all. It was the global epicentre of mass misinformation with buildings crammed full of trolls pumping out fake information on fake social media profiles with the sole intention of causing dissent and confusion.

Finland used to be a part of Russia. Well, it actually started off as being part of Sweden until, during the rather unimaginatively titled 'Finnish War', it was taken over by Russia. Using the Bolshevik Revolution in Russia as a useful diversion, it declared itself independent in 1917.

I got to the front of the passport line. The immigration guy stamped my passport. I checked the stamp, something I rarely did. It said 'Helsinki – Vantaa'. I checked my maps and discovered that Vantaa was a town just outside Helsinki where the international airport was located.

Damn . . . these people were good.

We got a taxi into Helsinki. My first impressions of the place was that it was clean, weirdly clean. It was all shiny and new, as though it had just been built. We drove past a hotel called 'Soros Hotel' and my mind went into meltdown. Soros . . . George Soros, a man who, like Bill Gates, got dragged into every conspiracy theory I'd ever heard. When arguing with anti-vaxxers online I was constantly accused of being a 'shill' paid for by George Soros.

Soros is a Hungarian-American who made a vast amount of money in finance and appears to be determined, like Bill Gates, to give a lot of that fortune away. Soros is Jewish and had donated a lot of money to people like Barack Obama and Hillary Clinton and their presidential campaigns. This had obviously annoyed a lot of people on the right who claimed that he was some sort of puppet master orchestrating global events. There was more than a tinge of classic antisemitic sentiments behind these claims.

And yet here, in a country that supposedly didn't exist, one of the first buildings that I spotted had the name of somebody that conspiracy theorists felt was behind a lot of the bad things happening in the world. It was a weird coincidence. I looked it up online to see if it was owned by the man himself only to find that the hotel was actually called 'Sokos Hotel'. I had misread it. I was an idiot.

Facts, it appeared, didn't care about my feelings.

We drove into downtown Helsinki. The buildings started to look a little older. It was late on a Saturday night but there was hardly anybody on the streets. It was a touch eerie. We checked into the Lilla Roberts, a rather lovely Art Deco hotel, and went to sleep almost immediately. It was 10.30 p.m. and still light outside.

The following morning, I woke up and pottered down to reception. A cheerful receptionist with pale skin and ridiculous cheekbones greeted me.

'Good morning, sir.'

'Good morning,' I replied.

'How may I help you today?'

'This might seem like a strange question, but where am I?' I asked.

'You are in the reception,' she smiled.

'No, I mean – where *am* I?' I asked a little too forcefully, raising a quizzical eyebrow.

'Ermmm . . . you are in your hotel.'

Her initial greeting smile was fading a little and being replaced with a slightly nervous frown.

'And where is this hotel situated?' I persisted.

'Helsinki,' she answered, moving backwards slightly.

'In which country?' I was not to be deterred.

'Finland . . .'

'Are you certain of that?' I asked.

'Yes . . . of course. We are in Finland,' she said slowly.

'How can you be certain?'

'How can I be certain that we are in Finland – this is what you are asking me?'

She looked confused. She briefly wondered whether this kind of weirdness would have been a daily occurrence if she had taken that enticing transfer to the Van Der Stoner Hotel in Amsterdam.

'Yes, how do I know for sure that I am not in Sweden but that you are telling me that we are in Finland?' I smiled in what I hoped was in a friendly but enigmatic manner.

'I'm really sorry, I'm not understanding you, sir. We are in Helsinki, the capital of Finland. I am Finnish. I speak Finnish, not Swedish.'

She looked around hurriedly for support. A tall, skinny man with translucent skin and bad acne walked over.

'Can I help you, sir?' he glowered.

'Only if you can prove to me that we are in Finland.'

He looked at the girl who looked back at him.

'Is everything OK, sir?' he said quietly.

From the look on his face, I concluded that I had taken this line of questioning as far as I could.

'Could you tell me where breakfast is served, please?'

He pointed to some double doors at the end of the long, stylish reception area.

'Thank you,' I started to walk away before suddenly turning back and firing off one final question. 'How do you say that in Finnish?'

'*Kiitos*,' said the man, staring at me strangely.

'*Kiitos*!' I exclaimed, nodding slowly as I turned away and headed off for breakfast.

Stacey was already in the breakfast room. She had bolted ahead the moment she had heard me start to talk to the receptionist. She claimed to be embarrassed by my behaviour but, deep down, I knew she was impressed and starting to realise just how much dedication I put into my writing trips abroad.

Hotel breakfasts are a conspiracy if you ask me. If you make the mistake of not booking a 'breakfast included' rate, then you have to eat the equivalent of about three days' worth of food to make the price good value.

Hotels are onto this technique and constantly attempt to thwart you by:

1. providing tiny, impractical glasses for all juices;
2. looking totally confused if you ask for anything but filter coffee;
3. doing something devious with the conveyor-belt toast machine, so that no piece of toast is ever to your satisfaction;
4. making scrambled eggs from the dried scrotums of dead squirrels.

After breakfast Stacey and I headed out to look around 'Helsinki' or whatever city it was that we were in. As with the night before, there were surprisingly few people about. We were headed for Market Square, the apparent centre of the city. Just below our hotel we crossed a large open square called Kasarmitori that was dominated by a vast shiny sculpture of what looked like a spaceman standing on top of a large metal ball. It looked out of place. Was this some sort of secret signal to those in the know? Who was this statue dedicated to?

In the far corner of the square sat a little concrete kiosk that looked like a tourist information booth but turned out to be the world's smallest Joe & the Juice outlet. Stacey, for some peculiar reason, adores Joe & the Juice, whereas it leaves me rather cold. She insisted on buying a coffee, despite having drunk her body weight in it for breakfast. As she ordered from an annoyingly handsome surfer-looking dude, I took the opportunity to ask him what the statue was about.

'Ah . . . I think it is in memory of the Winter War,' he said, looking none too certain.

He did not look like a gentleman that had been long troubled by education and so I did not pursue the matter, mainly because I was keen to get Stacey away from his handsomeness as soon as possible.

I racked my memory to remember what the Winter War was. I'd assumed that almost all wars in Finland were winter wars as the place was not known for its tropical climate.

Unsurprisingly, it involved the Russians again. The Soviet Union invaded in 1939, three months after the outbreak of the Second World War. Still irked at Finland going it alone, their plan was to install a friendly puppet government. Things did not go very well as the Finns fought incredibly fiercely in temperatures that reached -45 °C. The Soviets eventually gave up and a peace deal was signed that gave them some territory, but allowed Finland to survive as a made-up country.

Interestingly, it was the inability of the Soviets to succeed in conquering Finland that gave Hitler the impression that the Soviet Union was weak and could be easily conquered. This, of course, led to Operation Barbarossa and the subsequent Nazi military disaster.

Arriving in Market Square, we nosed about for a while. If I was honest, it was not exactly a market, more of a loose conglomeration of orange tents selling tourist tat and salmon soup.

We got a bowl of salmon soup, not because we were hungry, but because it allowed us to sit down and people-watch for a while. I'd never had salmon soup before, and after tasting it I had no plans to do so again. Hunks of, admittedly fresh-looking, salmon sat in some thin, murky liquid inundated with dill. It was not unpleasant but, like *Love Island* contestants, it was instantly forgettable once finished.

Sadly, the people were not interesting enough for a decent people-watch so we headed towards the cathedral that was perched on a little hill just behind the square. It was reached by an impressive set of steps that also served as another place for tired tourists to sit and people-watch should they not fancy the salmon soup. This did mean that the steps were a magnet for touts hawking an assortment of tourist activities.

Three representatives from three different hop-on, hop-off bus tours pestered everyone with the enthusiasm of vultures feasting on fresh roadkill. Stacey loves a bus tour. It is her way of getting her bearings in a new city. I am the opposite. I refuse to even countenance the idea of getting on one as, to me, an experienced, independent traveller, it's like admitting defeat.

It is possibly a silly attitude, but it's just one of my travel rules. Another is refusing to eat, drink or shop at any establishment in which people are stood outside trying to pull you in. I like a place that is either confident enough in its own excellence or too lazy to harass passers-by.

There is an infamous restaurant in Mykonos that regularly makes the headlines every two months or so when a forlorn-looking tourist couple are photographed brandishing a bill for eight hundred euros, having had a couple of mojitos, four crab legs and a Greek salad. The place, called dk Oyster, is famous for extortionate prices and getting physically intimidating when you complain.

The copious TripAdvisor one-star reviews are a car crash.

This is a con artist wet dream. Food is shifty, service is shifty, wait staff refused to let me leave without paying. I had to dispute charges with my credit card company. Avoid like the plague. EpsilonEm

$70 a beer, $200 for any food, its jaw dropping when you pay. They bully you into paying or you 'can't leave'. Fake prices on menus, it's almost comical.
COMPLETE SCAM!!!!
Everyone working here should be in jail . . . period
Mattl

TripAdvisor had even put a warning on the place's page, something I'd never seen before:

TripAdvisor has been made aware of recent media reports or events concerning this property which may not be reflected in reviews found on this listing. Accordingly, you may wish to perform additional research for information about this property when making your travel plans.

It is all very simple. Just follow my rules. If a restaurant has people standing on the street, waving menus and trying to get you to come in, keep walking. If you don't, you're a mug.

Back in Helsinki, Stacey and I climbed the cathedral steps fast, avoiding both the tourists and their circling vultures. Once at the top we entered the cathedral. I have no idea why I always go into cathedrals. I am an atheist and cathedrals are almost always pretty much the same. Like fireworks, once you've seen one, you've seen them all . . . but you always harbour that slim hope that something new might occur.

As it so happened: this cathedral with its gleaming, Orthodox-looking cupolas did surprise me. I was expecting the usual display of golden, ornate bling bedecking the walls. Instead, it was almost minimalist. The walls were smooth, bare stone with almost no decoration. It was rather refreshing and much more to my taste than the usual gaudy religious bling. It was like wandering into an Apple Store having mistaken it for a Versace outlet.

The cathedral, probably the most famous building in Finland, belongs to the Finnish Evangelical Lutherans. Apparently, Lutherans did not approve of excessive decoration and liked things clean and simple. It was deceptive. The outside was uber-Russian style whereas the inside was peak Scandinavian chic – sleek, elegant, restrained.

Most people, if they accept that Finland exists, assume it is part of Scandinavia along with Norway, Denmark and Sweden. This, however, is not strictly true. Although Finland, the Faroe Islands and even Iceland are often lumped in as all being Scandinavian, they are not.

The Finnish language is not a Scandinavian language, and Finns are ethnically distinct from Scandinavians. Things do get a touch more complicated if you start to talk about the 'Scandinavian Peninsula'. This does not include Denmark, but does include parts of Finland. I was not sure that any of this was important because we are actually discussing where a possibly non-existent country belongs . . .

I'd had some experience with Finland and religion before. When I visited North Korea for my book *The Dark Tourist*, one of the group was a strange Finn. He'd announced that he was a member of the Church of the Flying Spaghetti Monster.

Followers of this religion called themselves Pastafarians and, in an attempt to lampoon the craziness of mainstream religious views, insisted on their right to wear their religious outfit on their passport photographs. This consisted of a colander worn on his head.

The Church itself started out in America. A man called Bobby Henderson demanded that Pastafarianism should be given an equal amount of time by teachers as subjects such as evolution and intelligent design. Rather gloriously, the official history of the Church included the notion that the Flying Spaghetti Monster invented the universe after a night spent drinking heavily. For reasons not clearly explained, pirates were seen as the original Pastafarians.

The Church was often viewed as a more amusing, updated version of Russell's teapot. This has nothing to do with the increasingly conspiracy-minded gob-on-a-stick that is Russell Brand. It refers to the philosopher, Bertrand Russell, who came up with the teapot analogy to show that the burden of proof lay with a person making unproven claims as opposed to asking people to disprove the claim.

Russell's view was that if he claimed that a tiny teapot, too small to be seen by any telescope, was orbiting the sun between the Earth and Mars, he should not expect people to believe him just because they could not prove him wrong.

Russell's teapot is principally used to debate the existence of a god but it seemed to me that it was incredibly pertinent to conspiracy theories.

According to Russell's teapot theory, it was not for me to prove that Finland did exist, rather the burden of proof was up to the people who believed this to be the case. I should have maybe read a little more Russell before travelling to Finland. It might have saved me the journey. But, whatever, I was here now and determined to do my best.

Whether Finland existed or not, it would be fair to say that both Stacey and I were a little underwhelmed by Helsinki so far. It had more the feel of a large provincial town than a European capital and we were already wondering what on earth we were going to do for three days.

Secretly I found myself wishing that it had been Barbados or Bali whose existence had been questioned. But that would have been too easy. I was an intrepid investigator looking for truth. This, I reminded myself, was work, not an excuse for a holiday. One thing was for certain: I'd definitely picked the right work trip for my wife to accompany me on. Three more days of this and she would never ask again.

We walked back down the steps and returned to Market Square. I knew that Stacey really wanted to go on a bus tour but had been sweet enough not to force the issue. I decided to compromise. I'd spotted a boat offering an hour-and-a-half's tour of the islands and city coastline. This felt slightly less naff than a bus tour and I felt that we might get a better sense of the place from the sea.

So, we bought our tickets and sat on the open-top deck watching impressively aggressive seagulls dive bomb anybody foolish enough to attempt to eat something outdoors. Seagulls are the Vikings of the bird world, constantly plundering and looting with scant regard for anything but their ill-gotten booty.

The boat left dock with about nine other tourists on board. Over a speaker came a slightly scratchy narration recording in what was supposedly Finnish, and then English, informing us of what we were looking at. Because the Finnish version came first and was quite long, the English commentary was always behind and referred to something that we could no longer see.

This was no problem really as there wasn't much to point out – an island. Another island. An island with an 'old wooden house on it'. This was not going to be troubling the Tourist Experiences of the Year Awards.

The main draw was Suomenlinna, a vast sea fortress that spanned six islands in the bay. Originally called Sveaborg (Castle of the Swedes) after the country that built it in 1748, it was then renamed Suomenlinna (Castle of Finland) when Finland became independent (or non-existent) in 1917 having taken it back off the Russians who had nabbed it off the Swedes in 1808.

You had to really keep a good eye on your sea fortresses here.

As we drifted past the fortress, I couldn't help wondering why there were so few people about, both on our boat, but also on the fortress itself. It was supposedly Finland's most popular tourist attraction. I went below deck and chatted to the captain, a grizzled-looking man with violently ruddy cheeks and cold, grey eyes that looked like they'd seen way too much.

'Hello, Captain,' I said.

He nodded curtly.

'May I ask, where is everybody?' I gestured to the empty shores.

'Zombie attack,' said the captain, with just a hint of a smile.

'Ha ha. Very good. No, but this is a serious question,' I persisted.

The captain said nothing and looked over at his well-stocked bar with ill-concealed longing.

'It's midsummer. Surely this should be peak tourist season.' I was not going to let it go.

'It is,' said the captain, doing his best to break his steely fixation on a bottle of vodka.

'So, is this just a quiet year, or is this normal?'

'You are in Finland. Nothing is normal.'

The captain looked pleased that nothing was normal. He looked like a man that feared normality. This was a great attitude, and I was happy for him, but I wondered if he had let something slip.

'What do you mean by that?' I asked.

I was like the Columbo of conspiracy theories. Nothing got past me.

'I have to drive the boat now, please excuse me.' The captain turned away and walked towards what appeared to be his wheelhouse.

It came as quite the surprise that nobody was currently driving the boat. We were in a fairly tight channel between two islands, so I decided not to press the matter and to let him crack on with his job. I returned to the top deck where Stacey, being Canadian, had taken the opportunity of my absence to start chatting to a family sitting behind her.

They were Danes, but they spoke better English than both Stacey and me. I was a big fan of the Danish. I had made a TV show called *How Beer Changed the World* with a Danish production company and spent quite some time in Copenhagen. Danes were so nice that I was almost suspicious. No country could be that perfect. It worried me. I assumed they all did truly terrible things in the privacy of their own homes.

The Danish family were in Helsinki for the weekend.

'Why did you pick here to visit?' I asked.

'Because we had not been here,' replied the dad in cool Danish logic mode.

'And what do you think of the place?' I asked.

'Yeah, it's nice. It's quiet. It makes Denmark look like Ibiza.' He laughed.

'You are here on holiday?' the wife asked Stacey.

'Yes, sort of, my husband is also working,' she said, through gritted teeth.

'Aha, and what work are you doing here?' asked the wife.

I could feel Stacey's buttocks clench.

'I am trying to work our whether it exists or not,' I said.

There was an awkward pause.

'Aha. You are trying to work out whether Helsinki exists?' the wife said slowly.

'Finland, whether Finland exists,' I replied.

'And why would it not?' asked the man, intrigued.

'My husband is a writer,' interjected Stacey quickly.

'Ah. You are writing a fantasy book?' The man stumbled a little for the right word.

'No. I'm investigating whether Russia and Japan colluded in 1917 to fabricate the existence of this "country" in order that they could have sole fishing rights.'

I felt Stacey's leg give me a sharp kick.

'And what is your conclusion so far?' asked the wife, subtly drawing her children a little closer to her.

'I still have an open mind. We only arrived yesterday.'

The deck went silent. I looked out over the bay. I could see the cupolas of the minimalist cathedral and a smaller version of the London Eye. It was a big wheel that had a sauna in one of the gondolas. The Finns really love saunas. I felt that we would have to give one a go if we really wanted to crack the stone-faced Finnish psyche.

After a turgid hour and a half, the boat docked back in Market Square and we disembarked. The captain was at the passerelle to bid us farewell. He had the look of a headmaster, waving the kids off for school holidays, counting the seconds until he could lock the doors, dress up as a beautiful lady and dance erotically through the empty school corridors.

I winked at him, which in hindsight might have given off the wrong signal. He looked confused and then a little irritated.

I hurried down the ramp and straight into the middle of a seagull kill zone. A large American woman was having an actual wrestling match with a buffed-up gull who had grabbed one end of her hot dog and was not going to let go. The woman swung the bird violently, holding on to her end of the hot dog. I was not only fascinated by the unequal match-up, but also staggered by the strength of the sausage itself.

The woman's husband, a much smaller figure, was keeping his distance from the battle but shouting at her.

'Jesus Christ, Jean. Just let go,' he pleaded.

'No frickin' way,' said Jean, trying to punch the bird with her other hand.

'Why? You're never going to eat it now. It's had it in its mouth,' said the husband.

'Shut up, Shawn!' screamed Jean.

Shawn shut up. He knew better than to argue with Jean when she was involved in a physical altercation with a European seabird.

★   ★   ★

One way to really get to know a country is through its art. We decided to head to Kiasma, the Museum of Contemporary Art that was up by the railway station. We entered and paid for our tickets. It was expensive but, then again, everything in Finland is stupidly expensive. A pint is about twelve pounds and a flat white around six. This was not, to put it finely, a Ryanair country.

Kiasma was a long, thin modern building clad in zinc. Sadly, it was also currently buried under a wall of scaffolding. We made our way up a series of ramps to enter the first gallery.

It was shockingly bad. I mean laughable.

Particular lowlights included:

1. a tent, inside of which were some chairs with teddy bears on them;
2. some paintings that would have looked bad on the walls of a kindergarten;
3. a video of a naked man jumping around an empty room on a pogo stick.

I bloody love art, in all forms, but this place was taking the piss. If this was genuinely the best that Finland could produce, it only deepened my suspicions. It looked like something put together in about half an hour. We did the whole place in under fifteen minutes.

Once back in the reception area I approached the ticket desk.

'Hello, I'd like a refund please,' I said to the albino behind the desk.

'Oh! Why is this?' She looked dumbfounded.

'Because I made a mistake. I thought this was a modern art gallery, not somewhere that exhibited artwork by troubled children.'

She stared at me for a while as she took my words in.

'I'm sorry. I don't understand.'

'I want our money back. We just paid over sixty pounds to look at possibly the worst selection of art that I've ever seen.'

'I'm sorry, sir, we do not do refunds.'

'I can see why. You'd be bankrupt in a month.'

I found Stacey hiding in the museum shop. Normally, when I'm travelling, the modern art museum shop is your best bet for interesting, off-beat souvenirs and presents. Not this one, however. It was devoid of anything interesting. I spotted a kid's book. The title was *Can You Keep a Straight Face?*

'No,' was the answer . . . Truth be told, I had not been able to keep a straight face since we'd entered the museum.

Leaving Kiasma under the death stare of the ticket albino, we made a beeline for Helsinki Central Station. Now this was a seriously beautiful building, with more than a hint of New York's Grand Central about it.

Unlike everywhere else, the station was really busy. I assumed that this was because everybody was leaving.

We fought our way through the crowds, stopping occasionally to admire the stark beauty of the architecture. My favourite part was the Presidential Lounge – an enormous room, exclusively reserved for the use of the Finnish president and their guests. It had originally been intended for the sole use of the Russian tsar but, following Finnish independence and the murder of the entire Romanov family by the Bolsheviks in a cellar in Yekaterinburg, this became a touch pointless.

The current Finnish president was a rather dull looking fellow called Sauli Niinistö who looked like the sort of man who expected his own lounge. The current prime minister, on the other hand, was a rather cool-looking woman called Sanna Marin who, at thirty-four years of age, was one of the world's youngest ever state leaders. She looked like she'd be more comfortable hitchhiking. She reminded me a lot of the fictional Finnish prime minister Minna Häkkinen, played by the glorious Sally Phillips in *Veep*, although *Veep* was filmed before Marin came to power . . .

Hang on, what was this all about? Was this further evidence of some mainstream media conspiracy to promote the idea of Finland existing, but they had gone too early with the sexy young prime minister planned by the Illuminati?

As we exited, on the other side of the station, I remembered the lyrics of 'West End Girls' by the Pet Shop Boys. Was this the Finland Station that they had name-checked?

No, it wasn't. The Finland Station was in St Petersburg and was, of course, where Lenin returned to Russia from exile in Switzerland ahead of the October Revolution. This explained the Pet Shop Boys' lyrics. I was very relieved. I just couldn't handle the Pet Shop Boys being a part of all this.

That evening, Stacey and I headed off to a posh restaurant called Natura where I made the schoolboy error of suggesting we go for the tasting menu.

We stumbled out four hours later, considerably poorer and, curiously, still hungry after a nine-course meal. We ended up in a local falafel chain and finally got something substantial to eat for the same price as one glass of wine at the restaurant.

As we munched on our falafels, we both agreed that whether Helsinki was real or not, it was one of the dullest places that either of us had ever visited.

We made an executive decision.

The Baltic states were just across the Gulf of Finland and we decided to do a day-trip to Tallinn, the capital of Estonia, the following day.

On the face of it, this was not going to help my investigation into the Finland-does-not-exist conspiracy, but I felt that we might get a different perspective by visiting a close neighbour. More importantly, it was supposed to be beautiful and it wasn't Helsinki.

So, the following morning found us bound for the ferry port on the west side of the city. Neither of us admitted it but we were both happy to be leaving Finland. We were excited at the prospect of visiting a new country that actually existed.

The ferry terminal was packed. There must have been at least two thousand people squeezed into the vast glass-fronted hall. I was worried that we might not get onto the ferry but, when it came into view, it was astonishingly big.

Everything suddenly became very un-Finnish as the crowd jostled and fought to get through the ticket machines. I jokingly mentioned to Stacey that these must be the actors whose shift had finished, desperate to get on and kick into R&R mode. The couple next to us gave us a curious look and I kept my thoughts to myself.

Once on board we found ourselves in the aft of the ferry looking out through a three-storey-high glass window. The queue for the bar was already massive, and groups were sitting around tables pouring vodka into soft drink bottles. It was a two-hour crossing and it appeared that most of our fellow passengers were on a mission to be unconscious by the time we docked.

It was about thirty minutes into the journey when something clicked. Wasn't there some big conspiracy theory to do with a ferry in the Gulf of Finland? With little else to do, I went online.

In 1994, the MS *Estonia*, a ferry from the same company as the one we were on, had sunk in between Tallinn and Stockholm, killing 852 people. It was one of the worst maritime disasters of the twentieth century.

As per usual, there were all sorts of theories as to what had happened. Some people thought it might have hit a Soviet submarine. Others blamed a shadowy organisation called the Felix Group who had supposedly sunk the ferry using explosives because it was carrying secret Russian military technology, smuggled out of the disintegrating Soviet Union to the West.

The wreck was eventually discovered on the bed of the Baltic Sea. In 1995, the Estonia Agreement was signed by Baltic countries, designating it as a sea grave and making it illegal for anybody to approach it. Curiously, the United Kingdom was the only non-Baltic country to sign the agreement, which raised some eyebrows.

This struck me as an interesting and not entirely ludicrous conspiracy theory. Obviously, sometimes, shit happens. Boats sink. People die. But, given the geopolitical climate at the time, what with the collapse of the Soviet Union and the chaos of the emerging new democracies in eastern Europe, the idea that some kind of covert post-Cold War was still being fought was not crazy. Look at the downing of Malaysia Airlines Flight 17 over eastern Ukraine in 2014 – oh god, I'm doing it now! – we all know it was approved by Moscow.

In 2019 a Swedish filmmaker named Henrik Evertsson used an underwater drone to film the wreckage. He discovered a 13-foot hole in the hull that appeared to indicate some sort of explosion. Evertsson made a documentary, *Estonia: The Find That Changes Everything*, in which he alleged that the ferry had been used by Swedish forces to smuggle Russian military technology and that MI6 had been involved.

A loud beep from my mobile phone brought me out of my conspiratorial reverie. It was a message from the Finnish Telecom Company . . .

Welcome to FINLAND. Now, all calls, texts and data you use in our Europe Zone will come out of your normal UK allowance.

Strangely, I had not received a text like this when we landed in Helsinki.

'What are you looking at?' asked Stacey.

'I'm just looking at info regarding the sinking of one of these ferries.'

'You are seriously weird,' she replied.

'Just doing my job, ma'am,' I said, trying to somehow channel Bruce Willis at the airport in *Die Hard 2*. I had no idea why I did this. I wondered whether I was mentally ill.

Stacey returned to looking at info on things to do in Tallinn while I tried to identify which of our fellow passengers might be MI6 agents.

After an hour and a half, the coast of Estonia came into view and we were soon docked and ready to disembark.

There was no passport control. We just strolled into Estonia unmolested.

We walked out of the port and through a park in which we found a memorial to the MS *Estonia* disaster. The sculpture was called *The Broken Line*. It consisted of two large metal arcs separated by some distance. I couldn't quite grasp the significance of the piece. I assumed it was something to do with the ferry route, as shown on a map and now broken because of the sinking. But, frankly, your guess is as good as mine, and I was still sulking with the art world after the visit to Kiasma the previous day.

We passed through the walls of the old city. A friend, who had been to Tallinn for work, had described the place as being like 'on the set of *Shrek*'. He was not far wrong. It was like a miniature Prague, a city that I was all-too familiar with, having been a diplomat there for a year back in 1990–1.

As we meandered through the cobbled streets, we were accosted by a couple of locals in medieval garb. I spotted their game immediately. They were trying to lure us into some sort of naff, ye olde lunch experience. I swatted them away and gazed at the poor saps who had been ensnared with ill-concealed contempt.

We eventually came to the main square. It was surprisingly small. It looked like it had been scaled down to fit into some Disney version of Tallinn. Every establishment had an annoying man waving a menu at you. It was like some Baltic Mykonos.

Nobody urged us to go into the Depeche Mode bar. So, in we went. It was, as the name suggested, a bar entirely devoted to the Basildon-born electronica pop group. It was so incongruous that we could not resist. It reminded me of the Stone Roses Bar in York. Lead singer Ian Brown, one of the nicest men in music and a guy whose video for 'Golden Gaze' I directed in the early 2000s, was now a fully paid up anti-vaxxer . . . which was depressing, as were the fading photographs of Depeche Mode that were hung around the bar. We had one drink but it turned out that, unlike one of the band's greatest hits, you just could get enough. We moved on.

We lunched in a Georgian tavern, tucked away from the main tourist drag. We were the only people there, but the food was surprisingly good and the owners, possibly shocked at having customers, could not have been nicer. One of them, a rather sultry-looking Georgian woman, came over and had a chat.

'How long are you in Tallinn?' she said, her deep brown eyes scanning us for clues.

'We are just over for the day from Finland,' said Stacey.

'Well, we think it's Finland,' I added, watching her face to gauge her reaction.

Unsurprisingly, she looked confused and a little concerned as to whether we were going to be able to pay the bill.

'I am investigating whether Finland exists or whether it was fabricated by Russia and Japan.'

I was aware that this was not likely to clarify matters much, but she actually seemed to relax at this new information.

'Russia? Nothing is real in Russia.'

She almost spat out the word. Russian–Georgian relations were not exactly cordial.

'Have you been to Finland?' I asked.

'No,' she said, guffawing. It was as though I'd just asked her whether a small dog could do trigonometry.

After lunch, we waddled about town until we came upon the Russian Embassy. The Russians were not popular in Estonia either. The Baltic states had long feared that they might be next on Putin's Russian Empire revival tour. The recent Russian invasion of Ukraine had not calmed their nerves.

Crowd barriers outside the building were covered in Ukrainian flags, poorly executed anti-Russian cartoons and hastily scribbled notes of abuse. A hundred feet up the road, the Swedish embassy was flying a giant Ukrainian flag.

Following a recent petition, the Estonian authorities had changed the name of the street so that any mail sent to the Russian Embassy had to be addressed to Vaba Ukraina 1 (1 Free Ukraine). This was not a good city in which to be Russian.

There were only so many gift shops selling wacky hats and felt animals that one could pop into. After a while I started to wonder whether the medieval house experience might be worth a go. That was our signal to leave Estonia. We had lasted four and a half hours.

We bought a fridge magnet and headed off back to the ferry, leaving the magical kingdom for a fictional country.

The ferry terminal was already heaving. Either most of our fellow day-trippers had also tired of the place, or the replacement shift of actors was ready to head over to the set of 'Finland'.

We took our place on the ferry. We appeared to be the only passengers not to join the bar queue. Clearly these were method actors getting into their roles as hard-drinking Finns. This was curious as, despite their reputation for drinking, Finland was only ranked thirty-first in the list of the world's hardest drinking countries. Estonia, I discovered, was currently ranked number one. Maybe the Finnish reputation for drinking was only because the actors playing Finns had brought their hobby on to set?

For the record, the United Kingdom is currently twenty-fourth. The lowest drinking countries in the world? Surprisingly, it's not Saudi Arabia. Joint lowest are Bangladesh, Kuwait, Libya, Mauritania and Somalia. Ryanair, unsurprisingly, did not fly to any of these destinations.

Back on the ferry I checked out the new cast.

There appeared to be a couple of popular types for the character designers of *Finland: The Movie*:

1. The Emo-Finns. Essentially unisex versions of Lisbeth Salander from the film *The Girl with the Dragon Tattoo*, they travelled in pairs and must have had separate bags just to carry their eyeliner.
2. The Lumberjacks. Small but impressively built men with bushy, unkempt beards squeezed into tight, stonewashed jeans and impossibly snug sports tops.
3. The Amazons. Tall, high-cheekboned women of indeterminate ages, let down at the final hurdle by bad pockmarked skin. Each Amazon was accompanied by an anonymous-looking man sporting a baseball cap and wraparound shades.

If I had to name a defining faux-Finn factor it would be weird-shaped beards for men and amateurish colour-dipped hair for women.

We were all sat beneath the giant windows in what looked like a vast floating greenhouse. At the front was a kids' area with soft cushions, beanbags, *SpongeBob SquarePants* on a loop and, very randomly, a fake awards-show background for photos.

We were right next to the stairs that descended down three tiers into SpongeBob Land. Every five minutes or so, a different middle-aged man sporting a Bluetooth headset would wander in, stand a little too close to us and survey the scene below like some curious ornithologist.

I hadn't seen anybody use a Bluetooth headset for years. Suddenly, they were everywhere. Were these the production coordinators, keeping an eye on the cast as they readied for the curtain going up? Were they all in contact with each other? Were we the only non-members of the 'production' on board? Was this all for us?

Once you allowed yourself to go all *Truman Show*, your mind started playing very weird tricks on you. There was a curiously logical chain to it all, should you choose to go down that path. I could see how these theories got traction among the gullible and the confused.

The cast traipsed past us on the way to or back from the bar. A hunchbacked father in a tracksuit was followed by his shuffling wife and their awkward, incel son. Just sometimes, out of the blue, there was a wild card. An incredible beauty, elegantly dressed, would walk past, accompanying their mutant family with a slightly bewildered look as to how they'd ended up in this situation.

I was reminded of one of my favourite scenes in literature: the court scene in E. M. Forster's *A Passage to India* in which Adela notices an Untouchable, whose physical beauty is so striking that it makes a mockery of human hierarchies.

The Court was crowded and of course very hot, and the first person Adela noticed in it was the humblest of all who were present, a person who had no bearing officially upon the trial: the man who pulled the punkah. Almost naked, and splendidly formed, he sat on a raised platform near the back, in the middle of the central gangway, and he caught her attention as she came in, and he seemed to control the proceedings. He had the strength and beauty that sometimes come to flower in Indians of low birth. When that strange race nears the dust and is condemned as untouchable, then nature remembers the physical perfection that she accomplished elsewhere, and throws out a god – not many, but one here and there, to prove to society how little its categories impress her.

Eventually the coast of Finland came into view. This time, I received no notification from Finnish Telecom. We docked and joined the inebriated mass of humanity, all attempting to squeeze through the small exit. Once again, there was no passport control and we sauntered back into Finland.

We hailed a cab. Our driver was a Somali who claimed to have lived in Finland for thirty years. I resisted the urge to ask him how it felt to come from the lowest-drinking nation on earth to this, the land of vodka and saunas.

We were due to fly home the following evening. This meant we had another day to fill in Helsinki. I could tell that Stacey was impressed by my dedication to my work, but I felt that it might be time do something that she might enjoy. We decided that, to get under the skin of the place, we really had to try a sauna. There were saunas everywhere. There was one in the airport, in parliament and in every apartment block. We were spoilt for choice. We had spotted a place under the big wheel with a sauna that looked interesting.

The Allas Sea Pool was situated right on the harbour front in Market Square. An elegant wooden building, it contained a restaurant and bar with terraces that overlooked a platform below on which sat a couple of outdoor swimming pools, a sea pool and three huts containing saunas. Around these were arranged rows of sun loungers in which people relaxed in between sessions.

We had brought nothing with us, but we could rent towels, robes and swimming costumes. Saunas are normally nude in Finland, so I was relieved to find that swimsuits were mandatory at the Allas Sea Pool.

I was handed my rental option – a tight pair of budgie-smugglers. I would have felt more comfortable nude. I politely declined and forked out for a normal pair of swim shorts at the store.

We were then asked whether we wanted mixed or single-sex changing rooms? I was all up for mixed. Sadly, this was kyboshed by Stacey. So, I braved the male changing room alone.

I entered to be confronted by a superabundance of Finnish buttocks and penises. Swimsuits might have been mandatory in the sauna but the locals were clearly making up for this fact in the changing rooms. Everybody lounged about chatting to each other, breathtakingly unselfconscious. It filled me with anxiety.

I remembered an incident a long time ago, at a very posh gym in west London. I had done a pathetic workout and found myself in the men's locker room along with Peter Mandelson and Jeremy Paxman. Mandelson, then the so-called 'Prince of Darkness' as Tony Blair's spin doctor, came out of the showers modestly sporting a pair of Speedos. Paxman, the intimidating presenter of *Newsnight*, whose mantra was allegedly 'why is this lying bastard fucking lying to me?', on the other hand was letting it all hang out. He sat, legs akimbo, with everything on display, haranguing some underling on the other end of a phone about who the guests were on that night's show.

I undressed and hung my stuff up in a locker. The unisex sauna was out of order and so I entered the men's one. It was small, with two wooden benches on each side of the hot coals which sat in front of large picture window overlooking the harbour. It only fitted eight people at a push.

I sat down on the empty bench to my left.

Opposite me was a man and his two kids, both around seven years old. The man stared at me and said something in Finnish. Rather than admit that I could not speak Finnish, I did this weird thing that I sometimes do in these situations. I replied in gobbledygook, in what I thought was a local-sounding accent. My only point of reference in this part of the world was the Swedish Chef from the Muppets. So, I started making short, 'hurdy gurdy, puuut the chicken in de pot'-style sounds.

The man just stared at me in bemusement before looking away.

The man got one of his kids to ladle some water from a bucket onto the hot stones. A wall of invisible heat started to boil both the wooden walls and my brain. The Finn stared at me defiantly, as though urging me to quit. I didn't flinch. He motioned for his kid to ladle another serving onto the stones. A second wave of third-degree burns enveloped the room. We both instinctively understood what was happening. This was now a sauna-off and there would only be one winner. The first guy to crack was a pussy and I was convinced that he was prepared to sacrifice his kids for victory.

I tried to look as though I was enjoying the rivers of sweat that were now flash-flooding my body. The man looked impassive. I decided to up the ante. I stood up. For a millisecond he thought I was quitting and started to smile. I picked up the ladle and poured water over the side of the basket, where the stones were bone dry. This served to create something close to a pyroclastic flow. It took everything I had not to start crying. I sat back down, my eyes closed tight, so as not to let any tears slip out.

When I eventually opened them, the man was still staring at me but he was sweating way more than before. One of his kids was howling softly while the other looked weirdly unresponsive.

The man shifted a heavy chain off of his hairy chest. I noticed, to my satisfaction, that there was the faint outline of a burn where it had been resting against the skin. Not long now, I thought.

Keen to retain momentum, I leaned over to pour more water. The man beat me to the bucket and moved it next to his feet. He had taken back control. He had also shown the first sign of weakness. For the next three minutes or so, our respective worlds were reduced to this tiny, sweaty struggle. We both locked eyes. Everything was about this primal battle. The only interruption was the odd yelp of discomfort from the weaker child.

Finally, the child made a break for the door. The father muttered something harsh, but he was gone. The other kid said something and the father growled and nodded. That kid got up and slid out. It was now just the man and me.

He was younger than me, forty-something. I noticed that he was starting to get very red. I was increasingly confident that I could beat him. I leaned over and grabbed the bucket. He did not resist. I poured all the remaining water onto the stones. The sauna became literally unbearable, I could barely breathe. The man got redder but still maintained his death stare. I closed my eyes and tried to count to a hundred. I needed to break this battle down into manageable chunks. I couldn't give my opponent any hope that I might break.

'One, two, three, four . . .'

It was so hot that my Apple Watch appeared to have gone into emergency shut down. A message flashed up:

It looks like you've fallen into a volcano?

Press:

1. Emergency SOS?

2. I'm OK.

'Five, six, seven, eight, nine, ten, eleven . . .'

I squinted through my eyes at my opponent. He was definitely struggling now. Technically, I had an advantage. I had no idea how long he had been in the sauna before I came in. We both knew, however, that none of this mattered. The first of us to hit that door was a loser.

'Twelve, thirteen, fourteen, fifteen . . .' I started to lose awareness of my surroundings. I was finding it difficult to count. I was not feeling too good. I stared at a spot on the wall opposite and tried to slow my breathing down. It was no good. I started to panic a little. That awful, familiar pre-sensation I used to get just before the onset of a panic attack. At least here, there was no wondering what had triggered it.

'Thirty-eight, forty-two, forty-three, seven, seven, seven . . .' I was in trouble. I had to get out. Something inside of me refused to give up. Maybe I was testing the *Truman Show* theory. Production would have to step in soon, surely. I started to feel drowsy and weirdly calm. I had passed through the worst bit. My body seemed to be adapting.

I suddenly felt someone shaking me. I opened my eyes. I looked up. The man was holding my arm and trying to pull me up. I had passed out.

'Are you OK? You must get out. It is too long for you . . .'

The man looked concerned. I tried to refuse but I really did have to get out. I stood up unsteadily and he guided me to the door. In a last pathetic effort, I made sure he exited first. Technically, I won. It was a Pyrrhic victory. He sat me down on a bench next to a large naked man whose silver back hair would have been the envy of any band of gorillas. The man brought me some water that I gulped down greedily.

I was feeling a little better.

'Thank you,' I said.

'No problem,' he said in perfect English.

'I don't know what happened,' I said.

'You are not used to the heat. You should be more careful.'

He was not gloating. He appeared very nice. Had I imagined our mortal battle?

'When you are ready, we swim in sea pool, this will recover you.'

I started to feel another challenge had been issued. I was too weak to react.

'Yes, let's do that,' I said.

I got up and slowly exited the hut. The sensation of the sea air on my face was lovely.

The man and I walked around the corner to where a hole had been cut into the decking. Stairs led down into the dark, cold

Baltic. He descended the stairs and submerged himself in the water. Like an automaton I followed him. As the water hit my chest, I realised quite how insanely cold it was. I nearly turned round but my body was not fully functional. It was somehow easier to keep descending. Then I was swimming in liquid ice. My shell-shocked body was desperately trying to work out what was going on.

And then, after about a minute, I felt great. I felt alive. Every nerve-ending tingled. I was hyper present. This felt good.

The man spotted my change of expression.

'Now it makes sense, right?' he smiled.

'It's amazing,' I spluttered.

I meant it.

'Where are you from?' asked the man.

'England.'

He nodded as though this explained a lot.

'Are you here for work or holiday?' he asked.

'Work. I'm a travel writer.'

'Aha. What are you writing about?' he asked.

I hesitated. I had already made enough of a fool of myself.

'I am trying to find out if Finland exists or not,' I said.

The man did not look surprised.

'Ah yes, I have heard about this thing,' he said, smiling.

'Have you?' I was surprised.

'Yes,' he said.

'And what do Finns think about it?' I asked.

'How do you know I am Finnish? I might be pretending. I could be Swedish,' he looked serious.

'Are you?'

'Am I what?' he asked.

'Finnish?' I asked.

'Maybe,' he grinned.

'Who knows what anyone is?'

The man smiled and made for the stairs. His kids were waiting for him.

I realised that I could not feel my toes.

I got out and went to find Stacey, who was lying on a lounger reading a book.

'Hey, you took your time. How was it?' she asked.

'Fine – it was . . . fine,' I said, slumping down next to her.

I was almost looking forward to my Ryanair flight home. Almost.

I was actually keen to get home. Finland, or wherever it was I'd been, had seen me dipping my toe into conspiracy waters. I was now ready to dive in. It was time to visit the conspiracy motherland.

2

Colorado

Everything you can imagine is real.
Pablo Picasso

If there is one unassailable truth out there, it is that America is the spiritual home of the conspiracy theory. For a deep dive into conspiracy theories, I had to go to America. And the only way to properly get under the skin of America was with a road trip.

The real beauty of a road trip is that, despite the supposed destinations, it is the unexpected things that you bump into along the way that are often the most revealing.

I was keen to check out as many different conspiracy locations as possible. I wanted to concentrate on places that I hadn't been to before. I pored over a map of the country, sticking pins in the various places I wanted to check out.

Eventually, I decided on the best route: Denver, Colorado, to Houston, Texas. It was a big drive, with some great destinations, including New Mexico, a state I'd long wanted to visit.

I couldn't wait to get cracking.

I popped into my barber's in Cheltenham for a quick trim before I set off. I like talking to him. He is well travelled and always keeps me up to speed on the latest Cheltenham gossip. I told him that I was off to the States the following day.

'What a shag. Having to get the COVID tests again?' he said, teasing my quiff into a perfect triangle.

'You what?'

'The COVID tests . . . my wife went to New York last week for work and nearly got caught out.'

'But that's all over?' I said, with a terrible sense of dread rising inside me.

'No, they've brought them back in,' he said.

I hit the internet and he was right. I'd thought that the necessary nightmare of COVID tests and travel was over. I was wrong. America had just decreed that COVID tests were now required again before travellers would be allowed entry.

It was 4 p.m. and I was off the following morning. I started to panic. I rang around the travel clinics and pharmacies in town but none of them had any availability for a couple of days.

In desperation, I drove to the pharmacy near me where I'd got a test the last time I'd travelled. They were closing when I got there but, after much pleading, I managed to persuade them to help me out. All I needed was a simple antigen test. But because people had been cheating and using other people's tests, you now needed a certificate confirming that somebody had witnessed you taking it.

Armed with the certificate I headed home to get ready for my departure. If I was a conspiracy theorist, I would have assumed that somebody was trying to prevent me from getting to America. On the other hand, if I was a conspiracy theorist, I probably wouldn't have taken the test as I would have thought the pandemic was a hoax.

I had another reason to be pleased I was travelling. Quite a long time ago, I had stupidly agreed to be on an open-top double-decker bus travelling up the Mall in London the following Saturday. I was supposed to be one of the famous faces representing the noughties in a parade to celebrate the decades of the Queen's rule for her Platinum Jubilee. This trip gave me a get-out.

Admittedly, I had been chuffed to have been asked. I also suspected that I would have loathed every minute.

It turned out that I was absolutely right. I had dodged a bullet. I avoided sharing a bus with the likes of Heston Blumenthal and Gok Wan. I was not really made of the right stuff to be a D-list national treasure. I was happy to have an excuse to get out of the situation.

I could have used the occasion to find out a little more about the death of Princess Diana. Was the Duke of Edinburgh in the Alma Tunnel in Paris on the night of 31 August 1997? Had he been armed with a military-grade laser light that he used to blind the driver of the car carrying Dodi Fayed and Princess Diana?

I felt that it was unlikely that the Hairy Bikers, Mo Farah or money-saving guru Martin Lewis – some of the other luminaries that I would have been sharing the bus with – would have any inside information. You could never be totally sure, however. Maybe at the party afterwards, in the gardens of Buckingham Palace, the royal family would slip up. I might get a glimpse of carelessly exposed lizard skin. Maybe a sweaty Prince Andrew would give something away as he proffered trays of Pizza Express dough balls to the assembled glitterati?

Sadly, we would never know. This conspiracy tourist was bound for the USA.

I got to Heathrow and, having gone through security, settled myself down for my usual pre-flight ritual at the seafood bar: half a bottle of champagne and a prawn cocktail.

I'd started this poncey travel ritual a long time ago. It was so that, in the case of some terrible plane crash, my last meal on earth would not have been microwaved chicken and potato croquettes washed down with a mini can of Coca-Cola.

It had always been expensive, but it was now eye-wateringly ludicrous. I calculated that I was served one prawn fewer and charged one pound more every year. I still clung on to the tradition.

It was my last-gasp attempt at squeezing some form of glamour out of air travel. Pretty soon, it would be cheaper to fly first class than pay for this meal, but I was a creature of habit.

Normally, nothing excited me more than the idea of a road trip. This time, however, I had to admit to being a little road-weary. I'd just come off a three-month UK tour in which I'd driven to almost every part of the country. A road trip from Weston-super-Mare to Hull didn't quite have the same exotic excitement that an American equivalent would. I was pretty confident that the moment I got driving in the States, I would perk up.

I was starting in Denver, the moment I landed. For some reason Denver International Airport had more conspiracy theories about it than any other building I could think of. No serious list of conspiracy destinations was complete without DIA (as the airport is commonly known) on it.

I had been to Denver before. My memory of it was, to be honest, hazy at best. Marijuana had been legalised for medical use in Colorado back in 2000 and for recreational use since

2012. Weed had become a major part of the state's economy ever since. It had attracted a special type of tourist.

Upon checking into my downtown hotel, I'd been given a vaporiser at reception. Once in my room, I'd taken full advantage of it. I could remember very little of the next three days. I had a recurring anxiety dream about being in a restaurant where the walls were festooned with animal heads. I was alone and eating rattlesnake, prairie oysters and several other unknown items. I'm pretty sure this actually happened.

I think I'd ended up on some sort of micro-brewery tour. By that time, I was so high that I was eventually asked to leave as I couldn't stop talking.

So, for all intents and purposes, I was visiting Denver for the first time. I wondered whether excessive consumption of Mary Jane, Reefer, Ganja, Blaze, Stinkweed, Bud, Kush, 420, Broccoli, Cripple, Jefferson Airplane, Maui Wowie (insert your favourite moniker here) and a belief in conspiracy theories went hand in hand. I felt it must have some sort of link.

Back on the plane I was given my aeroplane meal. Chicken, rice and beans. A stale bread roll, an inedible salad and a tiny tub of Loseley ice cream. This could have been my last meal on earth had I not re-mortgaged my house for the seafood bar experience. I felt smug.

I ignored most of the meal but toyed with the ice cream. I don't have a sweet tooth, but I was intrigued. I removed the lid before wondering what to do next. How to eat the ice cream, should I wish to do so? Sure, there was the paper-thin plastic cutlery, but technically, I would have already used that on the poison chicken. The thinking behind all airline cutlery breaking on first bite was so that you didn't use it to hijack the plane.

Personally, should I have been hijack-inclined, I would have forced the pilot to eat the salad unless we diverted, immediately, to Hawaii.

I briefly considered just scooping the ice cream out with my fingers. Since the economy section of most planes was referred to by air crew as 'the zoo' it would not have raised many eyebrows.

I decided against it, however, and replaced the top onto the tiny tub. As I did so, I felt the lid shift slightly in a curious fashion. I touched it. There was something underneath the top of the lid. I looked around me nervously.

The gentleman next to me was engrossed in one of those endless Keanu Reeves action movies that were almost a sub-genre of cinema in their own right. The apex of these was *The Matrix*, a film that, personally, left me cold. A lot of conspiracy heads and stoners (Venn diagram time) seemed to have mistaken the movie for a documentary.

Whenever I ventured into any conspiracy-related topic online, my comments would be inundated with 'Red Pill/Blue Pill' references. According to Morpheus, the rebel leader in the movie: 'You take the blue pill, the story ends, you wake up in your bed and believe whatever you want to believe. You take the red pill, you stay in Wonderland and I show you how deep the rabbit hole goes.'

Conspiracy theorists were keen exponents of the red pill.

It seemed quite weird to me that they might take their inspiration from a mainstream Hollywood movie. If it actually was subversive and 'the truth', then surely, by their own logic, it would never have been allowed to be made?

To my right, a lady was watching Ricky Gervais make fun of transgender people and the idea that women could be funny.

Ricky Gervais was, of course, being ironic. The crowd were also laughing ironically. Irony appeared to be doing a lot of heavy lifting . . .

I slipped my finger under the rim of the tub. It came away easily. Looking around to check that nobody was watching, I lifted the thin round piece of cardboard off the tub top. There was a curious makeshift wooden spoon hidden within it.

Who had put this there? How had they known that I would need one? What strange force had guided me to discover it?

I ate the ice cream in a deeply pensive mood. This Loseley organisation was up to something and I intended to find out what that was.

I listened to *This American Life*, one of my favourite podcasts. Fortuitously, it was all about school shootings. It described how conspiracy theorists like Alex Jones and his crazily popular *InfoWars* had labelled the parents of a mass school shooting as crisis actors. He claimed that the kids involved were actually in the Bahamas on holiday.

People close to victims of mass shootings were warned that, should they talk about their experiences in public, they would be trolled remorselessly online by people claiming that they were liars.

How had the world got to this? How could a clearly deluded individual such as Alex Jones be taken seriously by anybody? Jones lived in Austin, Texas, and I decided to do my best to try to track him down.

Colorado had suffered its fair share of mass shootings, Columbine being the big one, in 1999. There had also been the hideous cinema shooting in Aurora, a kind of satellite city of Denver. In 2012, a guy dressed in tactical clothing entered the cinema during a midnight screening of *The Dark Knight Rises*. He set off tear gas grenades before opening fire. He killed twelve people and wounded seventy.

As it so happened, I was going to be staying very close to said cinema. I had booked a random Airbnb somewhere in the boonies as there was some sort of convention in downtown Denver and all the hotels were either booked or crazily overpriced.

I wasn't expecting great things but I hoped that it might be the sort of area in which I might stumble upon a conspiracy theorist or two.

The plane landed in Denver. I switched on my phone only to get the news that there had been a school shooting in a town called Uvalde, in Texas. Nineteen schoolchildren and two teachers were dead. No doubt Alex Jones and his underlings would be getting down to work slandering the dead even though Uvalde was near Austin, Texas, where Jones lived.

I deplaned and passed through immigration. Once I'd picked up my bags, I got to work. I was in Denver International Airport, ground zero for a plethora of conspiracy theories.

The stories started from the moment construction commenced. DIA was opened on 28 February 1995, more than a year behind schedule and supposedly 2 billion dollars over budget. People began to ask why construction had taken so long and what all that money had been spent on. The finished airport was the largest in the United States, taking up an area of over 53 square miles and it had the longest runway for public use in the country. Why would Denver, of all places, need an airport of this magnitude?

Conspiracy theories started to pop up everywhere. DIA, the theorists claimed, was clearly the intended destination for the

Illuminati when the rapture kicked off. An anonymous construction worker claimed that the delays were actually due to a vast network of underground buildings and tunnels. Rumours abounded that these tunnels linked DIA to places like Cheyenne Mountain, the vast underground complex that hosted the North American Aerospace Defense Command (NORAD), Space Force and various other secret US government institutions.

Cheyenne Mountain was outside Colorado Springs, about a hundred miles from Denver. These tunnels, if they existed, had to be on a massive scale. People asserted that the tunnels were prepped and ready to accommodate the entire global elite. This would allow them to survive whatever cataclysm it was that they anticipated.

Another claim popular with conspiracy theorists was to do with the amount of fibre-optic lines used. There were enough, supposedly, for an entire city. There were even rumours that Teflon-coated fibreglass had been used underground to counteract any potential ground-penetrating radar.

My particular favourite was that, when viewed from the air, the DIA runway network resembles a swastika. I checked this by looking at the airport on the map on my phone. I could just about see what they were driving at, but I was not convinced. You'd have had to have consumed quite a lot of the local wacky baccy to make that leap.

Also, just as with the Suez Canal ship, were you to be building a secret base in which to hide the New World Order, would you really build it in the shape of a swastika? Call me old fashioned, but this would not be the most effective way of hiding it. Maybe it was a double bluff. Maybe it was hiding in plain sight. Maybe it was nonsense.

Further conspiracy theories swirled around a time capsule that was buried in the airport. It was not supposed to be opened until 2094. The capsule was covered by a dedication marker that clearly contained Masonic symbols. It also mentioned something called 'The New World Airport Commission'. I had to admit, it was a very strange-looking dedication plaque.

Supposedly, the capsule contained a credit card, a Colorado flag, newspapers from the day the airport opened and some random items representing the year 1994.

What would represent 1994, I wondered? Here were my suggestions:

1. The closing of Aldwych tube station.
2. The discovery of the chemical element darmstadtium.
3. The sinking of the MS *Estonia*. (Coincidence? I think not.)
4. O. J. Simpson's low-speed highway chase.
5. Kurt Cobain committing suicide.
6. BBC Radio 5 being closed and replaced with BBC Radio 5 Live.

It is unlikely that these were the things actually commemorated in the time capsule, but you never know.

The Masonic symbols did intrigue me.

I'd received a message a few days earlier on Facebook. Would I like to come and look around the Cheltenham Masonic Lodge? I was vaguely aware of it, a handsome windowless building, not five minutes' walk from my house. I'd long wondered what the building was until, one day, I'd spotted the sign on the front door telling me that this was a Masonic Lodge.

Intrigued, I agreed and two days later I was outside, knocking on the door. The man who had messaged me opened it up. He looked like a roadie for Genesis and was very friendly. As I entered, I asked him why he'd contacted me of all people? He replied that he knew I loved history and thought I might like to have a look around.

He was right. I knew pretty much nothing about the Freemasonry except for the Monty Python jokes. It was all silly walks and secret handshakes. I'd also read something about them using secret phrases like 'the great architect' to let a judge know that they were a Mason. Apart from that, I knew nothing.

My guide walked me through the building. We peeked into a large dining hall with decorated shields on the wall. We then entered a robing room, where members apparently got changed for their ceremonies. I nodded politely but, so far, so uninteresting.

We climbed up the stairs to the first floor and entered a vast, high-ceilinged ceremonial room. It had a black and white tiled stone floor, wooden pews, various ceremonial objects and a large gold and red-velvet throne surrounded by red velvet curtains. Now this was more like it. This was the kind of thing I'd been hoping for.

'Sit in the big chair, if you want,' said my guide.

So, I did. He took a photo of me in it. It was supposedly for me but I couldn't help wondering whether that photo would show up somewhere one day alongside the headline ' "HELLO, NO I'M A MASON!" Dom Joly's secret Masonic shame.'

My guide started to give me a basic explanation of Freemasonry.

You were not asked to join. You had to ask to join. He told me that they raised a lot of money for charity and that you gained more secret knowledge as you rose through the ranks. I tried to find out what some of this secret knowledge was. He told me that this would ruin my experience were I to join.

I assured him, in no uncertain terms, that this would never happen. I was totally unclubbable. Like Groucho Marx, I would never join any organisation that would have me as a member.

Perhaps feeling that I was implying that the Cheltenham Lodge was beneath me, he told me, in slightly hushed tones, about a special showbiz lodge based in London.

'It's got a lot of members who are in your world,' he said.

'I always wondered how Keith Lemon kept on working,' I joked.

He looked back blankly at me.

'There is a famous comedian in that lodge,' he said.

'Oh – who is it? Is it Jimmy Carr? I bet it's Jimmy Carr – I bloody knew it.'

I was convinced I was right. It was either him or Bill Bailey.

'No, it's . . . oh, what's his name?' My guide wracked his brain for the name.

'Is he a TV comedian? A stand-up?' I asked, trying to help him remember.

'No, he's . . . you know, my mate Chalky . . .'

I stumbled for a moment. I had no idea who his mate Chalky was. Then I clicked.

'Oh, you mean Jim Davidson?' I said.

'Yes, that's it, Jim Davidson.'

I now knew for absolute certain that I would never become a Freemason.

'Do you consider yourselves to be a secret society?' I asked.

'We are a society with secrets,' he replied, trying to sound enigmatic.

'Oh,' I said.

We went back downstairs to a bar that looked like it belonged in a working men's club. I was offered a drink but I politely declined. I was still none the wiser about what this was really all about.

'Come to our Christmas lunch,' my guide said, smiling.

He was a nice enough fellow, but I loathed Christmas enough already without turning up to some festive function to find Jacob Rees-Mogg dressed up in an apron burning pictures of the poor.

I was sure this was not what would actually happen, but the whole 'secret society with weird rituals and outfits' thing felt like kindling to conspiracy fire-starters.

Back in Denver, I briefly considered sending a photograph of the time capsule to my guide back in England. Maybe he would know what they symbolised? I decided against it. He might think I was up for the Christmas lunch.

The walls of DIA were also a source of concern to conspiracy theorists. Well, not the walls themselves, but what hung on them. The artwork in the airport was supposed to contain secret messages to those in the know.

The one that really freaked them out was a 28-foot mural called *Children of the World Dream of Peace*.

The name certainly didn't sound too scary. It was by the Texan artist Leo Tanguma. He had four pieces hanging in the airport.

On first inspection, I had to admit, it was a bit weird. In the mural, a scary, gasmask-wearing, Soviet-looking soldier, brandishing an AK-47 and a large sabre, appeared to be trying to stab a white dove while some babies slept on rubble. To the side, a crying woman cradled a dead baby.

It was certainly a bold choice for public art but nothing that would trouble anybody who had ever been to an art gallery.

The conspiracy theorists had suggested that the sabre being brandished by the solider was the Masonic Shriners logo. Tanguma firmly denied any such links. After the first criticisms of his work started to be aired, he attempted to explain the meaning of the piece.

'I have children sleeping amid the debris of war and this warmonger is killing the dove of peace, but the kids are dreaming of something better in the future.'

If he had left it there, then he might possibly have calmed fevered minds. Tanguma went further, however. He claimed that the piece represented 'global catastrophe bringing the nations of the world together'.

He should have known not to use the word 'global' around conspiracy theorists. It was a major trigger. They saw this as a clear sign that the mural was part of some New World Order agenda in which global elitists orchestrated chaos in order to soft-sell a one-world government.

Naomi Klein wrote about a similar idea in her book *The Shock Doctrine*. She called it Disaster Capitalism. This was, Klein wrote, when neo-liberal free-market policies were foisted onto countries that had just undergone upheaval (whether human-made or a natural disaster) and were too distracted to resist or to propose alternatives.

This worldview definitely had some serious proponents. It was just the idea that the people involved would then commission an artist to paint a massive 28-foot clue on the wall of their secret base that was built in the shape of a swastika . . .

It seemed rather unlikely.

Denver International Airport authorities appeared to have a sense of humour as, in 2019, they installed an interactive talking gargoyle.

'Welcome to Illuminati Headquarters . . . I mean the Denver airport,' the gargoyle would electronically whisper to confused visitors.

Was this now a triple bluff?

I needed to pick up my rental car. It would hopefully take me all the way from Denver to Houston, from where I was catching a flight back home. I hopped on a shuttle bus and left the not-that-creepy airport. As we were about to exit the grounds, on our way to the rental compound, I spotted the final and possibly most intriguing of subjects of mass speculation for conspiracy theorists. Blucifer.

This was a 32-foot statue of a blue bucking horse, officially called *Blue Mustang*. It was the unofficial mascot of Denver International Airport and known to everyone as Blucifer. The nickname came from the pale blue colour of the statue and its seriously spooky, glowing red eyes. It looked batshit crazy at night.

The artist responsible for this piece, Luis Jiménez, said that he chose the blue colour in honour of the wild spirit of the Old West. I had no idea what this meant. Why would a blue horse represent the Old West? I wanted to contact Jiménez and ask him. This, unfortunately, was not possible, as he had died.

He was killed . . . by Blucifer. This was not a conspiracy theory. This was fact.

In 2006, while working on his creation, which was already eleven years behind schedule, a large section of the piece fell on Jiménez, pinning him to a support beam and severing his femoral artery. He bled to death on the floor of his studio. Blucifer was completed by his two sons and was finally unveiled in 2008, thirteen years late and at a cost of 650,000 dollars.

There was definitely more than a little weirdness in this airport. Combine that with excessive consumption of weed and it was little wonder that people had started getting strange ideas.

I drove to my Airbnb. It was one of those anonymous houses on a nondescript street in a seemingly endless housing development that you saw whenever Hollywood did a movie in the suburbs. I had to take a photograph of the street and the number as, a couple of drinks in, I knew I would never find the place again. Everything was identical. The only difference was the types of cars parked outside.

There was nobody there when I arrived. I pressed the video bell and a discombobulated voice answered and gave me a code for the front door. Once inside, I found a key hanging on my bedroom door. I let myself in. The room was small, had no windows and was almost entirely filled by a large bed. There were no decorations whatsoever. I got a brief idea of what life must have been like for John McCarthy when he was held hostage in Lebanon back in the day.

I didn't want to stay a minute longer than I needed to in this place. I showered, got changed and headed outside to wait for the Uber that I'd ordered. I wanted to get into downtown Denver as soon as possible. I needed people around me.

If had to cast my Uber driver, Matt, in a movie, I'd have gone with the role of Colorado Stoner Dude. He drove a messy old car, had long unkempt hair and he was a talker. A big talker. Normally I'd hate this but on this sort of trip it was gold dust. Matt was ex-US Air Force and now a wannabe actor. We got chatting.

'What do you do, man?' he asked.

'It's complicated . . . I'm a comedian,' I replied.

'No shit? I'm an actor, dude. You got any roles for me?' Matt was in networking mode.

'Is there a lot of acting work here in Denver? How come you're not in LA?' I asked.

'Everybody goes to LA, man. I figured I'd be a big fish in small town. *Art of War*, man. Sun Tzu.'

'I'm not sure that's a quote from Sun Tzu,' I said.

Matt laughed.

'Ha, no, that's not a quote but it's the same attitude, man. That guy was deep. The greatest victory is the one which requires no battle. Now that is a quote.' Matt smiled at me triumphantly.

'So, you have the battlefield to yourself here in Denver?' I said.

'Totally, man.'

'And, is there a lot of filming going on round here?' I asked.

'No, not much.' Matt looked sad for a second. 'When did you get to the States?' he continued.

I sensed he was wanting to change the subject.

'Today. I literally just landed a couple of hours ago.'

'Did you see Blucifer? That shit is crazy evil. If you go out there at night it has Satan's eyes, man, they look right through you. It's scary as fuck, man.'

Matt knew a friend of a friend who had worked on the airport construction.

'I don't know, dude. They were getting waaaaay too many materials for what was being planned. I've heard people talk about all sort of weird shit out there, underground prisons, alien autopsies. Tunnels, man. So many tunnels.'

As he waxed lyrical on a multitude of theories, the car stereo pumped out a steady musical bed of Guns N' Roses, Slipknot and AC/DC.

'I know a dude who wanted to blow up Blucifer because he blamed it for some bad shit that happened in his life.' Matt was looking less and less at the road, which was beginning to concern me. 'He'd lost some money to some dude and then his girl had left him. Anyways, he decided that all this voodoo was happening to him on account of Blucifer and so he was going to blow the thing up.'

Matt had turned around and was looking at me while the car careered down the freeway towards downtown Denver, whose high rises I could now see.

'Oh . . . right, and what happened?' I asked, pretending to see something exciting on the road ahead of us in an attempt to get him to turn round.

'I don't know, man. His dad was in construction so he had access to explosives and shit and he was fully going to do it.' Matt had thankfully turned his gaze back to the road ahead but was now talking to me in the rear-view mirror.

'So, what happened?' I looked at Matt and noticed that his eyes were quite dilated.

'What happened to what?' Matt looked a little confused.

'What happened to the plan to blow up Blucifer?'

'Oh right . . . this guy had access to explosives because he had a dad who was something in construction . . .'

'Yeah, you told me that already,' I said, smiling patiently.

'Oh, did I? Cool.' Matt smiled back and we kept on driving towards Denver in silence.

Finally, I couldn't take it any more.

'Sorry, Matt . . . so what happened?'

'Happened to what?' replied Matt, who I was now not certain should be operating a vehicle.

'The guy. Who wanted to blow up Blucifer . . .' I said, slowly.

'OH! Sorry, dude. Yeah, no, he didn't go through with it.'

'Why not?'

'I don't know. He likes to blaze so . . . probably forgot all about it. I never asked him actually. You want me to ring him now?'

I thought about this for a moment. I was loath to distract Matt any further from his driving but this sounded like a good story and this was why I was here.

'Umm, yeah sure, that would be interesting, if you don't mind,' I said.

Matt picked up his phone and started scrolling through his telephone numbers. His wide eyes now none too interested in the road. Finally, after what seemed like an eternity, he found the number and punched it in. The phone clicked onto the car speaker and I heard the soft American ringtone. After three rings the phone was answered.

'Yo, who is this?' said a very slow, stoned voice.

'Yo, MJ. It's Matt.'

'Matt?' MJ sounded none too confident in who Matt was.

'Yeah, Matt. Stop playing, dude. How goes it?'

'Who is this?'

'Yo, fuck you, man, it's Matt. I'm driving an English dude right now who is interested in Blucifer and shit and I was telling him about you planning to blow that shit up,' Matt laughed.

MJ stayed silent.

'What the fuck you talking about? Who is this?'

'It's MATT, man – from Lakewood!' Matt was looking at me despairingly in the mirror.

'Yo, what you asking about that shit for?' MJ was now a little more alert and seemed suspicious.

'Because I've got this English dude – he's a writer and he is interested about conspiracies, dude. I told him about Blucifer and shit.'

'What you telling him about me, man?' MJ's voice was rising slightly.

'Nothing, dude, chill. I was just telling him the story about you and Blucifer man. Nothing heavy, just wanted to get the end of the story for my man.' Matt was shaking his head at me in the mirror.

'There is no story – that is the end of the story.' MJ was definitely coming down fast off a previously pleasant high.

'No worries, dude. We were just talking and this story came up, man—'

Matt was interrupted by MJ: 'You are a fucking asshole, man. Don't be talking about this shit, man. What is wrong with you?' MJ hung up.

Matt stared out of the windscreen for a while and we drove in awkward silence. Finally, he looked into the mirror and our eyes met again.

'I guess he didn't want to talk about it.'

'Yeah, I got that,' I said, smiling.

'But . . . I don't think he blew it up . . .'

'No, me neither, because as I said, I just saw Blucifer today when I was at the airport.'

Matt nodded at this but I wasn't totally sure he had taken it all in. Thankfully, we had come off the freeway and were now driving into downtown Denver, past the baseball stadium. I asked Matt to stop and drop me off. He pulled to the side of the road and parked up.

'Pleasure to meet you, man. Good luck with your book and shit, man.'

'Thank you. I hope your friend wasn't too angry.'

'What? Oh no, man, it's all good. Remember, everything you can imagine is real.'

'Is that Sun Tzu?' I asked.

'No man, that's Picasso.' Matt smiled, a big lazy smile, and pulled away from the kerb.

I was alone in Denver.

I traipsed around downtown for a while, getting my bearings. Denver is the Mile High City and sits on a large plateau with snow-capped peaks visible in the distance. The first thing I noticed were the homeless. It was, in places, post-apocalyptic. Desperate, down-and-out human beings lay on the pavement in the cold shadows of the vast, anonymous, glass edifices that towered above them.

Walking in and out of the shadows, the temperature would peak and plummet dramatically. I ended up at place called the Water Grill, with the inevitable wall of TV screens showing live sport of all flavours. If your conversation should dry up, you could just nurse a beer and make occasional man noises at what was occurring.

Back home in the UK it was day one of the four-day Platinum Jubilee celebrations. The only non-sport screen showed Boris Johnson and his wife, Carrie-Antoinette, being booed as they entered St Paul's. When a Conservative prime minister has lost the Jubilee crowd they've lost the country. Boris was a dead man waddling.

Outside, through the glass, as if in some weird silent movie, gangs of marauding baseball fans stumbled over the homeless as they attempted to make their way towards the stadium. I felt happy in the Grill. In there, everything was OK. I could order lovely seafood and drink craft beer and ignore the real world. But this was not why I'd come to the States.

The next morning I awoke, showered and ordered another Uber to take me into town. Uber, I soon realised, was going to be a valuable research tool. My driver this time was Ernesto, a black guy who almost instantly informed me that he was a swing voter. I hadn't asked him a thing up to this point so it was a curious ice-breaker.

'It's just that, when I meet tourists, they always want me to get into Trump's face as they assume that I'm not a Trump guy.'

'So, are you a Trump guy?' I asked him.

'No, man, I'm not anybody's guy but I voted for him in 2016.'

We sat in silence for a while as I took this in. I was rankling at the 'tourist' moniker but, in a sense, that was what I was. Eventually, I couldn't help myself. I just had to know.

'But why did you vote for him?' I was genuinely bewildered by anybody who had made this decision.

'I don't know, man. I was just sick of the usual suspects and this guy was fresh; he tells it like it is.'

God, I hate that expression. It is such nonsense. It reminds me of a fabulous cartoon that shows a flock of sheep in a field beneath a large billboard. The billboard has a picture of a wolf in a suit, with the words 'I am going to eat you' next to him. 'He tells it like it is,' says one sheep to another. Online, the word 'sheep' or 'sheeple' is often bandied about for those who have no truck with conspiracy theories.

I didn't have the stomach for a Trump debate, so I asked Ernesto what he felt about conspiracies. Had he heard anything regarding Denver? This opened the floodgates.

'The airport, tell me you know about the airport? It's full of devils. That place is evil central.' Ernesto was quite animated on this subject.

'Where did you find out about this?' I asked.

'The devils? My eyes man. Did you land at that place? Did you not look around you? There's so much weird shit going down.' Ernesto, unlike Matt, kept his eyes fixed on the road ahead.

I told him about the guy who wanted to blow up Blucifer.

'Fuck yes, man. I'd blow up that shit sooner than never. That's not normal shit.' He was agitated but still laser-focused on his driving. I didn't want to, but I had to mention the Trump thing.

'But, Trump, as president, wouldn't he be in on all this stuff so he would know about all the secrets there?'

'No, man . . . Deep State. You know about Deep State?' His eyes flickered nervously in the rear-view mirror as though he might have said too much.

'Yes, I know about Deep State. It's supposedly a secret network of power that operates independently from the official government for their own nefarious purposes.'

I was quite chuffed with my explanation; Ernesto less so. I think he was quite freaked out by my knowledge of such highly classified material.

'Right . . . so you know about it, how?'

'I read about it online,' I answered.

There was quite a long pause as we both stared out of our respective windows. I decided to push on.

'The thing I don't get about Deep State is that surely Trump, by becoming president, is now part of it all?'

'No, man, he is the very thing they hate. He upset that shit. He bucked the system.' Ernesto smiled admiringly.

'But then, all of the other presidents were in on it, so it wasn't Deep State back then? Did Deep State only exist to fight Trump?' I was genuinely confused.

'Yes, man, they hated Trump as he wouldn't play ball. Deep State wanted to get rid of him and return control to themselves.'

'I don't want to be awkward, but you mean before Trump it wasn't Deep State; it was just "The State". But they went deep when Trump came in?'

'Of course, man. They hated Trump because he wasn't going to play by their rules.'

'So do you think Deep State made him lose the election?' I was in proper investigative journalist mode now.

'I don't know, man. I'm not sure he lost. I didn't vote for him this time but I think there were strange forces in charge.'

I nodded while I tried to take this information in.

'You heard about Columbine?' Ernesto was off on another tangent. I couldn't keep up.

'Of course,' I said.

'I went to Columbine. That was my high school.'

This was too good. I briefly considered returning my rental car and just taking Ubers all the way to Houston. These driver chats were insane. In the interests of full disclosure, however, I had taken a deeply dull Uber back to my Airbnb the night before. The guy had not said a single word.

'You were there when it happened?' I asked.

'No, man. That was way before my time. But they knew that shit was going to happen and they didn't stop it.'

'Sorry, who knew?' I asked.

'The government,' he replied.

'Deep State, or the government?' I asked.

'The government. They wanted it to happen so that they could take away the guns.' Ernesto was the most agitated I'd seen him. This was clearly a big issue for him.

'But surely you don't want guns in a school, right?' I knew that I sounded so British.

'Ha, we used to do school shooter drills at Columbine – can you imagine that? It was a bit fucking late, man. Hiding under a desk ain't going to stop no kid with an AR-15.'

'So, you want to arm the teachers?' I asked.

'I don't give a shit no more. I'm not relying on nobody to protect me. I'm self-sufficient.'

He looked at me and indicated down towards his seat. I looked over and he had raised his polo shirt to reveal a holster and a black handgun.

'If you can't beat them, join them, right?' said Ernesto.

'Is that . . . legal?' I asked, trying to sound like I was cool either way.

'Sure, it's legal, but if it was illegal the bad guys would still have them so I'd carry one even if it wasn't. Shit's gone crazy.'

I sat back in my seat and said nothing as I watched Denver wake up. It was about 8 a.m. and the homeless zombie army was on the move. They were packing their makeshift cardboard beds up into shopping trolleys as they were moved on by security guards preparing the entrances for the office workers.

I wanted chile verde, a Denver staple. I got Ernesto to drop me off at a diner on Curtis. The interior was peak Americana and rapidly filling up with a combination of workmen and delegates attending the convention. I knew this because they all wore oversized lanyards and travelled in packs. I grabbed a window booth and ordered.

Five minutes later, my food arrived. What looked like a ten-egg omelette accompanied a mound of hash browns, all covered in chile verde. This had to be my only meal of the day, or I would not survive the trip. The excess of food on every American plate not only accounted for the XXXL size of a lot of the population but also harked back to some primal fear. Possibly it was some subconscious return to hard times in the old country, or buried memories of the Great Depression. In America, food had to be plentiful first, tasty second.

I tackled my breakfast while trying not to stare at the hobos shuffling past the windows of the diner. Unlike the subjects in Edward Hopper's *Nighthawks*, possibly the most evocative artistic depiction of diner-life ever, we were Dayhawks. Nevertheless, I still felt strangely detached from the world outside. Waitresses floated around removing half-eaten plates from tables and refilled mugs with the bland filter coffee that was on perma-boil in places like these.

My phone beeped. It was a reply from a guy called Jeff Peckman. I'd sent him an email before I flew over. He was a local who had once attempted to create an 'Extraterrestrial Affairs Commission' within the Denver City government. This had been for the purpose of preparing the city for visits from

extraterrestrials. I'd come across his name when I'd been looking at all things Denver. I'd messaged him on a whim. He was
happy to meet up. We agreed to meet at a café in place called
Monument on my way down to Colorado Springs the following day.

A classic destination for a conspiracy tourist would be Area
51, a highly classified US Air Force base in the Nevada desert.
The road past it is known as the Extraterrestrial Highway and
has been something of a Mecca for conspiracy heads. But I'd
driven through there before and so had decided to focus on
Roswell, a place I'd never visited and another magnet for ufolo-
gists. I felt that a chat with Jeff would be a good way to kick off
this particular angle of exploration.

But first, I had to explore Denver. Barely able to move after
breakfast, I waddled out of the diner and into the long, cold
shadow-valleys of the high rises. Despite the sun shining, it
was freezing.

I probably needed to walk for five hours or so to work off
breakfast, but I couldn't resist the temptation of an electric scooter
parked right outside. It was owned by Lime, one of the many
companies competing for dominance in this new travel arena.

These scooters had taken over modern cities. I scanned the
barcode using the app and I was off.

A Limey on a Lime.

I zoomed around for a while to get my bearings. I found the
State Capitol that sits on a hill overlooking the state capital.
Denver is rather unusual for an American state in having its larg-
est and most well-known city as the capital. This is not normally
the case: Albany, New York; Sacramento, California; Tallahassee,
Florida, etc.

I lost my way a bit, suddenly finding myself in a rather insalubrious area where dodgy-looking men on corners started staring at me a little too hard. This is common in America. You can go from safe zone to no-go zone in a block if you don't know what you're doing. I didn't know what I was doing and it must have been very obvious. I looked like easy meat. I made my escape with as much speed and decorum as possible.

Once back in the long shadows of downtown, I dropped off my scooter and continued on foot. What I was really hoping to come across was a 'Birds Aren't Real' billboard.

These had been popping up all over the States and were the work of Bird Truthers. This was a spoof organisation mocking conspiracy theories by claiming that the United States government 'extinguished' more than 12 billion birds between 1959 and 1971, and replaced them with surveillance drone replicas. These drones now watch us every day. Some of the supposedly 'historic' details of the conspiracy in the movement's manifesto were wonderful:

It is believed that the initial plan for killing all of the birds and replacing them with flying cameras was thought up one weekend in May of 1956. Dulles and his team hated birds with a passion, and were heard on many occasions calling them 'flying slugs' and 'the scum of the skies' as they would often poop on their cars in the parking lot of the CIA head-quarters, and quite frankly all over the DC Metro area. I believe this was one of the driving forces that led Dulles to not only implement robots into the sky, but actually replace birds in the process. They did not need to kill all of the birds, and could have launched a quarter of the robot birds that they did, but the pigeons in DC at the time were absolutely ruth-less . . . they were eating very well. American morale was high – people were feeding them much more in public parks and on the street. This in turn created huge amounts of pigeon faeces, that would inevitably find its way to the wind-shield of many men and women – all of whom grew to not only hate pigeons, but all birds. In a stolen transcript from an ex-CIA deputy, she says, 'yeah, the higher ups were so annoyed that birds had been dropping faecal matter on their car windows that they vowed to wipe out every single flying feathered creature in North America'.

Unsurprisingly, according to Bird Truthers, the poisoned water bomb that was made to kill all the birds was designed and constructed in Area 51. A squadron of specially converted B-52 bombers was assigned to deliver the weapon. It only worked in the sky and dissolved before hitting the ground so as not to affect humans. In 1959, according to the Bird Truthers, Operation Water the Country was launched. The operation had massive repercussions on American history, including the Kennedy assassination:

On October 25th, 1963 Kennedy was shown a prototype of the Turkey X500, a robot that specialised in killing larger birds like eagles and falcons. The robot demonstrated its surveillance skills, as well as its ability to find and track escaped criminals. Kennedy was impressed with what he was shown but continued to demand the immediate shutdown of the operation. Less than a month later he was dead. Now I'm not saying that these events are correlated, but I am. JFK was murdered by the CIA because he was against the mass murder of every feathered flying creature in the United States. He was to be the first and only President to stand against the murder of the birds; from Lyndon Johnson to Donald Trump, every President we've had since has turned a blind eye to the atrocities that began in 1959. After Kennedy was killed, the CIA started rigging elections. They would only allow candidates who were anti-bird and pro-citizen surveillance to win the Presidency.

I love this movement. To be honest, their theories are no weirder than those circulating about Denver International Airport. They perfectly lampoon the often-dubious connections made by conspiracy theorists to further their theories.

I had tried to get hold of the spokesperson for the organisation, a Mr Peter McIndoe, after seeing him pretend to throw up in the middle of a confused live news interview. I felt that we had similar sensibilities, but there was total radio silence. Perhaps they had seen me dressed as a giant pigeon in *Trigger Happy TV* and suspected that I might be a double agent? All I could glean was that the organisation had started when he was a student in Memphis in 2017.

'We like to fight lunacy with lunacy,' said McIndoe in an interview.

Amen to that.

Sadly, there were no Bird Truther billboards in Denver. So, I decided to visit the art gallery.

It couldn't be worse than Helsinki and one often bumped into interesting outliers in these places. As my artistic tastes were pretty contemporary, I avoided the medieval armour exhibition, on loan from the Worcester Art Museum, Massachusetts. I made straight for the modern art.

It was pretty good. Standouts were a photograph of Tracey Emin, legs akimbo, attempting to shove a large pile of cash up her vagina. There was also a woman who had photographed herself naked while squashed against plate glass and an evil-looking baby standing in a cot surrounded by a room full of detritus. If the good people of Denver were concerned about the art in the airport, thank god they'd never set foot in this place.

I started to wonder whether I'd been right. Maybe there was a correlation between conspiracy theorists and people that didn't visit art museums much. If your only experience of art was seeing the stuff at the airport and you had no context or explanation for it, then you might very well think that something weird was going on. People fear what they do not understand.

I was the only person in the gallery. When I'd finished, I headed for the museum shop. I'd been hanging around in there, looking at stuff, for about five minutes or so when I was approached by a giant, overly tattooed, crop-haired woman. She was quite aggressive.

'Hey, sir, can I be of any assistance today?'

She spoke in that weird, half-friendly, half-aggressive way that American shop assistants often do.

'No, just looking, thank you,' I replied.

'Okaaaaay.'

She moved away a touch but continued to stare at me in an accusatory manner. I started to feel uncomfortable but didn't want to leave immediately because I felt that this might confirm her suspicions. I started to pretend to be interested in some jewellery.

'Would you like me to get those out of the case, sir?'

'No, thank you. I'm still just looking.'

'OK. Is there anything in particular that you are looking for?'

'Inner peace and an end to word hunger.' I smiled, hoping she'd enjoy my joke. She didn't.

'Sir, are you intending to purchase anything from this store?'

'I haven't made that decision yet, but you following me around and pestering me is making that very unlikely.'

I was a bit pissed off now, almost pissed off enough to buy something very expensive, just to prove her wrong. But maybe that was her plan in the first place. This was all getting very confusing.

'Am I doing something wrong? In England we are allowed to wander around shops looking at things.'

'You're from England?' Her tone softened.

'Yes, I am.'

'Cool – what brings you to Denver?' She was a touch friendlier now.

'I'm on a cross-country trip.'

'Nice, business or pleasure?'

'Mainly business,' I tried to sound enigmatic.

She took the bait.

'Oh, cool. What kind of business are you in?'

'Shoplifting,' I said, trying to keep a straight face.

Her face went through a range of emotions before ending up on whatever the emoji was for 'I'm too busy for this shit.' She walked off and sat behind the till, staring at me sullenly until I left.

I walked uphill and into an area known as the Golden Triangle. This was old Denver, with smart streets dotted with handsome stone mansions. I mooched around awhile before coming across the Molly Brown House Museum.

Molly Brown, I discovered, was an American human rights activist, philanthropist and actress.

After getting very rich through the discovery of gold at one of her husband's mines, Brown moved to Denver in 1894. While travelling around Europe, Brown got word that her grandson was ill and booked a trip back to the United States on the *Titanic*, famously surviving the ship's sinking. She later took up a number of activist causes, including women's suffrage and workers' rights. She died in 1932 in New York City.

Her life was interesting and the museum was decent. But what really fascinated me was the *Titanic*. It was no surprise that the sinking of the ocean liner had given rise to a plethora of conspiracy theories.

There was the insurance theory. This contended that it was not the *Titanic* that sank, but her sister ship, the *Olympic*, as part of some devious insurance scam by the owners, J. P. Morgan.

Morgan was the target of most of the theories. The most popular one being that the *Titanic* had been sunk on purpose. What with the maiden voyage being such a big deal, there were some seriously wealthy and important passengers on board. Some of them, luminaries such as John Astor IV, Isidor Straus and Benjamin Guggenheim, were rumoured to have been opposed to the formation of an American central bank.

The theory went that J. P. Morgan, who was promoting the idea of a central bank, had them liquidated by somehow organising the sinking of the *Titanic*. This theory was further fuelled by the fact that Morgan had a suite booked on the voyage but chose to cancel it at the last minute. This all seemed a very complicated and elaborate way of getting rid of your rivals.

It was ever thus, though. No important tragedy was ever spared a conspiracy legacy.

Interestingly, a man called Milton Hershey had also cancelled his trip on the *Titanic* at the last minute, having paid for a cabin. He was the founder of the famous confectionery company, best known for the chocolate bar of the same name. No conspiracy appeared to have been theorised about his no-show, which made for a refreshing change.

I moved on, soon finding myself surrounded by really lovely homes. Several beautiful couples passed me, out on a jog with their dogs. This is a very good guide to a city: the more joggers you see, the posher the area. As it so happened, the joggers didn't look the typical preppy-posh. This wasn't New York. Denver joggers had a kind of healthy stoner, digital nomad vibe that you see more and more as, because of COVID, people abandoned the mega-cities for minor-city living.

I stopped outside one brownstone house. A sign informed me that this was the Marijuana Mansion. It had played an important role in Denver history. It was where the Marijuana Policy Project, a pro-legalisation organisation, was based. It had been responsible for pushing through Amendment 64 which, in 2012, had legalised marijuana in Colorado.

The building was now a rather tacky, cannabis-friendly event space for hire. It had loads of 'crazy themes' like a Moroccan tent room but it looked naff as fuck. Around the back was a cannabis dispensary. There was an incredible amount of foot traffic going in and out. They didn't call this the Mile High City for nothing.

I ended up at Union Station, the loveliest building in Denver, a glorious Art Deco–style train station with stylish bars and eateries attached. I was disappointed to see that, unlike Helsinki, there was no Presidential Lounge.

I was meeting a friend called Nova. He was originally from Bradford and had been the keyboardist in a band called Scars on 45. He'd got stuck in the US while touring during COVID and had ended up marrying a local girl. We sat on a balcony overlooking the interior of the building and ordered whisky sours.

The overly charming barmaid asked me which bourbon I'd like in my sour. She seemed so sweet and obviously knew much more than me, so I let her choose. Big mistake. Every shot of bourbon she chose was forty dollars. I'd been well and truly suckered.

I should have known better. I'd just been watching an episode of *Better Call Saul* where the main character scams a loud guy on the phone with fifty-dollar tequila shots. I guess I had it coming . . . and she'd had such lovely eyes and a kind smile. It was an expensive lesson. I had little memory of getting back to my Airbnb that night and if I had talked to my Uber driver, I had zero recollection of it.

Morning came. It was time to hit the road.

I packed up my stuff and drove out. My head throbbed. I needed coffee and something to eat. I spotted a pleasant-looking place called the Moonlight Diner. I parked up and went inside.

It was early and they had just opened. I grabbed a booth with a view over the flat prairie towards the distant, snow-capped mountains. Moments after I arrived, an African-American family entered and sat at the table next to me. They were a mum, dad and their little girl who I guessed was about six years old. All three sported impressive dreadlocks. The dad was wearing a white T-shirt sporting the words 'MALCOLM X DIDN'T TAKE ANY SHIT'. The mum had on white socks in vivid orange sliders. The socks each had the words 'I don't give a fuck!' printed on them.

The door opened and five Colorado state policemen came in and sat down for breakfast. Their belts groaned with various types of restraint – spray, handcuffs, batons and large pistols. As the high-heeled, gum-chewing waitress approached me with the inevitable glass jug of filter coffee, Bruce Springsteen's 'I'm on Fire' played in the background. I was in peak Americana. However many times you visit this country, it never ever stops feeling like a movie set.

The next song up totally changed the mood. It was Bronski Beat's 'Smalltown Boy'. A melancholy paean to escaping small-town homophobia in eighties Scotland. I wondered if anybody except me in the diner knew what it was about.

After breakfast, I hopped into my car, the one I hoped would take me all the way to Houston without a problem.

It was a white Ford SUV. I had booked a compact car but American car rental companies were way more relaxed than their European cousins. I'd had to pay a three-hundred-dollar supplement to drop the car off in Houston but was then told to just go grab a car in the lot. All the keys were in the ignition, smiled the friendly lady. Technically, I think there were supposedly different areas for the different sizes of cars. People seemed to have taken very little notice of this, however, and simply parked anywhere. Thus there was a Ford SUV in the compact zone. It was most definitely not compact. It was bloody enormous. I jumped in and drove to the gate, chancing my arm. The guy in the booth asked me for my documentation. I handed them over and held my breath, waiting for the guy to point out my mistake. Instead, he just smiled, handed me my papers back and raised the barrier. I was through.

Outside was America.

I was headed south, towards New Mexico. But first, I made a detour and headed up into the hills. I wanted to check out Red Rocks. This was Denver's famous concert venue, a stunning natural amphitheatre nestled between ginormous red sandstone boulders. I remembered seeing a very early version of U2 playing at Red Rocks on TV. I had wanted to visit ever since. It didn't disappoint.

As I arrived, there was a massive traffic jam leaving the place. It seemed a bit early for a concert. All was soon revealed. There had been a dawn yoga session and the newly chilled techno-hippies were now driving their petrol guzzlers down to their workspaces. It was time to log in for another day's digital nomadding.

I left the Denver area and headed south towards Colorado Springs.

After an hour's drive I came to the town of Monument. This was where I'd arranged to meet Jeff Peckman of the ill-fated Extraterrestrial Affairs Commission. He was also an advocate for disclosure of UFO and extraterrestrial phenomena.

He had come to public attention in 2008 when he had invited journalists to view a video shot by a man called Stan Romanek. The three-minute video consisted of grainy images of a white creature with a balloon-shaped head and large dark eyes peering through a window that was said to be eight feet above the ground.

I'd watched this video. Shot in 2003 in what looked like night-vision, it started with Romanek, who claimed he'd just seen a UFO touch down in his backyard, shakily filming his window. He then put the camera on a tripod and repeatedly looked out of the window. Romanek then disappeared from shot for a while. Suddenly, an alien head popped up, as though on a stick, and stared though the window before disappearing rather quickly. It looked, to the untrained eye, incredibly fake.

Despite this, I was determined to try and keep an open mind. We'd arranged to meet at a coffee shop, just off the Interstate. As with most things in my life, I got there early, way too early.

I parked up and went in. Thankfully, it seemed a relatively unthreatening environment. I approached the counter and ordered a coffee. The owner, hearing my accent, looked up.

'You the guy from London?' she asked.

'I am – well, Cheltenham, but it really doesn't matter.'

'Jeff said you'd be coming in. He came in yesterday to check out the place.' She smiled to reveal three missing teeth.

'Oh, right. I presume it passed?' I said jokingly.

'Passed what?' she said, looking up fast.

'I'm joking . . . like it passed muster?'

'Mustard . . .?' she looked very confused.

'Muster. It's an expression. He thought it was OK?'

'Sure he did. Why wouldn't he?'

'No reason whatsoever. I was joking . . .'

'Lucky for you I get British humour. I lived over there for two years, in Edinburgh.' She passed me my coffee.

'Oh wow. If you can understand the Scottish accent, then you'll have no problem with mine.' I smiled, trying to look charming.

'Nooo if yee dinneee cause nay trouble?' she said in a surprisingly passable Scottish accent.

She passed me the card machine. On the screen were the tip options. Every time you paid for anything in America, you were faced with this deeply irritating ritual. I looked at my choices:

Add a Tip
15% 18%
20% 30%

So my minimum option was 15 per cent. I'd not seen a 30 per cent tip option before. This was clearly what news outlets were calling tipflation. If you wanted to tip less or not to tip at all then you had to go through a way more complicated process that made what you were doing crystal clear to the server. It was social pressure and you had to be pretty hardened to buck the system.

As it so happened, this lady had been perfectly pleasant and efficient, but it still rankled that I was being strong-armed into this. To me, a tip should be given when somebody goes out of their way to make your experience more pleasurable. I also always left tips in cash as you could never be certain that the management weren't pocketing it all. It was my choice. And, who decided who we tip anyhow? We didn't tip a nurse or a teacher but taxi drivers and hairdressers expected it. Where would it all end? Should we tip our landlords? Aeroplane pilots? I felt like Larry David in *Curb Your*

Enthusiasm, grumbling about having to tip everybody you ever met at a hotel.

I tipped 18 per cent. I didn't want to look like a cheapskate.

I sat in a corner and looked around. The inside was dark, the walls were wooden, augmented by the occasional badly printed photograph. By the door was what passed for a souvenir stall with some shitty T-shirts and a couple of fridge magnets. The place was nearly empty. A Hispanic family sat in one corner while a veritable mountain of a man in dungarees, with the largest beard I had even seen, sat staring at me from a table near the counter. If anybody remembers Giant Haystacks, the British wrestling baddy from the late 1970s — well, I had discovered his illicit offspring.

I knew instantly that this colossus of man must be Jeff. I also understood that I was in some sort of test that I had to pass in order to move on to the next stage.

He'd clearly been listening to me as I chatted at the counter. Everybody was obviously in on it.

Should Jeff feel uncomfortable or suspect that I might be there for nefarious purposes then he would disappear as fast as the creature in Stan Romanek's window. Jeff, in the words of the eighties loungecore star Sade, was a smooth operator. I needed to play this carefully.

The problem was that I had entered the game unprepared. I had to assume that Jeff was some sort of paranoiac who thought the government was watching him and that all Europeans were communist scum.

I would have to go with my instincts.

I raised my coffee cup in his direction and gave him a nod that I believed intimated both respect and an understanding that we were on the same level. One thing I was keen to convey was that we were both wary of 'them'.

Jeff, however, was not going to give himself away so easily. Rather than answering my subtle coffee greeting, he put his cup down and stared back at me even more intently. I smiled enigmatically. I was getting into this. This was how all covert meetings should go down. I was an obvious outsider and Jeff meeting me in public would set tongues wagging. I might be new to this particular game, but I didn't want to appear stupid.

I scanned the room in an over-the-top manner to further reassure him that I was aware of all possible threats and that I wouldn't do anything stupid. I gave him a long, theatrical wink. I was no newbie. He could trust me, but there was no reason that we couldn't also both enjoy the surreal insanity of our existence.

Jeff looked daggers at me. Was I being too flippant? Maybe he believed this stuff more than me. Maybe he genuinely felt that 'they' were watching us and that my behaviour was putting us in danger. To me, this was all fun and games. But I had to be cognisant that for Jeff, this was probably a lot more real.

I considered getting up and going over to his table. No. I was obviously the only Brit in Monument. I stood out like a sore thumb. It was clear that it was for me to make a move, but it had to be subtle.

I looked around the room. The Hispanic family were deep in conversation. The Edinburgh lady was chatting to a new customer. There was nobody else but Jeff and me.

In the corner to my right were the washrooms. I looked up.

Jeff was still staring at me intently, clearly waiting for me to make my move. I glanced around, nobody else was watching. I looked up at the signs for the washroom and then looked back quickly. In case he didn't get it, I indicated in the direction of the washroom with my head and raised my eyebrows. I assumed he'd get the message. It wasn't exactly subtle but I was confident that nobody else had seen it.

'Dom? Are you Dom? I'm Jeff Peckman . . .' A tall, grey-haired guy with big blue eyes shook my hand and sat down opposite me. It was the guy who'd been at the counter.

'Oh hey. Hello. Nice to meet you,' I said shaking his hand.

'Sorry if I'm late,' he said.

'Oh no, you're bang on time,' I replied.

I glanced over nervously at the giant bearded guy. He was glaring at me. I raised my hand in apology and pointed at Jeff sitting opposite me as though to explain. It didn't seem to work. It probably looked to the bearded guy as though my homosexual pick-up tactics had worked their magic on another customer. I no longer had need of his services. I tried not to look in his direction again.

The real Jeff Peckman was very friendly. He had that slightly distant look in his eyes of somebody who had possibly done a bit too much meditation. This turned out to be true. Jeff was an avid practitioner of TM, transcendental meditation. He was a charismatic guy. You could see why he had run for office. He'd run for the Senate on behalf of the Natural Law Party. Sadly, it had not been a massive success. He'd garnered 0.31 per cent of the vote.

Unfortunately for me, it turned out that Jeff was not very interested in UFOs any more. He had moved on, he told me.

Teaching TM was his thing now. I told him that I was headed Roswell way and he seemed happy to hear this. He told me that Roswell was the only place to go for proper UFO research, but I was not to just focus on the famous autopsy incident story. There were far more credible stories down there.

I quickly realised that I was going to get nothing interesting out of him. He was a nice guy but that was it. I had not come to talk about meditation. I had even put my phone on the table and had been recording the conversation as though I was some professional journalist. It was probably time to move on. After we'd had our coffees, I picked up my phone and turned off the recording. The meeting was over.

This was a textbook error. Never, ever turn off your recorder until you have left a meeting. The good stuff always happens at the end.

I was just initiating my goodbyes when Jeff started talking about somebody he knew in nearby Colorado Springs. He told me that this woman, 'an officer and a lesbian', who worked in one of the nearby military bases, had been driving her pick-up truck when she was abducted and raped by an alien. The US Army had then, according to Jeff, stolen the baby. When she'd made a fuss she was taken to NORAD and shown her foetus in a jar.

All this was suddenly pouring out of Jeff as though somebody had turned on a tap. And Jeff had not finished.

Next, he told me about a friend of his who was forced to donate semen in order to impregnate aliens and was taken to a large room where women were strapped to gurneys.

Jeff talked about this with a big dopey smile and kind eyes. It was as though he was discussing his drive from home to the coffee shop. He'd slipped from laid-back hippy to full-on loon imperceptibly.

When we'd first started chatting, he had mentioned that he was very interested in multiverses. It felt like there might be two Jeff Peckmans – the easy-going, hippy-dippy guy and then this other person who believed in crazy things.

It was fascinating just sitting with a person as they told you stuff like this. It was also a bit unnerving. He clearly believed what he was saying, and he appeared calm and rational. But it was difficult to know what to say back. What could you say to this? I was genuinely flabbergasted. It had been the sort of stuff I was after when I'd organised the meeting. But now I was hearing it from someone face to face, I just found myself staring at him wondering if he was all there. Was he dangerous? What the hell was I doing in the middle of nowhere talking to a complete stranger about alien rape?

I said my goodbyes and made my way out of the café, making sure to keep a good distance between myself and the large bearded man who was still staring at me aggressively.

I got back on the Interstate and drove south into Colorado Springs. It was a military town and most famous for the Cheyenne Mountain Complex, the massive installation and bunker under the mountain that used to host America's NORAD defensive systems but now also hosted the United States Space Force. It was like something out of a Bond film. The mountain had been hollowed out and was designed to survive a direct atomic attack, although the government now admitted that it might not survive a direct nuclear one.

Inside the mountain were fifteen buildings built on more than one thousand giant springs that would help them absorb an explosion. Inside the control rooms were screens displaying all manner of satellite images, every plane in the air and the constant location of the president and vice president. It was rumoured that eight hundred people would be able to survive in there for up to thirty days while being totally cut off from the world. It made you wonder why they needed Denver International Airport. In the old days you could take a public tour of the complex but these, like a lot of things in America, had been stopped since 9/11.

It had featured in the film *War Games* in which a young Matthew Broderick unwittingly hacked into the NORAD supercomputer while thinking it was some weird video game and ended up nearly starting World War Three.

Thinking of that film took me straight back to the paranoia and almost permanent sense of impending doom that hung over me growing up in the eighties. Granted, I was a goth, so this probably had a lot to do with it but there was a kind of omnipresent dread back then. Even fashionable gadflies Duran Duran sang about it with Simon Le Bon poignantly crying out, 'Don't say you're easy on me, you're about as easy as a nuclear war.'

Don't say we weren't deep back then.

I spotted signs for Cheyenne Mountain and turned off the main road. I started to wind my way up a smaller road towards what I assumed was the mountain itself. Soon, I was quite high up and had a good view of Colorado Springs and the valley below me. I wasn't exactly sure what I was going to do when I got to the entrance, but I had a tenuous plan. I was going to try to blag my way in. At the very least, I wanted to see the famous entrance. One for the 'gram and all that.

Pretty soon, however, I started to see more and more threatening signposts. At first, they said things like:

For official government business only

But then the signs started to threaten arrest for anybody who was not supposed to be there. Reluctantly, I had to admit that I was not supposed to be there. I turned around and started driving back down the mountain with my metaphorical tail between my legs. Metaphorical, that is, unless you happened to be the bastard offspring of a lesbian Air Force officer and an alien. I didn't want to take any chances.

I had planned to stop in Colorado Springs but, driving through it, it looked a touch dull. So, I decided to keep going. I was excited to get into New Mexico. If I was up for it, I could make Santa Fe that night. It was a big drive but, frankly, so was every drive in the States.

3

New Mexico

Two possibilities exist:
either we are alone in the universe, or we are not.
Both are equally terrifying.
Arthur C. Clarke

To get to Santa Fe, I would be following the famous Santa
Fe Trail. This was an important nineteenth-century route
through the centre of the country that, before the advent of the
railroad, linked Franklin, Missouri, with Santa Fe, New Mexico.
Quite why Franklin, Missouri, was of such significance was
beyond me. The current population appeared to consist of
seventy people. Maybe the rest had taken the trail and got out
of town?

It took two hours by car, or five days by covered wagon, to
reach the state line. Once I got into New Mexico the drive was
pretty straight and featureless. It was flat desert as far as the eye
could see. I had assumed that there would be plenty of petrol
stations but I was wrong. My fuel dial was plummeting towards
empty, and the further I drove without seeing one the more
nervous I became. The temperature outside was a balmy 46 °C
and I did not fancy breaking down in the middle of nowhere.
Finally, just as I really was considering my survival options and

wondering whether I could face drinking my own urine, I spotted a service station up ahead.

Actually, the word 'service' was not really appropriate. There was one pump that, like all petrol pumps in the United States, got totally freaked out by foreign credit cards. Everybody normal paid at the pump so the guy inside was already on edge when I walked over from my car and entered his desolate little domain.

The store was about as bare as could be. It looked like every dusty, ramshackle place that you'd seen in every American desert movie. There was the inevitable Confederate flag in the window that let one know that the owner was a bit racist. There were also a couple of Trump stickers and a 'Let's Go Brandon' sign on the door, just in case you needed clarification.

The 'Let's Go Brandon' thing was actually quite funny. In 2021, a crowd at a televised Superspeedway event in Alabama were chanting 'Fuck Joe Biden' during a live interview with the winner of a race whose name was Brandon Brown. The reporter misunderstood the chant and told viewers that they were saying 'Let's Go Brandon'. And so a meme was born.

The man behind the dirty counter was wearing seventy-year-old dungarees over a Guns N' Roses T-shirt. He would have cruised through any audition for a *The Hills Have Eyes* sequel.

'Howdy,' I said.

I immediately wondered why. I'd never used that word before in my life. The man behind the counter nodded imperceptibly.

'My card doesn't work in the pump,' I said.

'No card, no gas . . .' said the man in an impressively unfriendly manner.

'No, I have a card, just, it doesn't work in the pump.'

'Well, I guess you ain't getting no gas then.' He looked straight through me.

'No, the card works, but it's not an American card so it just doesn't work in the pumps. Can I pay in here?' I smiled.

'You not American?' asked the man, looking a little disgusted.

'No, I'm from England,' I replied.

'Is that right? And what the hell brings you here? You lost?' he laughed.

'No, I'm on the road to Santa Fe, and then onwards . . .'

He looked at me as though I was mentally ill.

'You on vacation?'

'No, work trip. I'm a travel writer and I'm writing about conspiracies. I'm off to Roswell and Dallas and then Austin.' I wondered how much he had taken in and whether he knew of these places.

'A writer, huh . . . you a journalist?'

'No, a comedian actually, but I write travel books as well. This one is about conspiracies – like UFOs and who shot Kennedy, that kind of thing.' I smiled at him. He didn't smile back.

'Well, you can write this: Joe Biden is an asshole, and he and Hillary Clinton should be in jail on account of the kids they murdered. Do you know about Comet Ping Pong?'

As it so happened, I did know about Comet Ping Pong. I was rather surprised that this guy, in the middle of Nowheresville, New Mexico, knew about it.

Comet Ping Pong was the name of a pizza restaurant in Washington, DC that had become the centre of a weird conspiracy known as Pizzagate. The theory was that the restaurant was a front for a paedophile ring run by Hillary Clinton and her old campaign manager John Podesta. The story had originated, as many of these theories did, on 4chan, a no-holds-barred website that revelled in spreading all kinds of weird nonsense.

After Hillary Clinton's emails were leaked, one email between Podesta and the owner of the restaurant, a Mr James Alefantis, in which they discussed hosting a fundraiser, was seized upon. The basement of the pizza restaurant, claimed 4chan users, was a place where kids were cannibalised and tortured by Clinton and her friends.

The only problem – well, not the only one – was that the place did not have a basement. This detail did not stop a guy called Edgar Welch, of North Carolina, from driving to Washington, DC in 2016. He entered the restaurant brandishing an assault rifle and opened fire. Nobody was hurt and Welch was arrested. But it was proof, if proof was needed, of how online speculation had real-life consequences.

'You heard of it?' the clerk repeated his question.

'Yes, I have heard of it,' I said.

'You going to write about that? That shit is evil and nobody is doing nothing.'

I briefly thought about arguing the case with him, but I remembered where I was and what my situation was. Without any petrol, I was screwed.

'Yes, I am going to look into it. It's an incredible story,' I said, truthfully.

'That's only the beginning,' he said, his eyes ablaze with right-eous anger.

'Where did you find out about this?' I asked.

'Alex Jones. You heard of *InfoWars*?'

'I have, yes – in fact I'm hoping to try and speak to him when I get to Austin.'

'That guy knows his shit and they don't like him telling his truth.' He was now way more lively than when I'd first walked in.

'So, can I pay by card in here?' I asked.

'You can try,' he said.

I stuck my card in, punched in my PIN and prayed. It took an age but it finally allowed me fifty dollars' worth of petrol. It was enough to get me to civilisation . . . or Santa Fe at the very least.

Santa Fe, founded in 1610, is America's oldest state capital. It was so different from anywhere else I'd been to in the US. As I drove in after a six-hour drive from Denver, the sun was setting and the dying light was bouncing off the distinctive adobe architecture. Gone were the verdant mountains of Colorado and the vast expanses of empty desert. The place had a mellow, Moroccan feel to it. The buildings were all low, thick-walled, flat-roofed and made of a sun-baked mix of earth and organic material. I liked the vibe instantly.

I had always wanted to visit, but I wasn't sure whether Santa Fe would be a great place for a conspiracy tourist. The home of people like Georgia O'Keeffe, it was a big art destination that attracted more high-end visitors than most Middle American cities. It would be a good place to spend the night, even if only for my own enjoyment.

It turned out that I was right. Santa Fe folk were good at keeping secrets.

Jeffrey Epstein was a man who'd launched a thousand conspiracy theories, some of which were definitely more than theories.

He'd owned a massive ranch called Zorro, 23 miles outside the New Mexican capital.

Trementina Base, a curious bunker owned by the Church of Scientology, was nearby. It was supposedly where all of L. Ron Hubbard's writings were etched onto steel plates in titanium containers and stored in inert argon gas, ready for his return.

Santa Fe clearly appealed to the dark side and appeared to have always done so.

Before supper, I went for a walk around town. I ended up, like most people, having a drink in the Plaza, Santa Fe's historic central square. Back in the day, there used to be a pharmacy called Zook's in the square. This had been a front for Russian spies. It was from there that they plotted an infamous assassination, that of Leon Trotsky in Mexico City in 1940. The Russians were in Santa Fe because they were very interested in obtaining US atomic secrets. Their pharmacy was only a forty-minute drive away from the Los Alamos National Laboratory, the headquarters of the Manhattan Project, America's secret atomic research facility.

The pharmacy, like Trotsky, was long gone, but Los Alamos was probably well worth a visit. I decided to drive that way the following day.

Santa Fe was quieter than I expected. As the evening progressed, the centre emptied out rapidly, leaving only street loonies for company. There were a lot of rather posh hotels dotted around the place, and I assumed that they acted a bit like cruise ships, luring their guests back home after a little excursion. I'd chosen badly. What had looked like a rather stylish establishment online had clearly used a very creative photographer. I slept fitfully, my head resting on a pillow made of discomfort.

If I'd known somebody to show me around, I might have enjoyed Santa Fe more. As it was, I was not sad to leave the following morning.

I, like a lot of people, had assumed that Los Alamos was in the middle of the desert. Possibly, I was confusing photographs of the Manhattan Project headquarters with those of the Alamogordo Bombing Range, two hundred or so miles south of Los Alamos, where the atom bomb was actually tested.

Los Alamos itself was a surprisingly green and pleasant place, perched high above the desert on a mesa, an ancient Indian site, the Pajarito Plateau. I could instantly see why, in 1943, the US War Department had exercised eminent domain (enforced purchase) over the entire town. It had turned it into Site Y, the headquarters for J. Robert Oppenheimer and his fellow scientists to try and build the first atomic bomb.

People down in Santa Fe only knew the place as 'The Hill'. Any deliveries to the place were falsely labelled to conceal their true contents. It was only after the bombing of Hiroshima and Nagasaki that any information about the project was released to the public. Had the secrecy surrounding it been a conspiracy? Or was it just sensible?

As I drove into town, I spotted signs proclaiming that Los Alamos was:

Where discoveries are made

I couldn't help but think about the consequences of those discoveries. I had visited both Nagasaki and Hiroshima, the apocalyptic end points of this atomic journey. My father, a young pilot in the Fleet Air Arm, had flown his Seafire over

Hiroshima the day after the explosion. He always found it difficult to talk about, although I think he was broadly in agreement with the deployment of the atom bombs. As a rookie pilot, he would almost certainly have been killed had a full-blown invasion of Japan been necessary.

I wanted to visit the museum, but it was closed. A statue of Oppenheimer, in his suit and trademark hat, stood very near the road. It was as though he was hitchhiking out of the place.

He had certainly had some regrets about what he had helped bring into being. He was interviewed in 1966, two years before his death, and recalled his thoughts at their first successful atomic detonation:

We knew the world would not be the same. A few people laughed, a few people cried, most people were silent. I remembered the line from the Hindu scripture, the Bhagavad-Gita. Vishnu is trying to persuade the prince that he should do his duty and, to impress him, takes on his multi-armed form and says, 'Now, I am become Death, the destroyer of worlds.' I suppose we all thought that one way or another.

I parked up in the main street and popped into Starbucks. There were two customers inside: a man wearing a 'FUCK BIDEN 13' T-shirt and a woman wearing a T-shirt with a large peace sign on it. They sat on opposing ends of the room. I ordered an iced coffee and sat awkwardly in the middle of a divided America.

Truthfully, there was very little to do in Los Alamos. I wasn't there for long. I got back in my car and drove on through the town. After a couple of minutes, I arrived outside the massive new laboratory complex in which modern scientists worked on becoming more effective destroyers of worlds.

I was stopped at a military roadblock and asked for ID. The soldier was friendly and asked me what I was doing in Los Alamos. I replied that I was a *Breaking Bad* tourist on my way to Albuquerque . . . biiitttchhhh. I didn't actually say the 'bitch' bit. I hoped that he wouldn't look in the back seat and see my pile of secret-site reference books or maps linking one weird site to another. He didn't. He lifted the barrier and wished me a safe trip.

I gunned the engine and started my way up a heavily wooded road that wound its way uphill fast. Soon, I came upon a vast slope of bare mountain, covered in tree stumps. It looked like there had been an explosion. Maybe this was where the current Los Alamos scientists came to have picnics and muck about with their new toys.

'Hey, Steve . . . did you bring the Treetoniser?'

'Umm, let me check . . . yeah, I got all three.'

'Cool, fire one off, man, let's see what it can do.'

'We're not supposed to . . .'

'Oh Jesus, have a fucking beer and relax, Steve. What is the point of working on this shit if we can't have a blast, so to speak?'

'OK, dude, but let's just use the little one, the Treetoniser Six.'

'Fuck yeah. Blow that sucker.'

'OK, here goes nothing.'

'WOOOOOOOWWWWWWW! Jesus Christ, you were supposed to use the Six! That fucker just atomised the whole hill.'

'That was the Six.'

'Dude, the trees are just gone!'

'I know, dude, I know.'

'We are fucking good at this shit, Steve. We are the baddest scientists in Scientist Land. Pass me a beer.'

'Shall we . . . do the Seven?'

'Totally, man, go for it. We have become Hellfire, destroyer of trees.'

'I fucking love science, man.'

'Me too, dude. Fuck coding, am I right?'

I summited the mountain and the trees returned. I was now driving through a beautiful forest. The sun was shining and the dappled light trickled through the branches. There was not another soul on this mountain. Lorde's 'Stoned at the Nail Salon' came on the stereo. Multiverses. I'd journeyed from darkness into light.

Life was good.

As I started the descent on the other side, I came round a corner and had to stop the car, just to take in what was in front of me. To my right, the trees disappeared and a steep, rocky slope descended a hundred metres or so down to a vast open grass prairie that sat in a gargantuan rock bowl. It was like a flashback to the Old West. It was like virgin prairie. I felt like the first human to gaze upon it.

America never failed to astound. This had to be some ancient volcano. It was the only explanation. I was right, and, as always in America, I was never far from an explanatory sign. This was the Valles Caldera, created a million years previously by a series of volcanic eruptions more than five hundred times more powerful than that of Mount St Helens.

This whole area had cataclysmic explosions in its genes.

As a kid, I'd been obsessed with *Arthur C. Clarke's Mysterious World*. It was a companion book to the TV series of the same name. Along with stories about Bigfoot and the Loch Ness Monster was an intriguing chapter about the Tunguska Event in 1908.

This was a 12-megaton explosion that flattened an area of about 2,000 square kilometres. It is thought to have been a meteor air burst and is still the largest impact event in recorded history. Unbelievably, only three people were reported to have been killed by the explosion. It just happened to occur over one of the least inhabited areas on earth, in Siberia. Had it taken place over a metropolitan area it would have wiped out a city or three.

If it had happened now, conspiracy theorists would have been all over it. It was a nuclear test gone wrong. Bill Gates testing his new death machine. Hillary Clinton destroying her email server.

I could have sat there all day. Except I couldn't. I was Albuquerque bound.

The first thing I saw as I entered Albuquerque was an electronic billboard with the photo of an almost comical-looking bad man. He was wanted for murder. By the looks of him, quite a few. This felt very appropriate for a city that, having recently binge-watched both *Breaking Bad* and *Better Call Saul*, was synonymous, in my mind, with crime.

I checked in at my hotel of choice, a hipsterised motel called El Vado.

I dropped off my bags and headed off to explore. It was fabulous – almost everywhere in town was a location for a scene from one of the two series. My first destination was no exception. The National Museum of Nuclear Science and History.

You could see it from the main road as it had several enormous nuclear missiles plonked outside the entrance, looming over the freeway. It would take a stubborn tourist not to stop.

I spent half an hour or so gawking at reproductions of the various atomic bombs produced by the Manhattan Project along with a multitude of different bombers used to deliver them. Inside, pride of place was given to a display on Werner Heisenberg, the godfather of atomic power. Heisenberg, of course, being the pseudonym used by Walter White in *Breaking Bad*.

Inspired, I drove across town to the location of Walter White's house in the series. I recognised it immediately, even though the current owners, clearly tired of fans like me making the pilgrimage, had erected ugly fencing around the front. Many fans had taken to hurling pizzas onto the roof of the house in homage to one particular scene. The new owners were clearly at the end of their tether. A large sign read:

> Please take photographs from the other
> side of the road. Do not disturb us!

I got a strong feeling that they would not take kindly to me ringing the doorbell and asking for a look round. I'm quite intuitive like that. I took my sad little photograph and left. It was a good thing I wasn't a sheeple. I later discovered that the owner had threatened to sit outside the house in a rocking chair and shoot the next person to try to throw a pizza.

Albuquerque was not a big conspiracy town, and I was really just passing through. There was one fabulous rumour that the 'anti-comedian' and star of *Taxi* Andy Kaufman was not dead and living a quiet life in the city. The idea that Andy Kaufman would ever live a quiet life, even in death, was ridiculous. In fact, if he wasn't dead, I'd be certain that he had started the rumour.

I headed back towards my motel. On the way, I drove past an SUV that was on fire in the middle of the street. Flames had completely enveloped the vehicle and a thick pall of black smoke floated up into the clear blue sky. People were just walking past, barely giving it a glance. Drivers didn't even stop to rubberneck, they just drove around it. I got the feeling that the locals had seen way worse.

I kept driving.

My motel was also a microbrewery, which was a result. I sat in the tap room and eavesdropped on a maths teacher telling the barman about how tired he was of living in Albuquerque. He'd had it with the crackheads. He talked unbelievably loudly. He was clearly used to having to project to a class of unruly students.

'IT'S GOT TO THE STAGE WHERE I JUST DON'T LOCK THE CAR ANY MORE, BECAUSE THEY KEEP BREAKING THE WINDOWS TO GET IN.'

I was tempted to butt in and tell him about my friend Sam who had the same problem in London and used to leave a note on the windscreen that said, 'Please feel free to come in and browse.'

I kept my counsel. Suddenly another man entered who was, extraordinarily, even louder. They were inexorably drawn to each other, like two foghorns on Grindr.

'YOU LIVE IN TOWN, BUDDY?'

'YEAH, I TEACH MATH.'

'WOW, BRAINS-TRUST, AM I RIGHT?'

'KIND OF.'

'YOU WANT A BEER, BUDDY?'

'SURE.'

'I'VE GOT THE DAY OFF. I'M GOING TO GET SERIOUSLY WASTED.'

'GOOD FOR YOU.'

'YEAH.'

'WHAT'S YOUR LINE OF WORK?'

'REAL ESTATE.'

'WOW.'

'YEAH, YOU GOT A PLACE TO SELL?'

'ACTUALLY, I JUST MIGHT . . .'

I was sure this was the guy who'd sold the Walter White house to the angry new owner. You'd sign anything just to get him out of your hair. After five minutes of this, I couldn't take any more. I retreated to my room where the air con was on full blast.

The sound of silence was heavenly.

That evening I took an Uber to what laughably passed for the 'Old Town'. It felt like Disney had constructed an Adobe Land. It was one long, tacky street and a shabby square full of bored-looking Latinos. I had asked the receptionist for a recommendation for dinner. He must have misheard me and thought I'd asked for the worst restaurant in New Mexico.

To make matters worse, I was seated next to another loud talker. This one was a daughter, about thirty-five years old, who had clearly decided that this was both the time and the place to tell her mother everything that she had been bottling up inside her for years.

'I DON'T THINK YOU UNDERSTAND WHAT I WENT THROUGH.'

'OK, honey.'

'I NEVER SAID ANYTHING. NOT ONE DAMN WORD ABOUT HIM.'

'OK, honey.'

'I HAD TO SIT THERE WHILE HE DID THOSE THINGS.'

'Yes, honey.'

'WHAT HE DID WAS NOT RIGHT, MAMA. IT JUST WASN'T RIGHT.'

'I know, honey.'

'DON'T JUST SIT THERE, "YES HONEYING" ME, MAMA. HE BEAT YOU. HE WALKED ALL OVER THIS FAMILY FOR TWENTY-TWO YEARS.'

'I know, honey.'

What was it with this town and volume control? I finished my plateful of Tex–Mex–Mush and asked for the cheque.

'IF I EVER SEE HIM AGAIN, MAMA, I'LL KILL HIM MYSELF. I'M NOT KIDDING. I'LL SHOOT HIM DEAD.'

'No, honey.'

'DON'T "NO HONEY" ME, MAMA. GOD HELP ME IF YOU EVEN THINK OF TAKING HIM BACK. I'LL KILL HIM, MAMA.'

'I know, honey.'

It was tempting to stay and see where this went, but the noise was just too much. I left the establishment and tried to get a cab. There was none. I checked my map and realised that, on foot, it wasn't actually too far back to the motel.

I started to walk.

It was 8 p.m. and 42 °C in the shade. The sun's rays were like a thousand little pinpricks. By the time I got back, ten minutes or so later, I was a dripping, sodden mess. I was soaked in sweat and feeling unsatisfactorily full. I'd had enough of Albuquerque. I could see why everybody took drugs there. It was a place you wanted to escape from, by any means necessary. I chose the open road. It was time to get back to work. It was time to go to Roswell while my car still had wheels.

The following morning, I walked to my car with fingers crossed. It was intact. I was going to be able to leave this curious town.

I could have taken the longer route, down through the White Sands Missile Range where the first atomic bomb was detonated under the code name Trinity. It was definitely an interesting place. Shortly after the Second World War, fast-tracked exonerated Nazi scientists were hard at work in the US with captured German V-2 rockets developing new technology with which to destroy other countries. This was not a conspiracy theory. This happened. It was the grim reality of realpolitik. My enemy's enemy is my friend. Communism was the new enemy. There was lots to look into, but I was slightly nuked out. I fancied some UFO action. I took the more direct route from Albuquerque to Roswell. It was about a four-hour drive across the desert.

There were the occasional distractions, such as the Musical Highway. This was a quarter-mile stretch of the road in which, if you drove at exactly 45 miles an hour, the rumble strips on the road played the tune of 'America the Brave'. I gave it a go but there appeared to have been recent roadworks as the whole tune did not play. I'll be honest, it was massively underwhelming, but you took what you could when driving though the desert.

Whenever a large truck came up behind me, I couldn't help but think of a very early film by Steven Spielberg called *Duel*. In it, a truck decided to pick on a random motorist and tried to run it off a desert road, very much like the one I was on. It was a brilliant film but, like *Jaws* with sharks, it had made me very nervous around lorries.

The vast majority of people have heard of 'the Roswell incident'. If you ask them what they know about it, the reply is that a UFO crashed somewhere near Roswell and that there was footage of an autopsy done on a strange grey-looking alien, supposedly by the US Air Force (USAF). Others claim that the technology gained from breaking the crashed craft down was used by the Air Force to further their knowledge. Most people know about it from movies like *Independence Day*.

What was known for sure was that, in 1947, debris from a crash was recovered from a ranch near Corona, New Mexico. The airbase in nearby Roswell issued a press release stating that 'a flying disc' had been recovered. This was quickly retracted and a new statement was issued stating that the object recovered was a weather balloon and that any 'alien bodies' that were spoken of were test dummies that had been dropped from high altitude.

The actual event itself made little global impact at the time. Then, in 1979, a former USAF lieutenant colonel named Jesse Marcel, in an interview with a ufologist, claimed that the debris he had retrieved from the ranch was of extraterrestrial origin. This caught the zeitgeist and Roswell became shorthand for governments hiding the truth about the existence of aliens.

The famous 'alien autopsy' footage, which most people assumed had been around since the incident, only emerged in 1995. The filmmakers had since gone on the record to admit that it was a hoax, although they preferred to use the term 'reconstruction'. All this had been lost and merged in the blur of time.

I am actually not a total sceptic as far as UFOs go. The idea that we are the only intelligent life form in the entire universe seems unlikely. There is also little doubt that militaries and governments keep things secret, for many reasons. What I find strange is that these alien visitors seem obsessed with landing in deserts and anally probing toothless rednecks. Why didn't they just land outside the United Nations and start talking?

I was curious to see how a town could turn a conspiracy theory into an international tourist magnet. Conspiracy theories, when managed well, could be big business.

I eventually arrived on the outskirts of Roswell. I was greeted by a green sign that said,

Welcome to Roswell

It had a flying saucer and three cows perched on top of it. The cement base of the sign was covered in stickers put there by visitors from all over this world . . . and possibly others.

I parked up and got out of the car. The heat was debilitating. It was like opening a pizza oven and cramming your head inside. I approached the sign and had a look. I took a couple of photographs and was about to move on when another car stopped and a couple got out. They walked up and also started taking photos.

'Would you like me to take a photo of you in front of the sign?' I asked.

They looked utterly baffled. I presumed they were not English speakers. I repeated myself slowly while making an old-fashioned camera clicking sign.

'Would you like me to take a photo of you two?'

It seemed to work.

'Oh . . . OK, thank you,' said the woman, who was, like her husband, quite large and wearing a sweatsuit.

'Aha, you're American? I thought you didn't speak English,' I said cheerfully.

She looked puzzled again.

'Could you speak slowly, sir? I'm having trouble understanding you,' she said.

'Sure, my apologies,' I said, taking her phone off her.

'Where are you from?' she asked.

'I'm . . . from . . . England,' I replied.

'Oh, you're a long way from home,' she said.

'Yes, yes I am.'

'Did you drive all the way?' she asked.

There was silence as I took in the question. Her husband, who appeared to be slightly more clued up, geographically, jumped in.

'He's from England, it's not in the USA.'

'It's in Europe – well, it used to be. We actually just left. You know, Brexit . . .' I said, trying to make a joke.

They looked totally nonplussed. I took a couple of photographs of them in front of the sign.

'Where are you guys from?' I asked as I handed the woman her phone back.

'We're from Missouri,' said the man.

'In America,' said the woman, as though talking to a simple child.

'Oh yes, Mark Twain country,' I said, proud of my knowledge.

'America . . .' repeated the woman.

'Yes, I know. But Mark Twain was born in Missouri. Although he was born in a town called Florida, in Missouri . . . so there could be confusion there.'

There was much confusion. I realised that neither of these people had ever heard of their state's most famous son.

'Would you mind taking a photo of me?' I asked, desperate to make this less awkward.

I handed them my phone and stood under the sign to pose for a couple of snaps. When they were done, I got my phone back.

'Thank you. What made you guys come to Roswell?' I asked.

'We're here to see stuff,' said the man.

'Aha! UFO-related stuff?' I asked.

'Could be,' said the man, looking a little suspicious of my questions.

'I'm here writing a book about that kind of stuff. May I ask, have you ever seen a UFO?'

'Maybe,' said the man.

'We don't want to talk to you,' said the woman suddenly. She started pulling her husband by the arm in the direction of their car.

'OK, well, bye then. Lovely meeting you.' I stood awkwardly by the sign as they got into their car and burned off in a cloud of dust. I was not a natural interviewer.

I drove on into downtown Roswell. It was a pretty bleak one-horse town. Driving down the main drag, it was clear to see that they had embraced the UFO thing big time. The McDonald's was a shiny chrome building shaped like a UFO. The Dunkin' Donuts sign was held aloft by a 20-foot green alien. Even the streetlights were shaped like an alien head with two black eyes stuck onto each one.

The only non-alien-related business I could see was a gun store. It had an enormous 'Let's Go Brandon' banner all along the outside wall that faced the parking lot full of large pick-up trucks.

I thought it might be a good place to start. I parked up and headed on inside. I couldn't help noticing that it was right next door to a bank. To my British sensibilities, this seemed to be tempting fate a little. But what would some snowflake Limey know?

I pushed open the door and went in. The sheer volume of unnecessary weaponry available was breathtaking. There were shotguns, rifles, assault rifles, handguns – so many handguns. Any alien landing in this town was undoubtedly going to meet stiff resistance, unless he was wearing a T-shirt with the slogan:

We're going to stage a comeback
the likes of which no one has
EVER SEEN
TRUMP
2024

I tried to write this T-shirt slogan here, exactly as I'd seen it on an actual T-shirt worn by an actual, shaven-headed, overly tattooed redneck in the gun-store car park. But however hard I tried, Microsoft Word would not allow me the option of using the correct font.

Looking at examples online, I think the T-shirt font was called Fraktur. Further research informed me that Fraktur had been the most popular early Nazi typeface. Hitler's *Mein Kampf* had used a hand-drawn version of it for the cover.

In 1941, things changed. Martin Bormann, Hitler's de-facto chief-of-staff, issued a circular to all public offices declaring Fraktur to be *Judenlettern* (Jewish letters) and prohibiting their further use.

From 1941 onwards, more modern, 'less Jewish' Nazi typefaces such as Tannenberg were now the accepted Nazi fonts. I tried, but couldn't get Tannenberg on Word either. Eventually I opted for Comic Sans. I didn't want to offend anybody.

We're going to stage a comeback
the likes of which
nobody has ever seen
TRUMP
2024

I was a bit annoyed that Bill Gates had made it so tricky for me to properly express other people's support for Trump in a genuine Nazi font. Why was he not allowing people on his system to use a typeface commonly used to promote genocidal views in the early mid-twentieth century?

It made you think. Maybe he was digging tunnels in which he would imprison hundreds of thousands of disappeared children?

A man with a large beard approached me.

'Hey, can I help you?'

'No, I'm just looking. I'm from the UK. We don't really have stores like these.'

'Ha, that I know. Your bobbies still just carry sticks, right?'

I could never get over the tendency for Americans to use the term 'bobbies' for the British police. It was a term that I, certainly, had never used and was last in popular use in about 1880.

I know better, however, than to correct armed men.

'Yes, they carry truncheons. It seems to do the trick,' I replied.

'Except in Birmingham, right?

'No, I think they carry them in Birmingham as well.' I was impressed with his knowledge of cities that weren't London.

'It's a no-go city, right? The bobbies have given it over to the Muslims.' The man looked like he was serious.

'Umm, I don't think so. I was there a couple of weeks ago for lunch and it all seems fairly . . . calm.' I wondered if there was anybody in America that would ever conduct a normal conversation with me; did I just attract these types?

'Really? I heard the whole city was no-go, run by sharia law and no Brits allowed there.' The man was friendly, but serious.

'Where did you hear that?' I asked.

'I've seen it said a lot on the TV,' he said.

'Well, no offence, but that's total nonsense.' I tried to look non-confrontational about it.

'There are no no-go cities in the UK?' the man said.

'Well, there's Swindon, that's a no-go for most people out of personal choice as it's a bit of a dump, but nothing to do with Muslims.' I smiled, to show him that this was a joke.

'What brings you to Roswell?' asked the man.

'UFOs, what else?' I smiled again.

'OK,' he said, totally unfazed.

'You ever seen one?' I asked.

'Sure. I've seen plenty. There's a lot of weird shit going on in the skies around here.'

'Really, and you think that it's alien activity, not military?'

'Could be either, but I've seen shit that can't be explained. Lights that move so fast and make turns that are just not possible for human craft. Ask anybody who lives here, they'll all tell you the same.' He was matter of fact about all this.

'It must help the tourism as well, am I right?' I smiled once more.

'You are correct. We get a lot of visitors off the back of it but that don't mean it's not real.'

I thanked him before wandering around the store, staring at more guns and wondering if there was any way I could smuggle a stun gun back into the UK. It would be useful the next time I played a gig in Swindon.

I got back in the car unarmed, and drove on down the main drag. Eventually I got to a place called the International UFO Museum and Research Center. Bingo. This was what I was after. UFO Ground Zero.

A large gaggle of tourists swarmed around the entrance, many of them drinking through straws from green containers shaped like aliens. I squeezed my way past them and entered the museum. There was a ticket desk. I approached it excitedly. An elderly woman sat behind the desk. She appeared a little less excited than me.

'Hello,' I said.

'Five dollars entry,' she said.

'Great, and what does that get me?' I asked.

'Entrance to the museum, the research library and the gift shop,' she replied.

'GREAT! I've come a long way to visit,' I said.

She didn't give a shit.

I spotted a sign behind her that let people know that tickets were five dollars each, except for military personnel who only had to pay three dollars. I pointed at the sign.

'I see the military only pay three dollars.'

'You in the military?' she asked.

'Conscientious objector from my school Cadet Force, ma'am. Total draft dodger.'

'Then it's still five dollars,' she said.

'What's the ticket price for extraterrestrials?' I asked.

'What?' she looked totally deadpan.

'Aliens. I'd imagine they'd be pretty interested in looking around here; would bring back a lot of memories.' I laughed.

She just stared at me.

'You gonna buy a ticket or not, sir?'

I handed over five dollars, got my ticket and went in. At the entrance to the museum was a large video map and a notice encouraging visitors to type in where they were from and leave an email address. I was the first visitor from Cheltenham. I added my email address: domjoly@bollocks.com

Curiously, I've not received any communication from the museum since my visit.

Opposite the map was a 3D mock-up of a crashed UFO and a couple of 'greys', as the classic grey aliens were known. One of them was standing while another sat on a rock, presumably still in shock from the crash. The latter looked in a bad way and I noticed grey gaffer tape wrapped around his neck.

A family of five were having their photo taken next to the aliens. I waited until they'd finished and then asked the dad whether he'd mind taking my photo? He seemed nice and took several photos of me standing in between the two greys. I took my phone back.

'Thank you so much,' I said.

'No problem. Where are you from?' he asked.

'The UK.'

'Cool.'

'Yeah. I've always wanted to come here. I thought it was all science fiction and then – BAM! – first thing I see are two actual aliens. I can't believe that I can stand next to them and get my photo and all. I presume they stuffed them after the autopsy to preserve them like this?'

I kept a poker face. He looked at me, trying to take in what I'd said.

'Those aren't real aliens, they're just models,' he said to me softly, as though to a dim child.

'Whaaat!? I thought they were the actual ones from the autopsy. Where are the real ones then?' I looked disappointed.

'I don't think they have them here,' he said, smiling sadly, clearly hoping this conversation with would end soon.

'I suppose your government probably have them. These are so lifelike. I could have sworn they were the real thing.'

The man ushered his family away from me and into the main room of the museum. I waited for a beat and then followed them in.

The museum display was a mixture of slightly tacky physical exhibits and lots of information and photographs stuck to the walls. There was a lot to take in. There was obviously a vast amount about the 1947 Roswell incident itself. There were interviews with people involved, people who'd found the debris, locals from that time. People had looked into this stuff in extraordinary detail but, to me, the photographs did seem to be explained away perfectly rationally as the remains of some sort of silver, high-altitude weather balloon – but what did I know? Maybe the Chinese were sending their spy balloons over America a lot earlier than people thought?

The time period when the Roswell incident took place was a curious one. The Second World War was not long over and the new Cold War was just heating up. Aliens were fast becoming a code for communists. Because of the Manhattan Project, military secrecy was probably higher in New Mexico than anywhere else in the country. It made sense to me that the government would be happy to have any new, experimental technology, often purloined from the Nazis, be explained away as UFOs or alien sightings.

Back in the museum, I was learning more about ufology. There were different degrees of close encounters, known as Hynek's scale:

1. Close Encounters of the First Kind: these are when people spotted stuff in the sky, a good example being the Phoenix Lights. These were a widely reported set of sightings of UFOs over Arizona and Nevada on the night of 13 March 1997. Thousands of people, including the governor of Arizona, saw large V-shaped formations of lights over Phoenix. The US Air Force attributed them to flares being dropped by aircraft on manoeuvres.

2. Close Encounters of the Second Kind: these tend to be physical events like crop circles and horse mutilations. Crop circles, almost everybody now knows, are the result of drunk

students armed with a plank of wood and some rope, mucking about in fields at night. Horse mutilations, on the other hand, are anybody's guess. Like anally probing rednecks, it did seem a weird thing for aliens to do, having travelled such long distances.

3. Close Encounters of the Third Kind: these have to include an alien figure of some kind. The museum had a big display about an incident involving a New Mexican police officer called Lonnie Zamora. On patrol in Socorro County, he'd spotted an object that looked like a big silvery letter O. Standing next to the object were two small humanoids. As he approached the UFO took off and roared away. Ever keen to turn these sightings into a tourism opportunity, the Socorro County Board of Commerce built stone walkways and installed benches at the site. Except they installed them a quarter of mile away from the actual site because of rumours that the actual site was now highly radioactive.

4. Close Encounters of the Fourth Kind: these are the ones you really want to avoid as they involve the abduction of humans by aliens. The museum opted for a non-redneck example: they used a biracial couple called Betty and Barney Hill. In 1961, the couple were returning by car to Portsmouth, New Hampshire, where they lived, from a holiday in Montreal and Niagara Falls. A flying saucer appeared above their car. They spotted humanoid figures in the craft. Things then became rather unclear. When they awoke, they found themselves 35 miles south of where the incident happened. When they got home their watches didn't work, there were weird

concentric circles on their car and a pinkish powder on their clothes. My favourite detail was when Barney attested that he was 'compelled to examine his genitals in the bathroom but found nothing unusual'. The couple were honoured with a roadside marker in New Hampshire at the spot where the incident supposedly took place.

I didn't know what to make of it all. The temptation was to write all these people off as mentally ill or attention seekers. But there had been multiple incidents of UFOs being spotted by fighter pilots, airline pilots and other people with fairly legitimate claims to mental stability. UFOs, however, were just unidentified flying objects and not necessarily extraterrestrial.

The museum soon ran out of ideas. There was a large exhibition of stuff about the TV series called *Roswell* followed by a hideous art exhibition with aliens as the theme. I could only guess that the artists were being anally probed at the very moment that they put brush to easel, because the work was truly painful.

I exited through the gift shop. It was nearly as big as the museum and no aspect of alien souvenir tat had been ignored. It was packed and they were clearly raking it in. I added to their coffers by buying a green alien fridge magnet. It would have been rude not to.

As the establishment was called the International UFO Museum and Research Center, I was curious to see what research was done there. I was keen to meet some critical thinkers.

Back in the main reception area, I spotted a door with a sign that read 'Research Library'.

This was it. This was where most of the real academic work on this subject must be going down. It looked like an unloved school library. There were rows of cheap, rickety bookshelves packed with thousands of books about UFOs. There were also a lot of *Star Wars* toys on display. To me, this rather undermined the credibility of the place.

It was totally empty save for one gentleman who was sitting at a table half-heartedly looking at a book. He was thickset, wearing stonewashed jeans and a large baggy blue T-shirt that displayed a cartoon of a red-haired woman and the words 'Stay Weird'. He looked up and I nodded towards him.

'Hey, how you doing?' he said.

'I'm good, thank you,' I replied.

'You here to do some research?' he asked.

'In a sense,' I said.

'You've come to the right place. They've got everything you need here. There's almost too much.' He looked around the room in awe.

'Are you a professional researcher?' I asked.

'Oh no. Just an amateur with an interest in these things. Where are you from?'

'I'm from the United Kingdom.'

'Oh! Anywhere near Suffolk?'

I was always thrilled when anybody knew where the UK was, let alone be so specific as to start referencing East Anglia.

'Gloucestershire. Why, have you been to Suffolk?' I asked.

'Oh no, but I would very much like to. I want to visit Rendlesham Forest.'

'Why?' I asked.

His look of total incredulity signalled that I was a total moron.

'Why? Why do you think?' he asked, quite aggressively.

'Because you like forests?'

'Are you serious?'

'Are you into trees?'

His tone had irritated me, so now I was teasing him.

'No, man, I'm not into trees.'

'Oh right. It's just that you really wanted to go to a forest that I've never heard of, and, what with there being a distinct lack of trees around here, I thought maybe you were a tree guy. I've got an app that tells me which tr—' He didn't let me finish.

'I'M NOT INTO TREES, OK? Do you know where you are? This is a research library for UFOs. Why would I be here researching trees?' He had gone a little puce.

'I didn't think you were here researching trees. It was just when you said you wanted to go to the UK to see a forest, I thought you might have another interest apart from UFOs and that interest might be trees, but I was clearly mistaken. I apologise for the misunderstanding.'

There was a long silence.

'So, you haven't heard of the Rendlesham Forest incident?' he asked, a little more calmly.

'No,' I said.

'It was back in 1980, just outside an RAF base called Woodbridge which had US Air Force personnel stationed there. The deputy base commander, a Lieutenant Colonel Charles Halt, reported seeing something landing in Rendlesham Forest. A patrol went to investigate – this was about three in the morning – and they saw a glowing metallic object. It was triangular in shape, with a pulsing red light on the top and blue lights underneath. It flew in between the trees and then disappeared when the patrol approached.'

He had the air of a lecturer now.

'That's it?' I asked. It didn't sound too exciting.

'That's it? That's the British Roswell. You come all the way here and you don't know about your own incidents?' He was angry again.

'Did anybody work out what it was?' I asked.

'It was a UFO. It made all the animals on a nearby farm go into a frenzy.'

'Yes, but when you say a UFO, do you mean aliens?' I asked.

'Of course, what the hell else do you think these are?'

'It's just weird that all these sightings always happen right by US Air Force bases.' I let my thought hang in the air.

'It's not weird at all. They are obviously investigating what military capabilities we have.' He was losing patience with me.

'Why do they keep abducting gap-toothed rednecks then?' I knew I had overstepped the mark before I'd finished my sentence.

'I think we have come to the end of our discussion, sir.'

The man turned back to his book and I was left standing next to a large plastic Yoda. I wondered if this was the moment to let the gentleman know that I'd never seen *Star Wars*. I decided against it. I quietly exited this palace of academia, nearly tripping over a Starship *Enterprise* on the way out.

Not for the first time, I remembered the great Bill Hicks.

'I feel like a UFO – because, just like a UFO I keep appearing in front of hillbillies in Southern towns, and just like a UFO, they find me incomprehensible.'

Back on the melting streets of Roswell, I needed to find somewhere to stay. Looking around, I realised that there would be no good options. I got into my car, now parked next to a large multi-coloured statue of an ostrich being ridden by a green alien, and started to cruise the cross streets.

Eventually I parked up outside a steak house called Cattle Baron. I had a large, tasteless plate of meat, potatoes and something deep fried and green. I scrolled through my phone trying to find somewhere to stay. I tried Airbnb and hit pay dirt. Somebody called Gary was advertising a place to stay in an abandoned ICBM silo. It was somewhere in the middle of the desert, about twenty minutes out of Roswell. I messaged Gary and prayed that it would be available.

Ten minutes later, he replied. The place was available. It wasn't cheap, but I couldn't not do it. He gave me directions, which involved turning off at a particular mile marker on the desert road going east out of town. I left Roswell behind with few regrets. Twenty minutes later, I spotted the mile marker and then the gently nodding oil derrick that was my signal to turn. I followed a track about half a kilometre into the desert until I came to a fence. The gate was open so I drove in and parked up next to a tiny building not much bigger than two telephone boxes. About fifty yards from the building was a large piece of flat cement that I presumed must be the top of the silo itself.

A man came out of the tiny building wearing a T-shirt saying 'Dunder Mifflin', the US version of Wernham Hogg in *The Office*. This comforted me. This was not Gary, but a friend of his who was there to welcome me.

We descended into the bowels of the earth via some metal steps inside the tiny building. The temperature dropped immediately. I relished the cool, slightly musty air on my face. We passed through several thick blast doors until we came to my quarters for the evening. I was to be staying in what had once been the crew control room. What must it have been like for them, sitting around in the middle of nowhere, waiting for the order to unleash Armageddon?

The complex had been built at the height of the Cold War in 1962 as part of the Atlas F project. The silos were only active for a couple of years until advances in technology rendered the Dart missiles redundant. The silos were decommissioned. The current owner, Gary, used to play in the abandoned sites as a kid. He eventually bought a couple for fifty-five thousand dollars each back in the mid-nineties.

There was a fully stocked kitchen, a bathroom, a large living room with loads of books on the Cold War, along with a comfortable bedroom. But the *pièce de résistance* was still to come. Gary's friend took me further down into the complex and through yet more blast doors. He then hit a switch and the silo itself was revealed dramatically. A cloud of bats, startled by the light, filled the void and the air was thick with the smell of damp bat shit.

I looked up to see the monumental cement blocks that formed the roof. These were what I'd seen on arrival. It was chilling to think that, had the order been given, these gargantuan slabs would have opened up on hinges, the missile lifted out of the silo by a counterweight and then launched at its selected target somewhere deep inside the Soviet Union. I wondered whether, back then, those men sleeping in my current quarters would have gone through with it.

I returned to my flat just as Gary, the owner, arrived. He lived with his wife in the silo in a flat beneath mine. He was a former military man and knew everything there was to know about the history of the US missile command. He told me that, although the silos were supposed to be secret sites, everybody knew where they were as they had all been built by locals.

I told him the reason for my trip and asked him his view on the Roswell incident. He knew many of the people involved and scoffed at the idea that they would not know the difference between a weather balloon and a strange craft.

Gary told me that a lot of people who'd been stationed in these missile silos liked to come and stay. Nearly all of them would tell him stories of having seen strange things in the night sky. They described peculiar lights and extreme aerial manoeuvres that were simply not possible for any craft they knew of.

Gary himself was dismissive of little green men but said there was a strong correlation between UFO sightings and nuclear installations. Why? He could not say. The truth was out there, but not down here.

Gary left me to go to down to his part of the facility. I had a shower, got changed and browsed through a couple of books on the Cold War. I hadn't brought any supplies and checked the fridge. It was packed with stuff that previous inhabitants had left. There was a case of hard lemonade. I'd had it before. It was deceptively potent. I picked up the case and headed upstairs to the entrance where I'd noticed one of those chairs you always saw outside desert trailers in the movies.

As I stepped outside, the temperature rose by about twenty degrees. It was about six in the evening and it took me a second or two to adjust to the fading light. I settled down in my chair, cracked open a can and watched the sun set over the desert.

It was beautiful.

I sat very still and watched as bats fluttered about. I cracked open another one. Soon, the last rays of the sun disappeared over the horizon and we reached that magic hour that TV people called bounce light. A small white owl landed on a fence post about seven feet away from me. It stared straight at me with large, hypnotic eyes. There was no noise save for the rhythmic creaking of distant oil derricks. The owl and I stared at each other, neither of us daring to blink.

Suddenly it spoke.

'You alwite?' asked the owl, in an unexpected cockney accent.

'Yes. Fine thank you,' I replied.

'You staying in the silo?' continued the owl.

'Yes. Just for one night,' said I.

'What's wrong with a faaakin' hotel?' snarled the owl.

'I just thought it would be interesting,' I replied.

'Interesting? What's so faaakin' interesting about staying in a metal tube underground? You want to get your faaakin' head examined.'

He was a very sweary owl.

'I just thought it would be a good experience. Something different,' I said.

'Something different? I'll give you something faaakin' different. Three months ago, I was out 'ere, about this time of night, minding me own business, when suddenly there's this faaakin' bright light, like some caaaant has turned a spotlight on me. I look up and there's only a faaakin' spaceship hovering above me. I try and move but me wings are like cement. I can't move nuffink but me eyes. Then this purple light comes down and I feel like faaakin' Westlife. I'm flying but without wings. This purple light effing pulls me into the spaceship and suddenly I'm

126

on a table surrounded by four little green caaaants in lab coats and I bloody know what's coming next.'

The owl tailed off and looked into the distance, deep in thought. A haunted look came over his large brown eyes.

'What was coming next?' I asked.

'What do you bloody fink? It's obviously 'appy hour at the anal probe clinic, innit? I couldn't move a faaakin' feather so I 'ad to lie there while all four of the little green caaaants had a go. Once they'd finished, I could hear the caaants laughing and making "too wit too woo" sounds and then, before I know it, I'm back down 'ere with a faaakin' sore arse and a severe case of PTSD.'

The owl stopped again and looked away for a second before recovering himself and turning back towards me.

'I'm sorry,' I said.

'That's all right. Weren't your fault. I'm just warning ya. If you're going to stay out here for a while, keep your faaakin' wits about ya.'

The owl spread his wings and took off. He went straight up for about a hundred metres before performing an elegant, swooping arc to the right. Then he was gone. I stared up into the perfect sky. Every star was visible. I could make out the Milky Way. Everything felt like it was in ultra-high-definition widescreen. I stretched my hand out towards the sky. I could almost touch the Big Dipper. I was alone in the desert. I was at one with the universe. I cracked open another hard lemonade.

This was seriously good stuff.

I awoke the following morning with a sore head and an empty case of hard lemonade. I made myself some restorative coffee and eggs, and got myself together. I had a long drive ahead of me to Texas. I was going across two time zones and through some of the most barren scenery America has to offer. I packed up my stuff, had one last look inside the missile silo itself and then left, slamming the heavy door behind me. I drove away slowly down the dusty track.

I was on the road again.

4

Texas

After an hour or so I crossed the state line into Texas and the Central Time Zone. I'd tapped my destination into the satnav. I was off to Dallas. It was pretty much a straight line for seven hours with the occasional one-street town along the way. I stopped at a gas station to fill up. The store was full of Big Gulps, Mega-Chips and Big-Dogs. It seemed that the rumours were true. Everything was big in Texas. Curiously the place also had a Bitcoin machine.

Driving through another one-horse town called Tahoka, I spotted what looked like a mass crucifixion. I parked up and walked over, unclear as to what was going on. About 200 feet off the road was a circle of poles with human beings seemingly attached to each one. As I approached, all became clear. It was where the people who maintained the tele-phone lines, which ran between wooden poles for thousands of miles along lonely roads, were taught their trade. About twenty of them were strung up on individual poles by harnesses, being taught by an instructor who stood in the middle of the circle. To pass the time they were throwing a football to each other. It was an intensely surreal scene and strangely beautiful.

About three hours into the drive, I stopped in a town called Post at a restaurant called George's BBQ. George might have been keen on BBQ but he was of Greek origin. The menu had a photo of the Parthenon, the Corinth Canal, plus a potted history of said canal's construction. It was gloriously random. Unfortunately, the menu also had photographs of the meals on offer, presumably in case the punters couldn't read. The food in these photos resembled a war crime. I was not expecting great things.

I ordered a plate of beef brisket. When it came, alongside crazy-generous portions of onion, potato salad, beans and pickles, it was delicious. I toyed with the idea of offering George my photographic skills for an hour or so. Instead, I contented myself with watching a man the size of a truck attempt to exit the restaurant by pushing the *pull* door for a good two minutes.

Back on the road, small Texas towns flashed past me. Each one had billboards that appeared to be trying to impress passing motorists.

The town of Snyder proudly proclaimed that *USA Today* had voted it the '48th best place to live in the USA!'

The town of Sweetwater announced that it was the 'Quail Hunting Capital of the World'.

I doubted there was much competition. Weren't quails tiny chickens? All I could think about was Dick Cheney shooting his friend by mistake while quail hunting – or tiny-chicken shooting, as it should be called.

A tiny quail of a car overtook me. This was something of a rarity in Texas. On the rear window was a sticker saying 'Vote

Beto'. Beto O'Rourke was the ex-punk, Democratic candidate for Texas governor. I rather liked Beto.

Suddenly, a monster pick-up truck with huge double wheels and a 'Let's Go Brandon' sticker roared into view. As it passed me, I spotted another sticker. 'I'm a Republican. Because not everybody can be on welfare.' The monster honked and flashed his lights at the little car, pulling right up behind it until it moved over. The monster zoomed on, black smoke belching out of an oversized exhaust. If ever a metaphor was needed for the great American divide, then there it was.

I drove past another mammoth billboard on the side of the road:

STOP GUN VIOLENCE!

I was pleased. At least there were some sane people in the Lone Star State. Then, I read the smaller print:

get a concealed gun license

America was a truly foreign land.

I finally got to Dallas. I was staying at the Lorenzo. This was the hotel Tina Turner went to when she'd finally had enough of Ike beating her up. It was near the big convention centre and was packed with dull-looking, laminate-sporting delegates. I checked out the pool. The temperature outside was 40 °C and rising but the water was tepid and smelled of chlorine. It was full of people trying to behave like they were at some Vegas pool party.

I headed out to a dive bar called Lee Harvey's, named after Kennedy's assassin (if you believed the mainstream version of events, which I did). The traffic was heavy and I put on a podcast, *The Rest Is History*, to pass the time. Coincidentally, the historians were discussing the end game of British prime ministers. They'd got to Spencer Perceval, the only PM to have been assassinated. He had been shot by John Bellingham, in 1812. I wondered whether Bellingham had a dive bar named after him in his home town of St Neots in Cambridgeshire.

Once at Lee Harvey's, I sat at the bar and ordered a beer and had a think about what to do in town. In a sense, the Kennedy assassination was the ultimate conspiracy theory. Millions of people saw this young, charismatic president get shot thanks to the Zapruder film. This was an 8-mm colour home movie, shot by Abraham Zapruder, who was standing on a plinth just below the grassy knoll on 22 November 1963.

There was something about people dying before their time that really triggered conspiracy theorists. When that person also happened to be the president of the United States then everything went into overdrive. Nobody was satisfied with the neat explanation that a lone gunman, Lee Harvey Oswald, had shot the president from the sixth floor of the Texas Book Depository as his motorcade swept past on Dealey Plaza. People started to talk about a second shooter on the grassy knoll. There was a person holding an umbrella – was that some sort of message? Maybe Lyndon Baines Johnson was responsible? He had never liked this young upstart and had been forced to take the role of vice president when Kennedy won the 1960 election by the thinnest of margins. Maybe he had a hand in it?

I couldn't help but think about the satirical site *The Onion's* fake front page:

Kennedy slain by
CIA, Mafia, Castro,
LBJ, Freemasons,
Teamsters.
President shot 129 times
from 45 different angles . . .

What was it about events like this that made people so desperate for some larger explanation? People just couldn't accept that, sometimes, shit happened. It reminded me of a quote by Zbigniew Brzezinski, President Carter's national security advisor (and also an advisor to Lyndon Johnson). He'd said, 'History is much more the product of chaos than of conspiracy.'

Humans seem to need to try to make order of chaos. This is tricky because chaos tends to be chaotic.

I awoke early the next morning. Despite having been before, I surprised myself by how excited I was. Dealey Plaza was only five minutes away in an Uber and it was already 28 °C outside. Nevertheless, I decided to heighten my anticipation by walking there. Back in 2010, I had woken up with exactly the same sense of excitement and had also decided to walk. 'Only the insane and the destitute walked in America', was what I'd written back then. This was still very much the case, even more so, if the truth be told.

I was wearing a T-shirt that I'd bought from the dive bar the night before. On it were the words:

Lee Harvey's
Dallas, Texas

133

I was already slightly regretting this. It was like turning up to the 9/11 memorial wearing a T-shirt saying:

Osama bin Laden
North American Tour

I walked fast, ignoring the stares of the homeless, pushing their shopping trolleys of despair towards nowhere.

And then, I was there. The mysterious energy that this place had emitted the last time I'd visited was still present. People often ask me why I like to visit these kind of places. Wasn't it a touch morbid? To me, there is no difference between this and spending sixteen hours queueing up along the Thames to walk past the coffin of a ninety-six-year-old woman that you didn't know. It was a way of touching history.

A couple of things had changed since I was last there. The white X painted on the road to mark the exact spot that Kennedy's head had exploded had been enlarged and tidied up. The Sixth Floor Museum had also been enlarged and tidied up. The entrance was now at the rear, just behind the grassy knoll, whereas before it had been on Houston Street. Back then there was a sign on the door banning firearms and photography. I'd always felt that the no-firearms rule was a little late, shutting the stable door once the horse had bolted. The new museum still banned them but photography was now permitted. This was progress of sorts.

I was there early and the museum was not yet open. I noticed a sign telling visitors that they needed to pre-book tickets and so I went onto their app and booked a ticket for when they opened at 10 a.m.

Pleased with my organisational abilities I strolled back down to the top of Dealey Plaza. As I got to the corner of Houston and Elm, directly below the window from where Oswald's position had been, I spotted a plaque on the side of the red-brick building. It had been put up by the Texas Historical Commission. They were obviously keen to emphasise that Dallas was more than just JFK. Two thirds of the plaque told the visitor about the, frankly, deeply uninteresting history of the building. At the bottom, however, they got to the pertinent stuff:

On November 22, 1963, the building gained national notoriety when Lee Harvey Oswald allegedly shot and killed President John F. Kennedy from a sixth-floor window as the presidential motorcade passed the site.

I had to check the plaque twice. It really did use the word 'allegedly'. Somebody had even scratched around it to highlight the use of the word. It seemed that, for the Texas Historical Commission, despite the findings of the Warren Commission, the facts were still very much in question.

I was pretty astonished at this. It was a bit like the National Trust getting involved in crop circles.

I sent them an email:

Hi

I am a British travel writer researching a new book about travelling across America. I was in Dallas recently and spotted the plaque on the Texas Book Depository.

I was wondering who made the decision to use the word

'allegedly' and what the thought process behind that was, as it seems to encourage a conspiracy theory?

Thank you in advance.

Dom Joly

After quite some time, I received a reply from a gentleman called Chris Florance, the director of the Communications Division. His answer was pretty simple:

Since Lee Harvey Oswald was murdered before he was charged or tried, our historians used the word 'allegedly' to describe the crimes commonly attributed to him.

This made sense. He had never been convicted. But they must have known that the use of the word would excite conspiracy theorists.

There were very few people about and so I took the opportunity to take some photographs of the site, including the new X, before walking up to the grassy knoll.

Dealey Plaza had been part of a new conspiracy theory recently. On 2 November 2021, a crowd of QAnon and Trump supporters gathered there because they believed that JFK's son, John F Kennedy Jr, who died in a plane crash in 1999, was going to appear and make an important announcement. Nobody was exactly sure what he was going to say, but many had their own theories. One QAnon supporter from Florida, interviewed on the day, had this to say: 'What we're learning is that JFK, when he was shot here, he was the second coming of Jesus Christ, and he was resurrected four days later, and he's been living in witness protection as well as his son and more than nine hundred others. And this is the route that he took, but now it's going to be the route that he'll finish.'

Another gentleman claimed that JFK Jr was going to announce that he was alive and was going to run as Trump's vice president in the 2024 election.

The big event was supposed to happen at twelve-thirty. The appointed time duly arrived and nothing happened. The crowd hung around expectantly for a couple of hours until it started to rain and they all eventually drifted off, many claiming that JFK Jr would now reveal himself at the Rolling Stones concert that was taking place that evening. Unfortunately for the believers, they couldn't get no satisfaction. JFK Jr was a no-show there as well.

As I reached the plinth where Zapruder had stood to film the action, I was joined by a guy wearing a T-shirt that read 'Occupy Mars'. I couldn't be sure which team he belonged to. He checked out my T-shirt and nodded admiringly. I did likewise. It was awkward. We were like two gate-crashers at a stranger's funeral.

'Hey,' I said.

'Hey,' he said back.

'First time here?' I asked.

'Yeah. You?'

'Second time.'

'Oh.'

This wasn't a great conversation. I was about to move on when he spoke again.

'You're British?'

'I am British.'

'I could tell by your accent.'

'Have you been there?'

'Where?'

'Britain.'

'No.'

'Oh right.'

'What are you doing in the USA?'

'I'm writing a book on conspiracies.'

At this, my new friend froze and stared at me for a while.

'Do you know about Q?' he asked.

I tried not to look excited, but I was. I'd hooked one. I'd reeled in a real-life QAnon supporter.

'Yes, I've heard a bit about him.'

'What you heard?'

'That he's somebody in Deep State who is leaking information about what is going on?' I was a bit vague, because I was.

'He's not leaking. He's telling patriots the truth. He's warning us about all the shit that's happening without our knowledge.' My new friend was now quite agitated.

'Wasn't there a meeting for QAnon here a year or so ago?' I tried to look nonchalant.

'The JFK Jr thing? Yeah, but he got spooked. Q explained that he wasn't ready.'

'Ready for what?' I asked.

'To reveal himself,' he answered.

'Q or JFK Jr?' I asked.

'JFK Jr. Q never wants his identity revealed or they'd kill him.'

My new friend looked around as though we might be being listened to.

'Did they kill JFK Jr?' I asked, looking serious.

'They wanted to. That's why he faked his death. The Clintons were in on it. They wanted him out of the way so Hillary could have a clear run for the White House.'

He made a weird face when he said Hillary, like he'd sucked a particularly sour lemon.

'I keep hearing this about the Clintons. They seem to have been very busy killing a lot of people,' I said.

'You don't know the half of it. There is so much shit that we don't know about.' He looked sad.

'Is Chelsea involved?' I asked.

He looked confused. 'Chelsea?'

'Chelsea Clinton, their daughter,' I said, clarifying.

'Oh right. I'm pretty sure she is. This goes way deep.'

He seemed, for all intents and purposes, like a fairly normal, slightly geeky guy, but a quick check under the hood was revealing an unusual engine.

'I'm confused. Why would JFK Jr return and support Trump. Wasn't he pretty famously a Democrat, as was his dad?' This was a genuine question.

'That was old-school Democrats. Things have changed a heck load since then,' he said.

'But JFK Jr died – faked – his death in 1999. He was a Democrat then, so he must have supported Bill Clinton, right?' I was actually interested to hear the answer.

'No, he saw how they were operating and was against them but had to pretend to support them. That's why he faked his death because he knew he was in danger.'

'Hasn't a lot of what Q predicted not happened?' I asked.

'People have misinterpreted what he said. He is just trying to warn us without giving away his identity to the Deep State.'

I said nothing for a moment. Not for the first time, it felt like we were in two different realities.

I had to try and understand why people followed this stuff.

'Can I ask you what you do for a living?' I said.

'Sure, I'm a day trader.'

'So, you play the stock market from home?' I asked.

'Yup.'

'How long have you done that?' I asked.

'Nine years or so, ever since I lost my job,' he said.

'What was that?' I asked.

He suddenly got a bit anxious.

'You going to write about all this? I don't wanna talk about this stuff.'

'No problem, I'm just nosey,' I said, truthfully.

'Sorry, I guess, I just don't feel comfortable.'

'Can I ask you one more question then?'

'You can ask.'

'What do you say to people who think that the stuff you are telling me is batshit crazy and that you are either gullible or insane?'

I tried not to sound like I was having a go. I was genuinely interested.

'You think that big corporations and the global elite don't conspire to retain their power and control? Are you honestly telling me that you are that naive? If so, people like you are the reason they succeed. Wake up, bro.'

I was sure he was going to use the word sheeple but, to his credit, he didn't.

'I accept that there is corruption, nepotism, common interests, criminal activity, dodgy shit that happens. But I don't think it's one big, organised conspiracy.'

Stacey and I, possibly in Finland.

The Russian Embassy in Tallinn.

The Cockney owl in New Mexico.

A whisky sour in Denver Union Station, Colorado.

Walter White's house in Albuquerque, New Mexico.

Roswell's fast-food street, New Mexico.

Me at the Roswell sign in New Mexico.

Deep underground in my missile silo,
somewhere near Roswell, New Mexico.

The crucifixion scene re-enacted in Tahoka, Texas.

X marks the spot where the fatal bullet hit JFK in Dallas, Texas.

What Lee Harvey Oswald saw in Dallas, Texas.

Grim scenes in Waco, Texas.

Gavin and Meg in Austin, Texas.

A gun demonstration in
Austin, Texas.

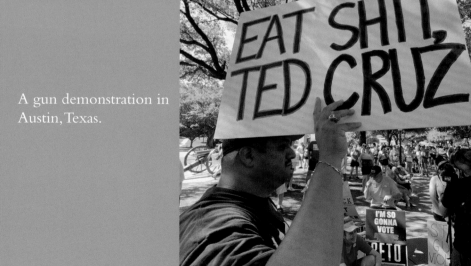

Ted at Camelot Castle in Cornwall.

Back to the fifties at Gander International Airport in Newfoundland.

Pete and I in Dildo, Newfoundland.

Abandoned flat earth museum
in Fogo, Newfoundland.

Underneath the Fogo Island Inn in Fogo, Newfoundland.

The edge of the world. Brimstone Head in Fogo, Newfoundland.

'The fact that you can't see it is the scary part, bro. That's the clever part.' He smiled sadly.

I really wanted to ask him about how, of all people, Donald Trump was the antidote to all this but I genuinely didn't want to fall out. He seemed like a decent enough guy. Also, it was interesting to chat to somebody like him IRL as opposed to arguing on social media where any attempt at balance or nuance was doomed. I did wish he'd stop calling me bro though.

'Do you think Oswald killed Kennedy?' I asked.

'Fuck no, man, he was a patsy. He said so himself before they killed him.'

'So, who did kill him?' I asked.

'Deep State. The military–industrial complex. Eisenhower warned us about it. You don't do what they want, you are gone.'

It became fairly clear that our conversation was now at an end. I nodded at him and then we drifted apart and went in different directions.

Maybe the Texas Historical Commission had got it right?

Still excited about my encounter with a real-life conspiracy nut, I headed off to get some breakfast in preparation for my visit to the Sixth Floor Museum. I found a place called the Corner Bakery and sat in the window. The breakfast options were slightly lighter and healthier here in the city, as opposed to the cardiac-arresting portions served on the road.

There was a handsome red-brick building directly opposite me, on the other side of the street.

A homeless man was lying on the concrete, in the middle of the pavement, right outside the front door. A couple of employees arriving for work, gingerly stepped over him and entered the building. A black guy ambled past. He was smartly dressed

and seemed in a hurry. As he passed by, the seemingly unconscious homeless guy raised his arm and clenched his fist in what
resembled a Black Power salute. The black guy glanced
awkwardly at the guy on the ground and walked on.

There was a commotion behind me. A homeless woman
had snuck into the restaurant. She had put her mouth over one
of the soda taps and was gulping it down like it was going out
of fashion. There was uproar. Three members of staff grabbed
her and she started punching them. A full fistfight broke out
with the homeless woman screaming like a banshee. Tables
were turned over. It was chaos. Eventually, the homeless
woman was overpowered, but not until after she had put up a
spectacular defence. She was frogmarched out of the place as
she screamed.

'I'm gonna come back and kill every one of you assholes!'

Not wishing to take a chance on this, I finished up and headed
back to the museum. As I rounded the corner into Dealey Plaza,
it had filled up significantly. It was now crawling with tourists
and conspiracy touts. A guy was approaching people and offering them some juicy alternative facts. I followed him and eavesdropped as he cornered a middle-aged couple.

'Hey, do you guys want to hear stuff you won't hear in the
museum?' he asked.

The man seemed receptive but the wife, less so.

'I know Oliver Stone. I also had Johnny Depp on one of my
tours just six months ago. He told me that Amber Heard was a
potential killer.'

He was in full flow now and the wife appeared a little more
interested now Mr Depp's name had been mentioned.

'He thinks Amber Heard killed Kennedy?'

'No, ma'am. She's too young for that but he said that she had it in her.' The man sensed a bite.

'Talk to him. He's the expert.' The wife pointed at her husband. 'He's been studying the case for forty years.' She rolled her eyes slightly.

'Oh yeah? Do you know about Lee Bowers?' asked the man.

'The guy in the tower?' answered the husband.

They were referencing a guy who had been working in a tower operated by the Union Terminal Company. It overlooked the car park and the grassy knoll. He had been a witness to the assassination. He'd said he had spotted two men he didn't know in the vicinity of the grassy knoll. He described a 'flash of light or smoke' from that vicinity as the motorcade passed.

'You know they killed him, right?' The man was interrogating the husband. 'He died in a car accident in 1966. Very convenient.' He was wide-eyed with derision.

'Yeah,' said the husband.

'And you know about the cell where they held Ruby, right?' He pointed to a building in the distance.

I love eavesdropping, but the door to the museum had opened. I didn't want to miss my slot so I slipped away.

The new museum was much improved. It had a fabulous recreation of the scene and an interesting virtual reality recreation of the motorcade. I also got to see the actual Zapruder camera. Thankfully, this time nobody stopped me taking a photo out of the window. Last time, the museum had suddenly got very realistic as I, like Oswald, had been forced to flee the sixth floor pursued by angry security people, having taken an illegal shot.

I spent half an hour in the museum before returning to the street again.

What must it have been like to have been a witness that day? This rockstar president and his wife driving past you. Hearing the gun shots. Taking in what had happened. And then, for the next twenty, thirty years, to be interviewed over and over again about those twenty dramatic seconds of your life. Your story had to change, expand, meander a little as it developed.

I had one other thought. What was it with assassins having three names? John Wilkes Booth, Lee Harvey Oswald, James Earl Ray. Somebody needed to keep an eye on Griff Rhys Jones.

I walked back to the hotel and got my car. I drove along the exact route of the motorcade. When I turned into Elm and drove over the white cross, I put my foot down and sped off. I was not, however, bound for Parkland Hospital, like the late president. I headed for the Interstate. I was headed south towards Austin, with a little detour along the way.

About an hour and half later, I drove into Waco.

The name was synonymous with one thing: the Waco siege, or massacre, depending on your viewpoint. In 1993 authorities surrounded the Mount Carmel Center ranch, headquarters of a religious sect called the Branch Davidians. They were led by a man called David Koresh.

The authorities suspected the group of stockpiling a large number of illegal weapons and attempted to search the compound. Six Davidians and four government agents were killed in the ensuing shootout and the siege began. It lasted for fifty-one days, only ending when the FBI launched a full-on assault that resulted in the compound catching fire. Seventy-six Branch Davidians, including Koresh, died in the ensuing blaze.

The siege was a catalyst for a massive increase in mistrust of the federal government. It led to the growth of militia organisations and events like the Oklahoma City bombing. It did appear to have been a vastly excessive use of force by the government against some religious nuts.

Waco itself is the home of Baylor University, which has a stadium that rivals Wembley in size. I found a place called Union Hall. It was one of those posh food malls. I had some chicken wings and a soft drink in a container the size of my car. Sated, I waddled back to my vehicle and drove for a further 15 miles east of Waco, through a poor, rural area, before arriving at the site of the siege.

I stopped at the gates. They were open but I was uncertain whether I could just drive in. America, as I knew from bitter experience, was not a country where you wanted to trespass without thinking it through. Eventually I drove in and parked up outside a couple of small buildings near the entrance. I knocked on the doors. There was nobody about. I got back into the car and drove on down the track further into the property.

I came to what looked like a church. It was a rather lovely setting. It was by a lake and a couple of horses trotted over to say hello. I walked over to the church and noticed what looked like brick foundations to the left of the building. There was a sign:

The vault area.
Where the mothers and
their children were
gassed to death.

This was it. I was standing on the site of the compound, burned to the ground in the siege. It was a creepy feeling. I walked up to the front door of the church and tried it. It was locked. I was about to leave when I spotted a side door. I gave it a go. It was open.

I went inside.

I entered a large room that resembled a village hall. There was a screen where the altar should have been and a projector showing a film of the 'government murders'. The walls were covered in T-shirts and posters that either supported Trump, slagged off Hillary Clinton, or just had a pop at the government in general. There were also graphic photographs of the charred bodies of children, presumably in the remains of the compound.

There was one T-shirt that seemed to be aimed at the tourist dollar. It was a map of Texas:

I VISITED MT. CARMEL
SITE OF THE 2 MASSACRES
Branch Davidians: 4-19-1993
Huaco Indians: 2-19-1835

I felt incredibly uneasy being in there. It was like I was on the set of a Louis Theroux documentary, just before the loonies arrived. Where was everybody? More importantly, how would they react if they discovered me in there, snooping about? I presumed that this place was intended to receive visitors, but I couldn't be sure. There was a white board in the corner. It had stuff scribbled on it. The aftermath of some lesson. Above a couple of pictures of the Tabernacle and the Ark of the Covenant was a roughly drawn human brain with arrows pointing to the different parts of it.

1. Frontal Lobe
2. Secret Holy Place

3. Prayers
4. Mechanical Reasoning
5. Holy Place

This was not a place I would rush to should I need brain surgery. I picked up a book called *Why the Deep State Massacred David Koresh*.

It was the Deep State again. They were very busy. I was joking to myself but I was feeling uneasy. Had I stumbled into some insurrectionist revenge convention? Were they all on a quick lunch break? Were they all about to come back in to find this English weirdo standing in the middle of their church? Would they suspect me of being a government agent? Random scenes from *Mississippi Burning* started flashing through my head. I really was a bit rubbish at this investigative stuff . . . I got spooked too easily. But there was something very spooky about this place. It wasn't just the extremist literature strewn about the place. There was something in the air. I'd felt it before in places – Auschwitz, Tuol Sleng, Sabra and Chatila, Swindon . . .

I exited the building. There was still nobody about. One of the horses was staring at me with big, nervous eyes. I took the hint. I needed to leave. I got in my car and drove out of the ranch, turning left and zooming off down the road until I was a good couple of miles away. I stopped by the side of the road to make some notes. I had parked right under a large yellow sign. It read:

When flooded, turn around.
Don't drown.

This seemed like sound advice.

I drove on until I spotted a petrol station. I was still feeling a touch paranoid. I'd seen so many flickering CCTV clips of these places being held up at gunpoint. I spotted a colour-coded measuring strip on the door. It was presumably so that CCTV could get an accurate read on a suspect's height as he fled the place having shot everybody dead. I paid up and walked fast back to my car. I was getting very jumpy in Texas.

I eventually arrived in Austin, the capital of Texas. It was a curious place. A college town and a liberal oasis, entirely surrounded by hicks. It was like West Berlin, marooned in the middle of East Germany. I'd half-imagined that the place would be surrounded by watchtowers with snipers primed to pick off any hippy or hipster that dared stray outside the city limits.

Austin's motto was 'Keep Austin Weird'.

I pretty much fell in love with the city immediately. I drove along green, treelined streets until I got to my destination for the next couple of days. I was house-crashing. During lock-down, I'd started a Twitch channel to keep myself amused. A guy called Gavin kept popping up and we became friends. He turned out to be a YouTube phenomenon as one half of the Slow Mo Guys. He and his friend filmed loads of stuff in super-slow motion and had become a massive hit.

Gavin told me that the reason he did what he did was because of *Trigger Happy TV*, which he said he had been obsessed with as a kid. I was obviously flattered, and I liked him. He seemed like a really nice guy. I'd told him that I longed to visit Austin. He told me that, should I ever do so, I should come stay with him. I was sure he didn't think that I would take him up on this.

He was wrong.

We'd been exchanging messages on WhatsApp and he had given me directions to his place. He'd asked me not to take any photos or footage of it. I thought he was being a bit dramatic, but seeing as how I was about to become an unwanted house guest for a couple of days, I wasn't going to argue.

I pulled up outside his place. We had never met. What could possibly go wrong?

Gavin and his girlfriend Meg came out to greet me. Meg, it turned out, was as famous as Gavin. She was a massive star on Twitch, famous for cosplaying, often as characters from video games. The house was lovely, but it turned out that I was not staying there. Gavin took me through the garden to the house next door. This was also theirs and where I'd be staying. Meg showed me her gull-wing Tesla and her Aston Martin in the garage. I was definitely in the wrong job.

I unpacked and had a look about. Meg had her studio on the ground floor. In my bedroom was a large pile of books featuring a naked Meg. It was an interesting introduction to my hostess. I made my way back over to the main house where I found them listening to a vinyl LP of Nintendo soundtracks.

I felt very old.

Hopping into the Tesla, we drove into downtown Austin. We went to a place called Stubb's for some BBQ. This could have been incredibly awkward, but it wasn't. Meg turned out to be quite the dark horse. She spoke fluent Japanese and her stepdad, who spoke Russian, Korean and Vietnamese, had worked in Area 51.

Everything for a reason.

Meg had little knowledge of what he did there as he didn't talk about it. But she was convinced that, had he worked with extraterrestrials, she would have known about it.

We eventually got around to Gavin's request for me not to take any photos or film of the exterior of the house. If he had stalkers, then he'd made it, I joked. Both he and Meg looked uncomfortable. I'd made a faux pas. Eventually, they told me the story.

An obsessive fan of Meg's, who lived in New Mexico, seriously objected to the fact that she and Gavin were together. One night he had driven all the way from New Mexico to Austin. This, as I could attest, was quite a journey. When he arrived in Austin, it was about three in the morning. Meg and Gavin were asleep.

The guy pulled up outside their house, turned off the engine and then sat there for about ten minutes. They knew this because Gavin had just installed a series of security cameras and they captured everything.

After ten minutes the guy, who looked a lot like Dwight Schrute from the American *Office*, got out of his car and walked up to the front door carrying a pistol. He shot the lock off the door and entered the house.

Luckily, Gavin and Meg's bedroom door was in an unusual position. It was directly to the left of the front door as you entered. The gunman did not notice it. He started to roam around the house, searching every room methodically, his gun raised and ready.

Meanwhile, Gavin and Meg had woken up, realised that somebody was in the house and had hidden in a cupboard. They were unarmed as they were not gun owners. Gavin had a taser that he held up in front of him as he watched the gunman walk around their house on his mobile phone.

When he was at the far end of the house, they called the police.

Eventually the intruder found their bedroom and entered. Gavin and Meg sat stock-still in the cupboard, hardly daring to breathe. The gunman looked around and then exited their room. He had one last look in the living room and then, apparently deciding that they were not home, went out of the front door and started walking towards his car. Gavin and Meg started to breathe again. Suddenly he turned and re-entered the house. He made for the far end of the living room. He picked up what appeared to be some form of cosh that he had left on the sofa.

That mistake probably cost him his life. He left the house again and got into his car. As he did so police cars pulled up, their lights illuminating him. On the footage, you could hear the police screaming at him to come out with his hands up. Then, a gunshot. The intruder had shot himself in the head. The bullet ricocheted off his skull and hit one of the police cars. The police, thinking they were being shot at, opened fire and peppered the gunman's car.

Then it was over. The police, confused by what was going on, took Gavin and Meg into separate rooms to interview them. By the time they got to Gavin, he had edited the security camera footage to give the police a full movie version of the events.

It turned out that the man's intention had been to kill Gavin and force Meg into some lesbian relationship with another online star.

Gavin pulled out his phone and showed me the footage. It was chilling.

'Wow. What do you do after something like that?' I asked.

'You buy a gun,' said Gavin, smiling wanly.

I had trigger happy fans, but in an entirely different way. I was glad I'd never made the move to the States when the occasion arose. I'd stick to the keyboard warriors I battled on Facebook. This was too much.

We drove back to their house and I triple-locked my guest house.

Before I went to bed, I told Gavin and Meg that should they decide I was an unwanted house guest then they should leave a towel hanging off their balcony. If I saw it the following morning, I would disappear and we would never speak of any of this again.

Come the next day, I was relieved to see that there was no towel on the balcony.

Nevertheless, I didn't want to impinge on them too much. I drove into town, to a place called Phoebe's Diner. I wrote a column, plotted out my plan for Austin and posted photographs of my breakfast in America.

That's the depressing thing about social media. Despite me posting a variety of what I considered to be thought-provoking and interesting photographs as I drove across the country, it was the photographs of my breakfasts, along with musings as to whether it was ever acceptable to order three eggs (it is), that were by far the most popular.

My vague plan was to try and hunt down Alex Jones. He was the face of *InfoWars*, the online outlet responsible for promulgating a vast litany of conspiracy nonsense. Jones lived in Austin. He could often be found on social media videos getting into altercations with punters in local restaurants. I'd asked Gavin to put feelers out to see if anybody he knew had any idea where I might be able to find him.

While I waited for leads, I took a look around. There was one historical event in particular that I wanted to learn more about. I wanted to visit 'The Tower'.

This was the main building tower at the University of Texas campus in the middle of town. It was the scene of America's first media-covered mass shooting.

On 1 August 1966, having stabbed both his mother and wife to death, Charles Joseph Whitman, a Marine veteran, took a load of rifles and other weapons up to the observation deck of the tower and started opening fire indiscriminately on people below.

Over the next ninety-six minutes he killed fourteen people and injured thirty-one. His killing spree finally ended when two people rushed the tower and eventually shot him dead. At the time this was the deadliest mass shooting in US history. I'd just seen a great documentary on the whole affair. It had used original news footage and mixed it, as so many documentaries were now doing, with clever animation to fill the gaps. I remembered a film that I'd seen as a kid called *Two Minute Warning* in which a sniper clambered up a stadium tower and started firing randomly into the Super Bowl crowd. This had to have been inspired by the Austin shooting.

I wondered whether there were any conspiracy theories around the Austin sniper. Nowadays, Alex Jones would have been all over it, claiming that the sniper was a government agent, or didn't exist. Even if a bullet had pierced his barrel of a chest, he'd probably have been lying on the floor screaming, 'This isn't happening. Nothing you see here is real.' Even worse: people would have believed him.

The official (and, as far as I could see, only) version was that Whitman had a brain tumour the size of a pecan, pressing on the part of his brain that controlled emotions. Alex Jones would have had a field day with that.

153

I walked over to the university campus. It was a beautiful place and anybody would be lucky to go there as a student. I wondered what would have happened had I attended an establishment like this, as opposed to my alma mater, SOAS (the School of Oriental and African Studies) in London, with its grim concrete architecture. Would I have spent more time at university? Would it have been a more fulfilling, enjoyable experience? By my third year I almost never went in. I hated the whole thing so much. The one day I did go in, when I had to hand in some excuse for work, there was a picket line outside. I was called a scab for crossing it. I tried to explain that I had been conducting my own personal boycott of the place for most of the last three years, but it fell on deaf ears.

I walked around the tower, trying to work out from which side the sniper had mainly been firing. Several of his victims had lain wounded on the burning concrete, unable to move to safety. I eventually worked out where this had happened. I stopped a student and asked them if they knew anything about it? She pointed me in the direction of a memorial garden.

If I was honest, it was a bit shoddy. Nobody seemed to be taking very good care of the place. Finally, I found a proper memorial. It was a 6-foot, pink granite monument with the names of the victims carved into it.

The Austin Tower shooting was a massive event in 1966. Along with the Vietnam War, it was the story of the year. America had just come to terms with the Kennedy assassination. This, however, was something new, something more random.

It was a warning of things to come.

In keeping with my sixties tour of Austin, I went to visit the Lyndon Baines Johnson Presidential Library. Every president, when they left office, had a library set up in which to keep their archives and document their term in office. The idea of a Donald Trump Presidential Library was hilarious. I presumed that it would store picture books only, with a Dunkin' Donuts attached.

The LBJ Presidential Library and Museum was an imposing modern building. It was packed with bored-looking schoolkids clutching clipboards. I ambled through the exhibition that laid out LBJ's life in a timeline. I particularly enjoyed the scaled down mock-up of the Oval Office. It was an eighth smaller than the actual one. It did make me wonder why they hadn't just gone the whole hog and made it the exact size.

LBJ had all of his telephone calls secretly recorded. This provided a fascinating insight into his presidency. I listened to one call at random and it was a doozy. LBJ was talking to Katharine Graham from the *Washington Post*. LBJ was obviously rather taken with her. I listened, slightly cringing at what, back then, possibly appeared charming. To modern ears, it was a touch creepy.

'I wish I could be like one of those young animals on my ranch – jump the fence just to see your sweet face,' drooled the president.

Overall, the LBJ Presidential Library and Museum had a touch of North Korea about it. I half-expected to see his embalmed body on display. My big takeaway from the place was that LBJ resembled a depressed bloodhound.

As I reached my car, I got a lead. I had a business address for Alex Jones. I drove over the river and headed towards East Congress. I ended up at a crummy-looking low-rise office block. This was not the multi-million-dollar media empire that I was expecting. I parked up behind the building and walked

round to the front door. I checked the names on the door buzz-
ers and found no *InfoWars* or Alex Jones. I pressed a couple of
them randomly and someone let me in. I went up some stairs
and found myself in a run-down, communal area. There was a
small kitchen to my right and a corridor leading to various
cramped-looking offices. The building appeared to be deserted.
Finally, I walked past an office where a woman was sitting at a
desk.

I knocked on the door and entered. She looked up, startled to
see somebody, anybody in this dump.

'Hi, sorry to bother you, can I ask you a question?' I said,
being as friendly and British as I could muster.

'Well now. Hi yourself. What can I assist you with?' She
smiled, probably assuming I was third in line to the throne and
that this might just be her Meghan Markle moment. Her ticket
out of there.

'Umm, I'm looking for *InfoWars*. I'm trying to speak to Alex
Jones?'

Her demeanour changed instantly. Suddenly, I was no longer a
rather long-in-the-tooth Prince Charmingish. I was now a pest.

'I have no idea about any of that,' she said sharply.

'I just had information that their offices were here?' I said.

'I think they maybe used to be. Not any more. Sorry.' She
looked back down at her computer.

'Do you happen to know where they moved to?' I asked,
turning up the Brit.

'I don't know. We get lots of people coming and asking.' She
looked uncertain.

'So, they were here. Did you ever see him – Alex Jones?' I
persevered.

'Sure. But not for a while. As I said, they moved. Too many people looking for them.' She looked at me accusatorially.

'I'm a writer looking to talk to him about his crazy theories,' I took a gamble and guessed that she was not a supporter.

It paid off.

'You can say that again. But I can't help you, I'm really sorry.' She looked around as though people might be listening in, even though we were clearly alone.

'Oh no worries. Thank you for your time anyhow.'

I was just about to leave when she started to write something down on a piece of paper. Without looking at me, she passed it over the desk. I picked it up and read it. It was an address. I nodded at her but didn't say anything. I was paranoid now. She smiled nervously and I left her office and headed back to the car. This manhunting was exciting stuff.

The address she had given me was only about ten minutes away. I drove straight over. It was a strip mall with what appeared to be a series of offices on top of some of the stores. Was this *InfoWars* HQ? Was America's conspiracy hunger being fed from this dump?

For a while I couldn't find the address. Then I realised that I was on the wrong side of the main building. I walked around and followed the numbers until I finally arrived outside the address.

It was a UPS store.

I was gutted. I went inside and asked an employee whether *InfoWars* or Alex Jones had a PO Box there. Surprisingly, she told me that they did.

I retreated to my car to think about what to do. Should I set up a stakeout? I was only in Austin for three days. This could be a total waste of time.

Just as I was debating my next move, Twitter came to my rescue. Somebody had found out where Alex Jones lived. Not only that, but they had an aerial photo of his house and GPS coordinates.

Dom Joly PI was back in business.

Then I realised that I wasn't actually sure how GPS coordinates worked. I spent an excruciating twenty minutes sitting in the car trying to find out. Eventually, I was pretty sure that I'd cracked it. An address on the outskirts of Austin appeared on my map. I gunned the engine and headed off.

Twenty-five minutes later and I was in a different Austin. This was a seriously plush part of town. Large, handsome houses squatted in the shade of treelined streets. My satnav took me to the entrance of a gated community. It looked pretty heavily fortified. I drove up to the gates and looked for an intercom. I wasn't sure what I'd say if there was one, but I was hoping that the bumbling British thing might work. It always did for Louis Theroux.

There was no intercom, just a keypad. I pressed the number of the house that I had found on Twitter, followed by the little bell symbol. There was no answer. This was Texas. There was no way I was going to climb over the gates and end up as target practice.

As I sat pondering my next move, a car approached the gates from the inside. They swung open to let it out. Then, ten seconds later, the gates in front of me swung open as well. I hesitated for a second, and then went in. I drove around for a while checking out the vast houses that made up the community. It seemed that the conspiracy business was a lucrative one.

I eventually found the number of the house that had been given to me. I parked up and looked at it for a while. I had no idea what I was going to do. I suddenly felt not too dissimilar to Gavin and Meg's intruder. Maybe I should forget it. I should get out of there. But I had come a long way for this.

I took a couple of deep breaths and got out. I started to walk up the drive. As I approached the building, I could see somebody on the phone through a side window in the front door. He spotted me at the same time as I saw him. I waved awkwardly but he blanked me.

Whoever it was, it was not Alex Jones. I'd heard stories that Jones supposedly shared houses with people so that they could fudge ownership and safeguard them from lawsuits. Was this one of them? The guy continued chatting on the phone as I stood awkwardly on the doorstep. Eventually, I pressed the doorbell. He opened the door. He was wearing a blue Lacoste polo, chinos and brogues. He still had his phone to his ear.

'What do you want?' he said.

'Hi, I'm from the UK,' I said before he interrupted me.

'Congratulations, what do you fucking want?' He was all Texas charm.

'I'd like to speak to Alex Jones.' I tried to sound nonchalant.

The man paused for a second, then spoke into his phone.

'I'm going to call you back.'

He put the phone down and stared at me.

'And who are you?' he asked.

'I'm from the UK. I'm a travel writer and I want to chat to him about *InfoWars* and conspiracy theories.'

'Yeah? Well, that's a no.' The man started to close the door.

'But he does live here, right?' I asked.

'You need to leave here now. How did you get in?' asked the man.

'I drove in,' I said.

'Who let you in?' he asked.

'The gate opened,' I replied, truthfully.

'This is a private community and you should not be here,' he said.

'Does Alex Jones live here?' I continued, starting to feel like a proper investigative reporter.

I had the bit between my teeth and I was not going to let go.

'Fuck off.' He was going a touch red.

'I want to speak to Alex Jones, now,' I said.

'Oh, do you?' said the man, opening the door a touch wider.

As he did, another person stepped into the large hall area behind the guy I was talking to. It was him. It was Alex Jones. His barrel chest was unmistakeable. He appeared surprised to find somebody at the door and stared at me. This was exciting. I'd tracked him down.

Maybe I would win the Pulitzer Prize for this.

'Mr Jones, could I have a quick word? I've come all the way from London. It's about the gay frogs . . .' I tried to talk over the first guy.

Jones said nothing, but the first man turned and looked pointedly to his left. I followed his gaze. There was a little side table and on top of it was a rather impressive handgun.

I looked at it. He looked at it. Then we both started looking at each other again. Alex Jones turned and went back into the main part of the house without saying a word.

'You're on my property. You've got ten seconds to get off my property. How does that sound?'

160

The first man looked like he was not fucking about. All thoughts of the Pulitzer Prize, even posthumous, disappeared and I started to back away fast.

'Thank you. Sorry for bothering you,' I said in my bumbliest, poshest English accent.

In America, the man with the gun is always right.

I got back into my car and drove out of the gated community. I wasn't sure that I was really cut out to be an investigative reporter. It was all quite nerve-wracking.

I drove to South Congress and had a restorative bite in the Magnolia Cafe, something of an Austin institution. While in there, I saw a flyer for an anti-gun rally outside the State Capitol the following day. It was in response to the recent school shooting in Uvalde. Alex Jones was often known to turn up at these events to harass people. The hunt was suddenly back on. I was leaving the following morning, but I decided to attend the rally before I left.

I met up with Gavin and Meg for supper in a crazily pricey Japanese restaurant in a strip mall. This was so North American. I could never get my head around the concept of smart, cool places being in strip malls. However beautiful and well done the interior, you were still in a strip mall.

During the meal I learned about being 'swatted'. This was the online phenomenon whereby people would ring the police and report some hideous crime taking place at the house of somebody who was livestreaming. They would then sit and watch as the house was raided by a SWAT team. This had recently resulted in a guy being shot dead.

I was really starting to understand why Meg and Gavin were not keen for their address to be circulated publicly. Meg was actually on a list with the local SWAT team as it was so likely to happen to her. This meant that they would do their best to check the hoax factor before sending an armed response unit smashing into the house. I couldn't help but remember that I was sleeping in the spare house, right above Meg's studio.

The next morning, I was up early and, un-swatted, I headed off for my final breakfast in America at Phoebe's Diner. I had chorizo hash and disappointing coffee. I'd parked outside the diner and was going to use one of the public scooters to get to the Capitol, which was, like me, just over the hill.

I found one right outside and set off. As I summited, I could see the Texan capital beneath me. I was really going to miss this place. I looked to my left. At the bottom of a steep slope was the Capitol building, the dome gleaming in the morning sun. I could see crowds, many with makeshift banners and placards, making their way up from the road along the treelined promenade that led to the main building.

I launched my scooter down the hill, only to discover, to my horror, that there were no brakes. These machines were designed to do about 15 miles an hour maximum. Due to the incline of the slope and the calorific value of American breakfasts, I had already passed this when I discovered the no-brakes situation. I was now hurtling down a main road, rapidly gaining speed on a tiny-wheeled, unstable scooter. I was fast approaching a set of traffic lights and a major intersection, currently packed with protestors crossing over to reach the Capitol grounds.

This had all the makings of the perfect TikTok video. Maybe my death would be my most watched piece of work.

I tried desperately to put my foot on the road to try to slow myself down, but this just rendered me more unsteady and I nearly came off. I looked to the side of the road. Everything was slowly going into slow motion. Except me. A man holding a placard that read 'Fuck your guns, protect our kids' was staring at me in total bemusement. A woman near him wearing a T-shirt that read 'Eat Shit Ted Cruz' was shouting something at me. It was around this point that I appeared to reach maximum velocity.

I was fast approaching the intersection. The lights were red and it was jammed with protestors. I screamed at the top of my lungs.

'GET OUT OF THE WAY!'

Several protestors squared up towards me, perhaps thinking I was some sort of kamikaze gun nut.

'FUCK YOU!' shouted one.

'I'VE GOT NO BRAKES!' I screamed. They finally seemed to get the message.

Just as I hit the intersection, the crowd parted for this portly Moses. I careered through them, bursting out the other side and into heavy morning traffic. I tried to turn away from a large pick-up truck. The scooter finally had enough. It flipped and I went flying off it, thankfully avoiding traffic but smashing my body into the high kerb of the pavement.

I lay crumpled on the hot ground, trying to catch my breath. Slowly, I started to try to feel my body for any breaks or terminal damage. I hurt all over but, unbelievably, it seemed that I had not done anything massively serious.

I felt my head. It was warm and damp. I was bleeding quite badly. I lifted up my T-shirt to mop it and it was soon soaked in blood. People had started to assemble around me. Nobody was really doing anything but rubbernecking. Finally, a man stepped forward. He had on a T-shirt bearing the slogan 'What would Jesus do?' over a picture of an AR-15, the assault rifle used in a lot of school shootings. I felt that Jesus might help me get up. This guy had other ideas.

'What the hell do you think you were doing, dude?' He looked livid.

'No brakes,' I replied weakly.

'Yeah? Maybe don't go down steep hills with no brakes? That's an idea, right?'

'I didn't know there were no brakes,' I said. My head was pounding.

'You're a fucking idiot,' shouted a woman.

For a bunch of liberals, they weren't massively . . . liberal.

I got up unsteadily and walked away from the small crowd, pushing my broken scooter as well as I could. When I'd got a decent distance away, they seemed to lose interest. I tried to end my ride but the thing refused. The app clearly thought that I was still cruising carefree around Austin. I parked it up and hobbled into the Capitol ground from a side entrance. I wanted to at least catch a little of what I was there for.

There was a makeshift memorial for the kids lost at Uvalde where people had left candles and flowers. I hobbled up to the Capitol building where a crowd of about two to three thousand had gathered to hear a succession of speakers, from survivors of school shootings to local politicians.

I enjoyed the placards. One, carried by an old lady, read. 'You pissed off this grandma, Greggy Boy.' This was aimed at the governor of Texas, Greg Abbott, a local bogeyman.

I listened to a schoolkid talk about the insanity of high-school shooting drills being the norm. She started to get very upset.

The crowd roared their support for her. I looked around and spotted a guy livestreaming while interviewing an old lady. I went over and eavesdropped. He was pro-gun and was trying to rile this old lady live on air. It made me angry. I couldn't help myself and I started to heckle him from the sidelines.

Spotting this curious, blood-spattered Brit, he turned his camera to me. We started bickering but I really didn't know enough about the gun control debate. Like most zealots, he had stats coming out of his ears and, it being impossible for me to verify any of them, he just bulldozed me.

As I tried to absorb his incoming fire, I found myself mesmerised by his cold dead eyes. They were intensely black and flickered from side to side in his sockets.

He paused briefly and I asked him about assault rifles. Were they honestly necessary?

'You're the guy on the scooter? I saw that. You could have killed somebody. Should we ban scooters?'

I was speechless. He'd got me. My head hurt. I was suddenly very tired.

I walked away and out of the Capitol grounds, blood still dripping hard from my forehead. There had been no sign of Alex Jones. It was time to go home to an unarmed Britain.

5

Camelot Castle

Conspiracies are the way non-complex
people make sense of a complex world.
Dom Joly

So far, I'd been travelling abroad to do my conspiracy touristing. I decided that it might be worth looking at something
a little closer to home. I wanted to go and visit somewhere in
the UK so that people didn't think that I was being too xeno-
phobic. But where to go?

The answer came when I was staying with some friends in
Cornwall.

Now, I'd always had a bit of an issue with Cornwall. Firstly, it
was just not designed for visitors.

The little coastal villages had no parking and the tiny roads
didn't allow for two modern cars to pass each other. Even worse,
you had to be organised. Any decent restaurant, hotel, beach
had been pre-booked about two generations ago. So, you found
yourself in a constant state of paranoia trying to find a parking
space, a seat in a restaurant, a drink in a nice bar.

I'd done quite a lot of filming in the county and they were
always a bit touchy. In fact, it might be another place that I was
banned from. It was so hard to keep track. I'd once stayed at a

terrible hotel in Padstow and had written about the experience in my newspaper column. As ever, local media pounced on the story. Some minor celebrity had not totally loved their area. There was a radio phone-in about whether I had ever been funny and the local newspaper started a petition to have me banned from the county.

I was pretty used to this stuff. Local media love nothing better than a 'comedian slams town' article. I said something derogatory about Weston-super-Mare once (who wouldn't?) and they went nuts. The local newspaper went to town. They interviewed the local MP who said that I was 'a disgrace'. Then they went around the town market and asked stallholders what they thought about my comments. 'He was never funny.' Then the mayor got involved and an effigy of me was burned at some town celebration. Finally, I was officially banned. I think I'm also still banned from Hastings. Their pier burned down and I woke up, read about the story on Twitter and posted a joke: 'Had a great night out in Hastings last night, can't remember too much but woke up smelling of petrol.' I thought it was funny. The local paper begged to differ.

'SICK COMEDIAN BOASTS OF BURNING PIER DOWN!'

I'd recently slipped back into Weston-super-Mare on one of the final legs of my *Holiday Snaps* tour. I'd made a couple of jokes on Instagram about my coming, as part of the never-ending attempt to drum up ticket sales. I was informed that the mayor who had banned me had long gone. The town had changed and I would be more than welcome.

The people at the theatre were lovely but, as I was signing books afterwards, there was a massive kerfuffle in the street outside. The security man rushed inside and closed the theatre doors. A mob was rampaging outside. They seemed angry and were hitting cars and shouting. I sat frozen behind a pile of my books. Was this it? Was this how I was going to go, torn apart by a frenzied mob in Weston-super-Mare? I steeled myself for death. I'd had a good life. I was going to go out with dignity. Well, about as much dignity as one could muster in Weston-super-Mare.

The sound of the mob grew louder. They were right outside now and I could hear individual voices raised in incoherent anger. I felt like Salman Rushdie. I was the victim of a West Country jihad and I must stand firm. I must stick up for my freedom of speech, my right to write. Let them do their worst.

And then the mob passed by, moving on down the street, smashing more cars as they went. The security guard peered nervously out of the window before indicating that we were safe. It turned out to be a large and highly intoxicated stag party that had got out of control. They had not come for me. They had come for the cheap booze and bright-ish lights of Weston-super-Mare.

Back in Cornwall, however, I was coming to the end of a restorative break with Dan and Rachel, some friends who had a place in St Mawes. I'd loved every minute of it. St Mawes was at the tip of the Roseland Peninsula. This meant that there were far fewer day-trippers and a minimal number of shops selling tourist tat. It had a prelapsarian holiday feel about it.

On our second day there, we'd driven to St Just in Roseland to visit what was supposedly the most beautiful church in England. The church sat on the edge of a tidal creek, surrounded by an almost tropical garden. It was very pretty, but what really fascinated me was the story that this little hamlet was famous for. It was rumoured that St Just in Roseland was where Jesus Christ first set foot in England.

Now, it might be news to you that Jesus ever visited England at all. It certainly was to me. I had sung 'Jerusalem' as a kid, and Blake's words 'And did those feet, in ancient times, walk upon England's mountains green' were projected with gusto, but I had not been aware of the story that Jesus supposedly travelled to Cornwall with his uncle, Joseph of Arimathea, a tin merchant, to purchase Cornish tin. He had also supposedly travelled on to Glastonbury but I had no idea who was headlining that year or who he had gone to see.

I got chatting to a fisherman by the creek and asked him whether he believed the story? He didn't know, but he liked the idea of it.

'There's no harm in the story, is there? It's possible.' He patted his wet dog.

'But there's no actual proof, I presume?' I also patted his wet dog.

'No, it's just a story, isn't it? It's not like that idiot in Tintagel, it's just a bit of fun.'

'What idiot in Tintagel?' I asked.

'The Mappin fella. The one in Camelot Castle. He spouts all sorts of nonsense all the time.'

The fisherman seemed to assume that I knew who he meant. I didn't. When I got back to St Mawes, I looked him up. It was paydirt.

The 'Mappin fella' was John Mappin, the heir to the Mappin and Webb jewellery company. He owned Camelot Castle, a hotel in Tintagel, the place on the north coast of Cornwall where King Arthur's Camelot was once supposedly based.

Mappin had made national headlines when he flew the QAnon flag from the top of his hotel and offered discounts to guests who were not vaccinated. He ran a weird YouTube channel called Camelot Castle TV Network whose motto was 'freedom is the grail'. On it, Mappin and his Kazakh wife, Irina, promoted conspiracy theories ranging from mainstream to the bizarre.

According to the hotel's own website it was one of the 'finest hotels in the world'. I decided that I should stop off there on my way home. I looked the place up on TripAdvisor and some people clearly loved it. One guy, called Charlie, wrote this:

(All spelling reviewers' own . . .)

The owners have nailed the ambiance of the British articocracy with a touch of Russian class to achieve something of a divine experience; the gandeur decor with emotional art using the most memorising of colours which fills the entire place with even more light. when you come down the stairs from your room if you don't choose the lift, and get few steps before the bottom it feels like being the ship with a 120 view of the ocean and west facing sunset in the of the most hisoritacl places of fascination on the entire planet is the an experience of anyone.

Another fan of the place was a Jacek M from Leatherhead:

The owners are a fine example of Britishness. Not like most who earn money in the UK, they will be decorated by the Queen and flee to Monaco to die with their fortune. John, Irina Mappin and Ted Stourton are heroes of our time. They save the historic hotel building and begin to restore its splendour. Very elegant service, Great food, for desserts I recommend the Russian honey cake. Human soul Ted paints wonderful pictures that universally rejuvenate you spiritually. Ted has time for you to help you choose one or two images. To leave there without any painting would be a pity for ourselves. At the moment this is the best place we visit in the UK.

So, there were clearly some fans of the Mappins and whoever Ted Stourton might be. A lot of people, however, were slightly less complimentary.

Aileen Pearce, weirdly, even mentioned me, despite spelling my name wrong . . .

Absolutely shocking rude & obnoxious behaviour from the 2 co-owners we were enjoying a quiet dinner when he decided to hold a business meeting on speaker phone it was like Dom Jolly we tolerated for over 10 minutes then asked the waitress if we could move to the bar 4 our desserts the other owner approached us & proceeded to berate us saying he was an important man who had averted 3 world wars???at this point I asked him to go away never experienced such bizarre behaviour very odd we couldn't get out of there quick enough talked to locals afterwards & they told us the owners were always upsetting customers & had trouble retaining staff will not be returning

Another, Gary from Cheltenham, was more succinct:

Go camping on the cliff edge rather than stay here.

On Twitter, a man called George Tait wrote a review that could be considered either good or bad:

My weekend at this hotel was easily the most memorable stay of my life. He locked me out in the pouring rain and he and his wife stood at the door arms folded looking quite deranged. And he plays the harp. Quite well.

The plot thickened. As far as I knew, Ted was not the owner of the hotel. It was John Mappin and his Kazakh wife, Irina. I had, however, never read more entertaining reviews of a place. I continued to browse until I found this one:

In the lounge there were albums of Ted Stourtons paintings and another small album full of people praising the 'LIGHT BOX'. I have to say that I was intrigued. The staff were very sparing with the info they imparted about this particular 'mystery' and so I asked at reception about seeing it. one evening (BIG MISTAKE!!!) after returning from a local pub where mum and I dined out . . . The young chap at reception said he would see if Mr Stourton was available . . . after a few minutes he emerged, dressed in a cream dinner suit with white polo neck, took my hand, kissed me on the cheek and told me how lovely I looked (also my mother) then took us downstairs into the bowels of the castle. We were brought into a room where we sat down and were told a sorry story about the hardship of artists, then brought into another room where our photo was taken, (which I believe will be sent to my e-mail address, have not checked yet as just got home) Then we were taken into a further room where a guitar was produced and we were serenaded with a song. Finally, the room with the light box. A black box with a dimmer light behind it. Very good effect, we were shown pictures whose perspective changed depending on the amount of light behind it. Mother and I were polite and made complimentary murmurings, as some of the effects were very good. HOWEVER . . . after the showing Ted asked which pics we thought were the nicest and we innocently told him (there were 3 we liked, but not to buy). He then turned on the lights and started his sales pitch starting at around £ 1700 . . . er . . . I was shocked, looked at my mother and felt totally SICK in my stomach. He had been so nice that I felt physi-callly AFRAID to refuse . . . I spoke up and said I was a single mum in the NHS and did not have that sort of money. He completely disregarded my comments and just brought the price down and down until we felt compelled to say yes . . . as we ascended the stairs out of the underground rooms, RIGHT ON CUE, out came Mr and Mrs Mappin to congratulate us on our purchases, shaking our hands and tell-ing us how very lucky we were to even have Mr Stourton staying at the Castle . . . (er, he does actually live there . . .!!!) Anyway, we were told we could settle up before we left and staff would wrap them for us but I never actually wanted them and felt intimidated into agreeing to buying them. On the day of leaving, I bundled all our stuff into the car, got the dogs in and went to pay for the room. They then got the pics, at which point I said I couldn't afford them and did not want them. The chap at reception then said I should wait while he went to get Ted Stourton. I was TERRIFIED! I knew he would try to force me to buy them, so, on the pretence that I had to get something from my car, I fled!! (so fast that I still have the room key, which I'm sending back today.) I loved the Castle and surroundings but not the 'light box;' experience of hard sell. YOU HAVE BEEN WARNED!

So, Ted appeared to be a painter who lived with the Mappins, and they all seemed to be involved in some hard-sell thing with his paintings.

If I was honest, the whole art-selling thing seemed no dodgier than a skilled and determined shopkeeper in a Middle Eastern souk. It did add an extra dimension of weirdness to my forthcoming stay but I was mainly interested in the conspiracy angle.

I couldn't wait to get in there and meet the Mappins . . . and Ted.

I sent Mappin a request for an interview, but nobody replied. So, I took matters into my own hands and booked a room for two nights. I was thinking of doing this under a pseudonym. I toyed with Napoleon Bonaparte. An over-zealous tour promoter had once asked me what false name I wanted my hotel bookings to be in. I think she was under the false impression that I was constantly harassed by crazed fans. As a joke, I'd suggested we use Napoleon Bonaparte. It had turned into a nightmare.

I was very absent-minded and often forgot room keys. Whenever I'd approach some poor beleaguered receptionist, they would ask for proof of identity before handing over another key. As I was unable to provide any ID proving I was Napoleon Bonaparte, we were at loggerheads. Any attempt on my part to google Napoleon and show him to the receptionist only complicated matters further. I was not sure how top celebs did this but I was rubbish at it. So, for Camelot Castle I was booked in totally above board as Dom Joly.

Bidding my friends farewell, I drove for an hour and a half across Cornwall, from the south to the north coast. It was night-time and my route took me over spooky, pitch-black moorland. It was all very *Hound of the Baskervilles*.

My car squeezed itself through lanes that just got narrower and narrower until I got seriously worried that I would get stuck. My family had a name for these tiny country lanes, where the hedges and trees almost converged over us like some eco-roof. We called them trunnels.

These trunnels were primeval. The sides were covered in ancient moss and water gushed down from every wooden artery. It was like I'd gone back in time. Curious shapes started to form in the darkness. My imagination played impressive tricks on me as my headlights bounced off the surroundings. Eventually, I burst out into a vast expanse of open blackness. Far below me, I could see the twinkling lights of a couple of fishing villages. I had traversed Cornwall alive. I had reached my destination.

Camelot Castle was certainly in a beautiful location. A brown, pebble-dashed Victorian pile, it sat, isolated, on a windswept hill overlooking Tintagel. As I drove through the dark, battened-down village towards it, it looked warm and inviting. A shelter from the storm.

It was just before midnight when I parked up outside. As I got out of the car, the wind was howling and the rain pummelled me. Despite this, I stopped for a second to stare at an Aston Martin, parked on the grass, that had been covered in paint. Parts of the castle had scaffolding up. I assumed that some careless builder had dropped paint onto the vehicle. That was an expensive mistake. The car was ruined. Somebody was in trouble.

I rushed inside. In the porch were children's toys and a motley collection of waterproof jackets and wellington boots. So far, so cosy country house. Maybe I had misjudged the vibe of the place?

Then I stepped into the main hall. The first thing I spotted was a large collection of crystals. To me, crystals were the gateway drug to madness. The moment you spot crystals anywhere, you should run. Best-case scenario, there were vegans about and you were going to be inundated with new-age mumbo-jumbo. Worst-case scenario, you were entering a conspirituality zone. This was a term I'd recently heard to describe hazy New Age thinking blended with beliefs in bizarre conspiracy theories.

Then I noticed the art. It all appeared to be by the same artist. It was, not to put too fine a point on it, appalling. Now, I'm more than aware that art, like comedy, is subjective, but this . . . it was truly mesmerising in its awfulness. It felt like somebody had been force-fed hallucinogens, exposed solely to the work of the Impressionists and then left alone in a dungeon with an endless supply of paint. It turned out that I was not too far off.

There were signs telling the visitor that the artist responsible, Ted Stourton, whom I'd read about in the reviews, was 'The Master of Venice'. I really needed to check Mr Stourton out.

That would be for tomorrow.

Turning away from the art, I checked out the rest of the hall. The walls were packed with badly framed, fading photographs of a gentleman that I recognised as John Mappin. In the photos he was posing with an assortment of celebrities, ranging from a shifty-looking Al Pacino (*Scarface, The Godfather*), Tom Cruise (*Risky Business, Top Gun, Mission: Impossible*) and John Travolta (*Saturday Night Fever, Pulp Fiction*) to Christopher Timothy (*All Creatures Great and Small*).

Mappin had gone to Hollywood in the 1990s in an unsuccessful bid to become a movie star. He did land a part in a soft-porn movie, sharing the screen with the gloriously named Julie Strain. Sadly, this did not lead on to Hollywood glory. While Mappin was not discovered by Hollywood, he made a discovery of his own: Scientology.

Suddenly the major Hollywood movie-star photos made sense.

Trying to take all this in, I approached the reception desk where a surly-looking woman sat staring at me. I was about to say something when I stopped. On the wall, right next to the reception, was the *pièce de résistance*. It was a humongous, framed photograph of Mappin standing next to Donald and Melania Trump. In the photograph, Trump was holding up some article that Mappin had clearly given him. I tried to see what the article was about, but the quality of the photograph was surprisingly bad and I could not make it out. Trump had scribbled on the photograph in gold marker pen:

To all our friends of Camelot! Thank you for all you have done to MAKE CAMELOT GREAT AGAIN! Continue in all your great deeds and works. Love Donald Trump.

John Mappin had been a fan of Donald Trump for a long time. In February 2016, just after Trump announced his bid for the presidency, the Mappins went onto Camelot Castle TV Network and, with straight faces, bestowed an honorary knighthood on the real estate mogul. Mappin announced that this was 'An historic and noble award, an honorary Camelot Castle knighthood in which, from this day forth Donald Trump shall be known at Camelot Castle as Sir Donald Trump of Camelot Castle.'

The phrase 'at Camelot Castle' was doing a lot of heavy lifting there. It would be akin to me saying that 'From this day forth, Donald Trump shall be known at Joly Towers as the Orange Shit Gibbon of Joly Towers.'

However ludicrous the ceremony, the flattery appeared to work. John Mappin was the third Briton to meet Trump after his inauguration. This was when the photograph in the lobby was taken.

I had hit paydirt. This was Valhalla for conspiracy theories. We had everything – New Age bollocks, Scientology, Donald Trump, QAnon and anti-vaxxers – all in a hotel on the site of King Arthur's court, with a nutty artist in the basement as a bonus. I couldn't wait until the next day.

I checked in. The slightly grumpy receptionist came out from behind her desk and showed me to my room. As we waited for the creaking old lift to make its way down from the top floor, I checked out the large living-room area. There were more, even larger Ted Stourton works. At the far end, a door led towards a dining room. The centrepiece, however, was a large round table that the receptionist was clearly very proud of.

'This is the round table. The table from King Arthur times,' she said.

'This is the actual round table?'

'Yes, this is where King Arthur and his Knights of the Round Table would have meetings around a round table.' She shrugged.

I was silent for a moment. Did she actually believe that this, obviously fairly modern, table was over one-and-a-half-thousand years old? It was very unlikely that King Arthur and the court of Camelot ever even existed. Did she really believe in the myth itself? The round table never actually featured in the original Arthurian tales. It was first mentioned in the twelfth century by the Norman poet Wace in his Norman French translation of Geoffrey of Monmouth's Latin *History of the Kings of Britain*. Wace appeared to have added the Round Table story, as it did not appear in the Latin original.

'Sorry, just to be clear: you are saying that this is the original Round Table around which King Arthur, Lancelot, Merlin, etc. all sat?' I stared at her incredulously, but ready to share the joke.

'Yes, this is Round Table.'

'A Round Table or *THE* Round Table?' I persisted.

The awkward silence that followed was interrupted by the lift beeping and the doors opening. She gave me my key and room number and I ascended on my own. I'd been warned by the reviews that the rooms were pretty shocking, but I was actually quietly relieved. It was hardly in the 'finest hotels in the world' category, but I'd stayed in far worse. My room seemed to have been recently refurbished as it was not in the shabby state of many others I'd seen in reviews.

I unpacked and threw myself onto the bed with a couple of brochures that has been left for me by the kettle.

The first brochure was a sort of homemade magazine called *Camelot Castle News* and I was instantly hooked. It was like some shitty Kazakh knock-off version of *HELLO!* If the person editing it was ripped to the tits on mushrooms. There were a lot of photographs of Irina Mappin in ballgowns and a potted explanation of why John Mappin was so classy:

> Being born into a jewellery and silver family who served the Royal Houses of England and Europe continuously since the 1700s, it can be said, almost literally, that John Mappin was introduced to the preferences of nobility and luxury from an early age. Keen, however, to make his own way in the world, the teenage John Mappin and a friend sold silver balloons outside the famous London store, Harrods.

It was pretty impressive, if you thought about it. Who would have thought selling silver balloons outside Harrods would allow you to purchase a castle in Cornwall? Never give up, kids!

There were random articles about Kazakh business opportunities, blurry 'society' photographs of visitors to the castle and a lot of articles about how Ted Stourton was rapidly becoming the greatest artist in the world. On a page adorned with the blurb 'TED STOURTON STUNS FINE ART WORLD' was a photograph of Ted and a slightly stunned looking Nicolas Cage being given a seemingly all-blue canvas. Ted had a restraining arm around the actor, presumably to stop him bolting.

The reader was urged to ask about Ted's 'Light Box', which I still hoped was not some euphemism. There were also a couple of pages of New Age guff regarding the Pyramids and a page about the danger of anti-depressants being given to children. It was one of the most random things I'd ever read.

The magazine had a sticker on the front telling me that I was not to remove it from the hotel. I put the dog-eared and heavily thumbed publication to one side. I picked up the second brochure.

This one was a little more official looking. It was called *Excalibur, Mappin Private Family Office Services & Consultancy.*

I flicked through it, but could make very little sense of the whole thing. It appeared to be pitching the Mappins as people who could offer consultancy services for other rich families with ugly castles and helipads. They offered help in education, legacy planning, philanthropy.

Then shit got very weird very quickly. The Mappins, it turned out, would also give you help with 'Survival Planning, Conflict Resolution' and, the big one, 'The End of War'. This was quite the service they were offering.

It wasn't clear what the survival planning involved. Perhaps it was a type of Bear Grylls survival course? Maybe they were selling one of those insane five-star bunkers that billionaires buy in New Zealand to survive the coming apocalypse? I was tempted to contact them and find out how much it would cost to end the Ukraine War. I decided to send an email asking for a quote when I got home.

This had all been very exciting and I decided to call it a night. I turned off the light and lay in the darkness listening to the sound of waves crashing into the shore below. There was another sound jostling with that of the Celtic Sea. It was an intermittent but insistent tapping on pipes somewhere in the bowels of the building. It sounded like somebody was trying to tap out a message. If only I had bothered to learn Morse code beyond SOS, but who on earth ever did?

'Tap, tap, taaaap, tap, tap' went the lone piper. Was it some kind of message? A warning? I now knew that QAnon believed that thousands of children all over the world had been kidnapped and were being held hostage in a secret network of underground tunnels in various cities around the world. The people doing this kidnapping were some sort of shady cabal of international Satanic paedophiles of whom Hillary Clinton and Bill Gates were often the purported ringleaders. Jeffrey Epstein's plane seemed to be the key to the whole affair, according to the believers. There was no doubt that Jeffrey Epstein was a phenomenally seedy individual who used his ill-gotten wealth to groom and abuse underage girls, but it was a pretty big leap to the underground Satanic tunnel network theory.

The tapping continued. 'Taap, tap, tap, taap, taap taap . . .'

What if I was wrong? What if the whole thing was a double bluff and there was a secret tunnel underneath Camelot Castle and people needed my help? Maybe the whole QAnon flag-flying thing was a false flag? Maybe there were children in a tunnel under the castle? This was all so confusing. My mind was now racing. I went online and looked up Morse code. I started to try and decipher the taps by writing them down. I took a short tap as a dot and a longer taap as a dash.

-.. --- / -. --- - / ..-. --- .-. --. . - / - --- / -.-. --- -- . / .- -.
-.. / ... . . / - .... . / .-.. .. --. .... - -... --- -..- / --- ..-. / - . -..

I found a Morse code translator and entered my findings, not expecting to get anything coherent back, but at least it would hopefully make me stop thinking about it and allow me to get to sleep. I waited a millisecond and then the screen flashed up a translation:

DO NOT FORGET TO COME
AND SEE THE LIGHT BOX OF TED.

I closed my eyes and tried to get some sleep. I had weird dreams involving Ted dressed as King Arthur and, randomly, a spray-painted dragon digging a massive tunnel with a digger. How the dragon knew how to operate the digger was unclear.

I awoke around nine-thirty, fairly well rested and jumped out of bed ready to do some investigating. I was a man with a purpose. But first, I wanted to enjoy the one, undeniable plus point of Camelot Castle: the view over Tintagel. It had been dark when I'd arrived the night before, so I was looking forward to this. I was on the top floor and I imagined that the view was going to be pretty spectacular. I opened the curtains with a dramatic flourish to reveal a startled workman, standing on scaffolding about two feet from my window. I was most surprised to see him. He seemed equally surprised to be faced with a naked man staring at him. Naturally startled by my physique, he took an unsteady step backwards before grabbing a scaffold rail to regain his balance.

Mortifyingly, I think he suddenly recognised me. His face started to light up and I could see he was gearing up to do the shouting 'HELLO!' thing. I rapidly closed the curtains. I went into the bathroom for a shower. The refurbishments had been done on the cheap. The bath was so flimsy and plasticky that I worried that it might crack. I had a makeshift, low-pressure shower and got out gingerly. I got dressed and headed on down to breakfast.

I opted not to take the lift and so took the stairs. Every inch of wall space was covered in large Ted Stourton pieces. I started to wonder whether he had a team of Oompa-Loompas churning the stuff out.

When I got to the ground floor, I went to reception to ask whether John Mappin was available for a chat?

The receptionist asked me what I wanted to chat to him about? I explained that I had left a message a couple of days ago wondering whether I could talk to him for my book. I had heard nothing back. She said she would enquire. I asked whether I could write him a note.

That would be fine, she said. I scribbled a quick note explaining that I was writing a book on conspiracies and that I would love to have a chat with him. I handed the note over, and she said that she would make sure that he got it.

I thanked her and headed off to breakfast. Just before the entrance to the dining room I noticed, underneath a particularly large Ted Stourton piece, a box where guests were encouraged to 'write a letter to Merlin'. It turned out that Merlin was pretty tech-savvy as guests were also urged to leave their address and email. I'd read in reviews that Merlin took this opportunity to send you Scientology literature.

I scribbled a quick question.

Dear Merlin, I hope this note finds you well. I'm a big fan. Have you seen Ted's Light Box?

I popped the note into the box in the manner of a politician posing for cameras in the polling station and entered the dining room. It was almost empty save for a couple of European-looking couples who were clearly having trouble equating the hotel website with the grim reality. I chose a table by the window and finally got my view of Tintagel, which was rather magical. It was a glorious, sunny day and the rain had disappeared. On days like these you could see the appeal of Cornwall, if Gordon Ramsay didn't have a house there.

Having finished breakfast, I wandered through the lobby and into the bar. Inevitably there was a plethora of Ted Stourton artworks on the walls. These, combined with a mirrored bar and heavy gold wallpaper, gave the whole place the feel of a faded brothel. I spotted a framed notice regarding Ted that felt rather defensive. It read, 'Beauty is whatever you consider to be beautiful, NOT what someone else says is!'

As someone who had faced critics myself, I felt a certain level of sympathy for Ted. 'Critics,' in the words of Kenneth Tynan, 'are the people who know the way but can't drive the car.'

I wasn't sure whether to wait to be summoned by Mappin or to go and do my own thing. I'd left a phone number so I could technically be contacted anywhere. I ordered a coffee and sat down in the bar to have a think. I'd been there for about ten minutes when he strode through the room. I looked up but he paid me no heed. He opened a set of doors that clearly led into his private quarters. Through the doors I could spot a large desktop Mac and some comfy-looking sofas.

The doors closed behind him and then, a minute later, music started to play loudly from within. Quite wonderfully it was Frank Sinatra's 'Call Me Irresponsible'. Sometimes, these things wrote themselves.

The coffee was rather good, but very strong and I started to get a bit spacey. I didn't fancy sitting around and waiting all day like some lowlife courtier. I decided to go outside and have a walk around Tintagel itself. As I got up, another song came on to the Mappin set list. It was George Michael's 'Careless Whisper'.

I headed towards the front door and stopped at reception to ask whether there had been any feedback from my request? They told me that he had received my note. I thanked them and turned to head outside. As I did, a bald man in a slightly shabby white suit popped out of a door on the other side of the hall. He looked a touch unwashed and was smoking a cheroot.

I approached him and introduced myself.

'Hello, are you Ted?' I asked.

'Yes, sir, I am. How may I help?' replied Ted. He had shifty eyes.

'I'd like to come and see your Light Box,' I said, hoping that this wasn't some secret sexual code.

'Of course, sir. Just check in with reception and they will organise a time.' Ted looked a little distant, almost disassociated from things.

'Thank you. I shall do that and I shall see you later.' I smiled.

'You certainly shall, sir,' said Ted enigmatically before disappearing outside to smoke his cheroot.

I was slightly weirded out by the encounter and by the way he kept calling me sir. Nevertheless, I returned to reception and asked to make an appointment with Ted. She told me that he would be free after lunch. I thanked her and went outside. The sun temporarily blinded me as I stepped through the doors and I stopped right next to Ted, who was tucking into his cheroot.

'Everything OK, sir?' he asked.

'Yes, fine. I'm seeing you after lunch.'

'Looking forward to it already, sir,' said Ted.

I walked away, towards the paint-damaged car that I'd spotted the night before. As I got near it, I realised that it was not damaged. It was a Ted Stourton installation piece. There appeared to be some form of pattern to the paint and the number plate read 'TED 4 ART'.

It seemed like a massive waste of an Aston Martin but I remembered the words of the poster inside: 'Beauty is whatever you consider to be beautiful, NOT what someone else says is!'

I walked on, doing a full circuit around the castle until I was standing on the far corner that afforded the best view of Tintagel. It was a rocky island linked to the mainland by a rather dramatic pedestrian footbridge. There were what appeared to be the remains of some construction on the island itself. If I was a king and going to build a castle, this was definitely where I would have chosen to do so. I felt pretty confident that, back then, the pedestrian bridge had not been there to assist them.

I wanted to join the path that took me down the winding route onto the island. As I passed the final window of the castle, I spotted another Ted book on the windowsill. This one had a Ted quote on the front:

'There are no art experts.
Who owns all the light and colour in the world?
You do.'
Ted Stourton

I was starting to get the strong feeling that Ted had been given a savage kicking by the art establishment.

I looked up at the castle. I wanted to see if the QAnon flag was still flying. It wasn't; it had been replaced by a flag with Excalibur on it. It was flapping frantically in the strong wind that seemed to be a permanent feature of the location.

On New Year's Eve 2019, Mappin flew a QAnon flag from the roof of the building. The flag featured a large Q on a white background. He tweeted to his 155,000 followers:

Q arrives at CAMELOT. Happy New Year to all the great truth seekers throughout history. Greater than standing armies is the power of an IDEA who's time has come.

In April of the same year, Mappin appeared to get even more excited about QAnon after getting some 'inside news'. Once again, he tweeted to his devoted followers:

I began this first day of April sobbing like a baby for over an hour, after having the news confirmed at 2am by two independent first-hand sources, that the underground kids were coming to the surface in Manhattan and elsewhere. Some of them will be seeing daylight for the first time in their lives. They have been bred, butchered, raped and had their life-force inverted and stolen. Theirs is the story of the atomseed of evil within our civilisational wheel.

This was clearly batshit crazy and, unless anybody had spotted a sudden plethora of traumatised kids wandering around, blinking in the sunlight, looking for their parents, total bollocks.

Mappin had been kicked off Twitter for a while until Elon Musk reinstated him.

I wasn't sure that I was looking forward to our chat, but I was grimly fascinated. I started walking away from the hotel. Someone started shouting from above. I could barely hear them in the wind but they persisted. I eventually got the message.

'HELLO! I'M ON THE PHONE! I'M NOT WEARING ANY CLOTHES!'

It was the builder from earlier. He was leaning over the scaffolding and waving at me while two of his mates laughed their heads off. I turned away rapidly and walked on briskly down the path towards Tintagel, attempting to do so with a modicum of dignity.

I spent half an hour or so tramping over Tintagel, but it was not terribly interesting. Was the court of King Arthur a conspiracy theory? There were a couple of homemade videos online hosted by people who look like they had failed *Time Team* auditions. I tried to watch a couple but they were deadly dull.

I huffed and puffed my way back up to Camelot Castle. The receptionist looked at me awkwardly. I could see that she was already getting tired of me.

'Any luck?' I asked.

'Maybe this afternoon,' she answered in a decidedly non-committal fashion.

It was about eleven in the morning and so I decided to go out for lunch. I couldn't face the depressing hotel dining room again. I decided to visit Port Isaac, a little fishing village not too far away. It was made famous by the TV series *Doc Martin* starring Martin Clunes.

I'd noticed a photograph of a confused-looking Clunes on Ted Stourton's website. He was standing next to Stourton in the lobby of the hotel. The website had a lot of photographs of dazed members of the public standing next to Stourton like awkward hostages. Clunes, along with Nicolas Cage, was one of the few celebrities actually photographed with Stourton, although his picture gallery was peppered with random, individual photos of celebs.

These included Nigel Mansell, John and Norma Major, Dame Joan Sutherland, The Lord Bishop of Southwark, Stewart Granger, Larry Adler, Richard Harris, Prince Albert of Monaco and Liam Gallagher's underwhelming post-Oasis band, Beady Eye. The implication seemed to be that all these people were big fans of Ted. It was weird, given Ted's insistence on getting a selfie with everyone he had ever met, that they had not posed for one. Whatever, should he get them all together it would make for a cracking drinks party.

I drove to Port Isaac and parked about five miles outside the village, in the nearest car park. I walked down into the picture-postcard bay and had lunch at a place called Outlaw's Fish Kitchen overlooking the detritus of a working fishing port, coexisting with herds of gormless day-trippers. The meal was delicious and I savoured a brief return to something approaching normality.

I was on high alert, however, as this place was the home of the Fisherman's Friends, a motley group of seafaring types who sang sea shanties. They had just had a second movie made about them. The name Fisherman's Friends was, in my book, an unfortunate one. I'd always been told that the skate fish was the true fisherman's friend. You only ever saw skate wings on sale in restaurants. The round tubular body was rumoured to offer much comfort to a lonely fisherman on a cold night at sea.

I focused on the narrow entrance to the bay, transfixed by a little boat struggling through the waves as it attempted to make its way back home. For a while I didn't notice the man waving frantically at me from the other side of the window. He was wearing a sweatshirt that said 'Golf is Life' and sported a back-pack that appeared way too big for a day spent ambling around a village.

I tuned back in and looked at him. Our eyes met and he smiled. I smiled back. He had a weird look on his face and I supposed that he must have slipped away from whoever was taking care of him. But why, then, the backpack?

He pointed at the door and then to himself. He appeared to be asking whether he could come in? As this was not my restau-rant, I had no way of stopping him, but I wished I could. I pointed at the door in a non-committal fashion and started star-ing out to sea again.

The door burst open and 'Golf is Life' man almost fell into the restaurant through the tiny door. The place was very small with only about seven tables and everything went very quiet. The man looked around, like a simple cat, hurled into a lift full of smug chihuahuas.

'Are you Dom . . . from *Little Britain*?' asked the man, stum-bling up to my table. Everybody else looked at me with disdain as though I'd somehow invited this guy in to show off. To make things worse, I was actually a bit miffed that he'd got the wrong comedy show.

Rather than say hello, or politely correct him on the show, or do something, anything, vaguely normal in this, most abnormal of situations, I went into bewildered foreigner mode. This was something that I often did when somebody annoying approached me in public and I wanted to make a quick exit. It invariably complicated things, especially when my wife was present as she would say things like, 'Yes, it is him, thank you for coming to say hi. Dom, say hello . . .' All while I continued to pretend to be something vaguely Scandinavian. I had no idea why I did this sort of thing. Possibly, it was because these sorts of encounters always made me uncomfortable. More likely, it was because I was an arse.

'It is you? Right?' 'Golf is Life' guy persisted as the other diners started to subtly up their level of scorn.

'Ehhh . . . mi ne komprenas, kion vi diras,' I said, in what turned out to be Esperanto.

'Whaaaat? Come on! It's definitely you.' 'Golf is Life' was getting louder, but I was now committed to my role of international person.

'Šajnas esti ia miskompreno? Mi estas eksterdeĵora fiŝkaptisto.' I was dying on the inside.

Why did I get myself into these situations?

The other diners were now looking at the waitress as though to have us both thrown out of the restaurant for disturbing their meal.

'I know it's you.'

He was right up in my face now. The other diners, although looking mock-embarrassed, were now all-too-clearly enjoying the impromptu show.

'Bonvolu simple foriri kaj lasu min ĝui mian tagmanĝon . . . kaj ĝi estis *Trigger Happy TV*, ne *Little Britain* . . .'

I was, secretly, quite impressed with my Esperanto, although my accent was flying fast over the European continent, careering from Dutch to Czech to Greek in the span of a sentence.

'Golf is Life' guy finally gave up and turned to exit. As he did, his backpack swept a glass of wine off my table. He made for the door but his strap got caught in the door hinge and he struggled desperately to release himself. I looked around the restaurant.

People were now looking for hidden cameras and clearly wondering if this was one of my skits.

I waved at the waitress and asked for the bill. Life as a private investigator masquerading as a television prankster was a complicated role . . .

I walked back to the car and drove slowly back to Tintagel. It was time for my Ted Talk.

Back in the hotel, I looked at the receptionist and she looked back at me. No words were exchanged. Three minutes later Ted appeared out of his door. He shook my hand and asked me what had brought me to Camelot. I briefly considered making up some bollocks about having to remove a sword from a stone, but decided against it. I told him the truth. I was a comedian and I was writing a book about conspiracies. Ted raised a lascivious eyebrow and told me that he loved comedians. I smiled carefully.

Ted clearly lived 'below stairs'. As we went further into his underworld, we passed signs of the hidden demands of petulant wealth – dumb waiters, complicated bell systems and elegant stone steps worn down by years of endless scuttling up and down to sate every whim of the daylight master.

About three floors down, we got to a basement corridor off which was a string of rooms. Ted announced that I must have a tour.

First up was Ted's photo studio, then a small art studio, followed by a sort of office in which Ted pointed out pictures of Laurence Olivier and Ringo Starr, both of whom, Ted informed me, were massive collectors of Ted's work.

'How did you meet the Mappins?' I asked Ted.

'I was travelling the world doing odd jobs when we met and they gave me the inspiration to be an artist,' replied Ted.

I had already read various theories. One was that Ted had been discovered by Irina when she was an art student in London. Another was that the Mappins had used the healing powers of Scientology to bring Ted's brother out of a coma.

Ted then took me into a large room at the end of the corridor. This was clearly Ground Zero Ted. The room was circular and everything in it, and I mean everything, the wall, the ceiling, the guitars, was covered in paint. It was as though Ted had consumed gallons of different coloured paint and then simply exploded in the room. On the far wall were the words:

Are you a friend of Ted?

Whatever else one could say about Ted, he was certainly productive, almost possessed.

Ted led me into the final room. This was where I finally set eyes on Ted's legendary 'Light Box'. Fortunately for me, this did not involve the removal of any items of clothing. He sat me down and told me that photographs were not allowed. He spoke in slightly hushed terms, as though the Light Box should not be disturbed.

The Light Box was bedecked in velvet, possibly to make it appear a little more magical than it was. He started putting his art onto the box and the light highlighted the work a little but with no obvious improvement. This was the moment, when, in the reviews, I knew that Ted commenced his hard-sell technique. I was rather looking forward to it.

But it never came.

Instead, Ted put a painting of a circle with two figures in it (a common motif for Ted) onto the Light Box. He asked me to close my eyes and picture my best friend. I was undecided as to who my best friend was. It varied, depending on mood. I was also a little nervous about closing my eyes for too long down there. I scrunched my eyes.

'Open your eyes,' commanded Ted.

I un-scrunched them.

'Did you see yourself, sir?' Ted asked.

'See myself?' I replied quizzically.

I was definitely a tad egotistical, but I was not sure that even I would consider myself as my best friend. I was curious as to why I would see myself.

'Yes, sir. Did you see yourself? In your mind?' continued Ted.

'No,' I replied.

'Oh,' said Ted.

Ted seemed disappointed. I was confused. There was quite a long, uncomfortable silence. I eyed the exit nervously.

'I would like to give you this painting as a gift, sir.' Ted looked at me straight in the eyes.

Firstly, I definitely didn't like the painting. Secondly, I was worried that this was a clever sales technique, like the lucky heather ladies, who gave you a sprig of lucky heather and then aggressively harassed you for money claiming it was a purchase.

Ted signed the painting and started wrapping it up in bubble wrap.

'This is a gift. I'm not paying for this, right?' I found myself slightly embarrassed to be asking this. I felt cheap.

'It is a gift, sir,' said Ted, finalising the wrapping and handing it over to me.

We climbed back up out of the dungeon and ended up in reception where Ted insisted that the receptionist took a photograph of us both. I assumed that I would now join the long list of 'Friends of Ted' on his website. Who knew, I might even make it onto the walls of the lobby.

Dom Joly, Comedian (*Little Britain*) – a friend of Ted.

I said goodbye to Ted and he did a little theatrical bow before retiring downstairs. I handed the painting to reception and asked them to look after it for me.

There was a lot of noise coming from the dining room. Mappin was hosting a lunch. I headed back to the bar, ordered another coffee and waited. 'My Way' by Frank Sinatra drifted out from his empty chambers.

After about half an hour, Mappin and his dining companions walked through the bar and entered his quarters. The last person in left the door slightly ajar and, as I was sitting very near the doors, I could catch snippets of conversation between the music. It appeared mostly to be the guests agreeing vehemently with whatever Mappin was saying. Sycophancy hung heavy in the air.

After another half an hour, the meeting ended and Mappin came to the door with his guests to say goodbye. He looked at me for the first time and indicated that I could come in and have a chat. As I stood up, one of the departing guests, a blonde woman, exclaimed loudly.

'Oh, hello, it's Dom Joly. What are you doing here?' She came up to me in a strident but not unfriendly manner. 'We've argued online,' she said, as if by way of explanation.

I had no idea who she was. Arguing online with somebody did not narrow much down in my world. I presumed she was some anti-vaxxer. She looked the type, but I could not put a name to the face. I thought she might kick off, but she was actually quite pleasant and Mappin did not seem overly concerned.

Mappin ushered me into his drawing room. He sat down next to his wife as though on two thrones. Their dog Monty bounded about and I immediately softened up as I instinctively like dog people. Hitler, of course, was a massive animal lover so I knew that this was not a fail-safe personality test, but hey-ho.

Mappin asked me if the conversation was being recorded? I wasn't very good at this sort of thing, and I said that it wasn't but then wondered whether I should be. I just wanted to have a conversation and see if I could work him out. I took the occasional note.

We started talking and my immediate thought was that he came across as less nutty and evil than I'd anticipated. He was a classic type. The slightly arrogant, public school sort who had the chutzpah and the confidence to wax lyrical on any subject, even if he didn't have the qualifications. I was probably guilty of this too.

I asked him why he had flown the QAnon flag from the top of the castle. What was he hoping to achieve and did he really believe in it?

He told me that he had raised it on the evening of New Year's Eve 2019, tweeted about it and then went to Lidl because they had run out of canapés. He said that by the time they got back home the thing had gone viral with people announcing that Q had arrived in the UK. He said that the most unbelievable thing about the whole story was that people were shocked he shopped at Lidl. He seemed to find this very funny. I chuckled politely.

He had not answered my question at all and I had done nothing to pressure him on it. I was so bad at this.

I asked him what he thought about people calling him a conspiracy theorist? He countered with a question. A classic tactic. What was a conspiracy, he asked?

Considering I was writing a book about it, I should have been ready with a zinger. But I didn't. I just sat there and listened to him hold forth on a series of increasingly crazy topics.

'The problem with conspiracies is that they are constantly hijacked by the lunatic fringe, which appeals to the media.'

I gathered from this that he saw himself as the more sensible, intellectual type of conspiracist.

He riffed on how interested he was in the speed in which memes of alternative ideas spread. As an ex-commodity broker, he said that it fascinated him. All he was doing, when he'd raised the flag, was signalling that Q was a coming force.

I nodded like an idiot. Honestly, what was there to say?

Then he really got into his stride. He liked Trump. He thought he had done great things, especially in exposing how fake the news was.

I was about to ask him whether he thought Trump had won the election when he segued into an extraordinary story about North Korea. Mappin claimed that a North Korean delegation had come to Camelot to ask him for advice on how to get Trump back to the negotiating table after the breakdown of the summit between the two leaders.

I wondered where they had heard of his skills. Maybe they had picked up the Excalibur leaflet promoting his services in international conflict resolution while on a dirty weekend? Maybe Kim Jong-un was a friend of Ted?

Mappin ploughed on. He claimed to have told the North Koreans how to deal with Trump. Subsequent to his sage but confidential advice, America had returned to the negotiating table. John Mappin, he announced, had been directly responsible for preventing nuclear war on the Korean Peninsula.

I really wanted to press him on what advice he had given them, but he was off on another subject. This time it was about the COVID vaccine. He told me about this doctor who had given him hydroquinone and zinc. He said that it was recommended by the Chinese government on an official website.

The same doctor, according to Mappin, had given this treatment to Rupert Murdoch and Jerry Hall. He announced this as though it was conclusive proof of the evil of the vaccine and the efficacy of his preferred and much-hyped COVID treatment.

When I asked him what the website was, he replied that it had subsequently been removed. I dimly remembered a story from the time in which there had been mild uproar when it was revealed that Rupert Murdoch had received supposedly preferential treatment and had jumped the queue to be given his vaccine.

I brought this up but Mappin swatted it away dismissively.

'Lots of rich people pretended to get the vaccine,' he said.

'Why?' I asked.

He didn't reply, but launched into another story about studies that had been carried out in Cedars-Sinai hospital regarding injecting disinfectant. Apparently, Trump wasn't stupid.

I was getting lost. Drowning in what seemed like a shifting ocean of wacky misinformation. It was like sitting in a real-life, crazy Twitter thread. He was not foaming at the mouth. He was not wild-eyed and screaming. In fact, he had a calm, authoritative air. His upbringing and wealth had given him this ability to seem very credible. He was a stupid person's idea of what a smart person was.

Because, all the stuff he was saying was stupid . . . really stupid. The problem was, you couldn't argue with stupid.

'There are three things that the Deep State will not let you attack without being silenced . . .' Mappin was off on another tangent. 'The military–industrial complex, Big Pharma and psychotropic drugs.' He was on a roll. 'Every Washington power player has been lured into sleeping with underage kids. This is then used as *kompromat* so that they do the bidding of the Deep State.'

I sunk into the sofa and stroked Monty. He looked equally desperate for this to end. What Monty, and more importantly Mappin, really needed was a long walk. A very long walk.

Now he was onto paedophiles and tunnels, the lifeblood of QAnon. He told me how thousands of children were being kept in tunnels before segueing into something about his old Winchester science teacher. He had taught him how to think critically with the help of something to do with boiling water. Then we were onto anti–depressants and how they blocked the ability of human souls to transfer to another body after death.

It all just became too much to take in. It was as though somebody had programmed a random bollocks generator with conspiracy terms.

And yet people listened to him. People believed this nonsense. Gullible people looked up to him. He *was* the elite that he raged against so ferociously. He must have special, inside knowledge, they all assumed. He was a resistance fighter, leading the revolution against tunnels and experts and peer-reviewed science.

There was no point arguing. Even if I had all the counter facts to hand, they would not work. Once facts became malleable – 'alternative facts', in the infamous words of Kellyanne Conway – once all news you disagreed with was 'fake news', there was no right or wrong any more. There were no more experts. There was just your truth.

Monty and I clung on to each other. I wondered how I could extricate myself from this situation. It had gone from being weirdly interesting to deeply depressing. I just wanted to leave and get back to normal life.

Finally, Mappin drew breath and Irina, who had sat impassively and silent next to her husband, leaned in.

'And who are you? What is your story?' she asked, suspiciously.

I tried to explain my life journey in a nutshell – grew up in Lebanon, became a Westminster TV producer, dressed as a squirrel, shouted into a mobile phone, now travelled the world writing books. Oh, and I was also vice-president of the Bill Gates fan club . . .

I could see from her puzzled expression that she was none the wiser.

'I have been to Kazakhstan,' I said.

'Why?' she asked.

'Why not?' I replied.

There was silence. It was a long awkward silence. Both Monty and I felt that this might be the time to bring proceedings to a halt. I didn't feel too bad. There had definitely been worse social events in this place.

I'd seen a toe-curling YouTube clip of when, in 2010, Mappin and his wife had thrown a birthday party for the then president of Kazakhstan, Nursultan Nazarbayev. Nazarbayev was the leader of Kazakhstan from 1991 until 2019 when he was finally forced out after mass popular demonstrations. His rule had been authoritarian, with an appalling human rights record and elections that were deemed neither free nor fair by the international community.

The birthday party was at Camelot Castle. Nazarbayev didn't show up. A representative from the Kazakh Embassy did. They cut the cake and then everybody listened to the Salvation Army choir sing 'Happy Birthday' to a dictator. It was beyond peculiar.

I said goodbye to the Mappins and went to the bar. I ordered a stiff drink and tried to write up as much of the strange encounter as I could muster.

That evening I dined alone in Irina's Restaurant, as the dining room was known. The whole vibe was starting to remind me of the hotel in *The Shining*. I'd actually stayed at the original hotel once: the Stanley Hotel in Estes Park, Colorado. The whole schtick was 'can you spend the night in America's most haunted hotel?' The short answer was 'No.' I tried my best but checked out at about three in the morning.

Back in Camelot Castle, Ted appeared at the dining-room door. He proceeded to wander around the room chatting to the three or four tables of diners like some needy restauranteur. Finally, he alighted at my table. I looked up at him. Our eyes met. I felt that we both clearly understood where we stood.

'Have a good evening, sir,' said Ted, bowing before marching out of the dining room. I took another spoonful of the thin, weak borscht and prayed for the sweet release of morning.

I needed to get as far away from here as I could. Fortunately, I was about to do just that.

6

Newfoundland

The Flat Earth Society has members all around the world.
Actual tweet from the Flat Earth Society

Of all the conspiracy theories, there was something about flat-earthers that intrigued me the most. It was possibly because they were so often the butt of people's jokes. Or maybe it was because the whole concept was just so outlandish and extreme that I wasn't convinced that it was all some surrealist joke.

One day, I'd stumbled upon an article about the supposed four corners of the flat earth. These were actual, physical places that you could go and visit. One of them was on a remote island called Fogo, in Newfoundland.

In that moment, I knew that I just had to go. I'd long joked about taking a flat-earther up in my hot-air balloon. This was one better. Imagine if I could actually take one to the supposed edge of the flat earth. What would happen?

It would not be my first visit to Newfoundland. I'd been before and had done so for another interesting reason to visit back then.

On that first trip, I'd been greeted at St John's International Airport by an incredibly friendly immigration officer. A rare thing in this world, but one of the lovely things about Canada.

'Hello, sir! Welcome to Newfoundland. What is your reason for visiting us, sir?' asked the smiling official.

'I'm here to frighten an Eskimo,' I replied, smiling back.

The official did not blink.

'I'm afraid that we have no Eskimi on the island, sir. Was there any other reason that you might be visiting us?' He smiled warmly.

'Tourist,' I replied, meekly.

'Welcome to Newfoundland, sir. Enjoy your stay.' The official stamped my passport and waved me through.

This was in 2003. Even back then, I think the term 'Eskimo' was probably a bit dodgy. I wasn't lying, however. I had persuaded the BBC to send me and a camera crew all the way to this large, remote island off the Atlantic coast of Canada to fulfil a desire I had scribbled onto a yellow Post-it note that had been stuck to my computer for a couple of years.

We ended up driving five hours out of St John's, across the frozen, barren tundra that was most of the island, until we came across a vast expanse of frozen lake. Sitting on said lake was a gentleman ice fishing. He might not have been an Eskimo, but he was definitely Eskimo-esque. He sported a Kenny-from-*South-Park*-type hood and was hunched over the hole in the ice on a small stool.

We parked up, the camera got into position and I crept across the lake towards the man carrying a large pair of cymbals. I finally got right behind him and smashed the cymbals together. He jumped out of his skin and stood up in surprise. I turned and ran as he watched in befuddlement. I jumped back into the van, along with the crew, and drove the five hours back across the barren frozen tundra to St John's, where we boarded a plane back to London.

When people asked me what made me laugh, I would reply, 'Travelling vast distances and making an enormous effort to do something totally pointless.'

I think we could all agree that there was little more pointless than the Eskimo incident. It still made me laugh.

Twenty years later, and I was off to Newfoundland again.

Most people would only ever have visited Newfoundland if they had been hijacked over the Atlantic. A hijack would have been useful as, since COVID, there were no direct flights to the island from the UK. My choices were to fly to Halifax or Montreal and then catch a connecting flight.

I'd been to Halifax. It was a place defined entirely by an explosion.

On the morning of 6 December 1917 a French cargo ship, laden with 6 million pounds of TNT, picric acid and aeroplane fuel, bound for the Allied war effort in Europe, collided with a Norwegian ship. The crew of the French ship, the SS *Mont-Blanc*, abandoned ship when the collision ignited the aeroplane fuel on board. They knew what was going to happen. The burning fuel was like a fuse to the main event – the TNT and the even more volatile picric acid.

The primed ghost ship floated into a pier in Halifax Harbour, attracting spectators to gawk at this floating fireworks display. Then the fire reached the explosive cargo.

The explosion created a two-mile-high mushroom cloud and destroyed half of Halifax in a millisecond. Until the atomic bombs were dropped on Japan, it was the largest human-made explosion in history. It killed 1,782 people and injured up to 9,000 others. It also disrupted all communications between North America and Europe.

Conspiracy theories inevitably started as to who was 'really' to blame. Suspicion fell on the Germans as the First World War was under way in Europe. Rumours abounded of German spies having been spotted near the shore just before the explosion. Any unfortunate German who happened to be in Halifax at the time was beaten up in the streets.

I chose the Montreal connection. I was nervous of a second German attack.

On the plane I was surrounded by members of the British swimming team on their way to Montreal for a training camp. They were all, understandably, wide-eyed and bushy-tailed, but they made me feel old. My joints ached. I felt mortal. For a couple of minutes, I thought I might have got lucky, as the seat next to me was empty.

I hadn't actually cared too much, until I noticed. Then, I got anxious and scanned every new passenger, nervously trying to work out whether they were headed my way. For a moment, as the steward made to close the main door, I thought I might be home free. Then, a passenger slipped in, just as they were closing up. The moment I spotted him, I knew he was the one.

A large man, he wore a crumpled excuse for a suit and carried hand luggage that was fit to burst. He squeezed his bag into the overhead locker, his crotch thrusting way too near my face for my liking. Once he had stowed everything to his liking, he turned his attention to the seat next to me.

He pulled out a pack of wet-wipes from his back pocket and started to feverishly wipe down every surface he could find. He wiped the armrests, the seat, the table, the screen, the remote control. If this man ever viewed the world with the assistance of a UV lamp, he would have a cardiac arrest.

He sat down and immediately tried to take control of our shared armrest. I was ready for him. I pulled an old Kleenex from my pocket, blew my nose and laid my hand, still holding the tissue on my lap, near his arm. He recoiled likes a wounded snake. I took ownership of the armrest. No germaphobe was ever going to win a dust-up with me.

I wondered why, if germs were so clearly an issue for him, he wasn't wearing a mask. Masks had almost become a political statement since COVID. Some people seemed to equate wearing one in confined public spaces with being some form of political prisoner. I was pretty relaxed about mask wearing. If somebody really needed me to wear one, I would, no problem. I was not, however, a mask obsessive. If I had a bad cold or flu, I would definitely pop one on. It was called common courtesy.

I peeked through the gap in the seats in front of me. A man was using the in-flight entertainment and had turned on the map feature. Using his fingers on the touchscreen he was slowly rotating a 3D map of the globe. A flat-earther would have flipped their lid. This was blatant promotion of mainstream science.

The original idea for this trip was to find a flat-earther in the UK and to bring them with me on a trip to the edge of the flat earth. I never got round to inviting one. I think, subconsciously, that the idea of spending such an extended period of time with one was daunting. I had a couple of leads in Newfoundland itself and hoped to persuade a local believer to come to Fogo with me.

I looked out of the window, over my obsessive cleaning neighbour, to see if we were high enough to see a provable curvature of the earth. We were not. I noticed that he was now watching a superhero movie. This was the final straw.

I could sum up my people preferences very easily. I like people who say 'bumper cars' and loathe people who say 'dodgems'. I also hate adults who watch superhero movies.

We landed in Montreal.

I loved this city, a weird French outpost in the middle of North America. I always equated the place with one of its most famous sons, Leonard Cohen. It was quietly cool, intellectual, idiosyncratic. I'd once been chatting to Jools Holland, formerly the keyboardist of Squeeze before becoming a kind of curious cockney national treasure and host of BBC's *Later . . . with Jools Holland*. Through that show, Jools must have met almost everybody there is to meet in music. I asked him who was the coolest person he'd ever met. He didn't hesitate for a second:

'Leonard Cohen,' he said.

'Why?' I asked.

'Just pure charisma. Like nobody I've ever met.'

High praise indeed.

In a very curious coincidence, Leonard Cohen had spent a lot of time living in one of the other four corners of our flat earth. He had a house on the island of Hydra, in Greece. I was pretty sure that this had not been the reason Cohen had chosen Hydra, but it was a nice coincidence.

The term 'four corners of the earth' appeared to have come from Miles Coverdale's 1535 version of the Bible, the first complete modern English translation: 'And after that sawe I foure angels stode on ye foure corners of the earth, holdinge ye foure wyndes of ye earth, yt ye wyndes shulde not blowe on ye earth, nether on ye see, nether on eny tree.'

Although it was very possible that Mr Coverdale might have believed the world to be flat, it was more likely to refer to the four compass points. The modern 'official' four corners of a flat earth formed a rather odd, triangular shape. They were, rather randomly, Fogo Island, Hydra, the Bermuda Triangle and Papua New Guinea.

I'd contacted the Flat Earth Society in the hope of being able to talk to somebody about the whole thing. I never got an answer.

Back in Montreal, I'd found an airport restaurant. I sat killing time, waiting for my connection to St John's in Newfoundland. Despite being fluent in French I could barely understand my waiter. Québécois is the equivalent of sixteenth-century French being whispered through a cheese grater. Sitting at the table next to me was a veritable bear of a man in full combat gear. He looked like a cartoon baddy, capable of killing a man with his bare hands. When the waiter approached him, however, he was softly spoken and polite. Thanks to COVID, it had been a while since I'd been in Canada, the Ned Flanders to America's Homer Simpson. It was rather wonderful to be back.

I ordered poutine, the Canadian national dish. It is essentially chips and gravy with little bits of cheese curd to make things weird. Because I was in Montreal, they had added a local touch: smoked meats and chopped up cornichons. Were I, perchance, to be incredibly stoned with high-level munchies, this would definitely be the holy grail. Distinctly non-stoned as I currently was, it resembled a glutinous mass with waaaaaay too much cheese curd. I had a lot of time for poutine, but this one was a disappointment.

After a three-hour wait, I started to trudge through the endless corridors of Montreal–Pierre Elliott Trudeau Airport to my gate. The international side of the airport was all shiny and exciting. The domestic area, however, was positively third world. I reached my gate only to find that there was another two-hour wait. By the time I hit the hay in Newfoundland, it would have been a solid twenty-four hours of travel, door to door. This was already starting to feel like a voyage to the edge of the world.

It was discombobulating, being in Canada, looking at conspiracies. Somehow, Canadians seemed too decent, too nice for conspiracy nonsense. Of course, this was not true. Canada, like everywhere else, had its own fair share of fruitcakes and nut jobs.

Romana Didulo was a Canadian of Filipino descent who had recently appointed herself as Queen of Canada and ruler of the world. She was big in Canadian QAnon and had been a militant anti-vax campaigner during the COVID-19 pandemic. She had urged supporters to 'shoot to kill' any healthcare official involved in giving vaccines. She claimed to be from another planet. She was, according to her, an Arcturian, with shape-shifting powers and access to all the money in the Vatican.

Her big beef was that she believed Chinese communists had been building a tunnel network under Canada. They would use these tunnels, according to her, to smuggle children for the elite paedophile organisations. Tunnels again? If these conspiracists ever found out about the London Underground, it would completely freak them out.

Didulo was a grifter and very big on fundraising. She was constantly asking her social media followers for money so that she could buy more RVs. She was obsessed with these vehicles. And you can't have too many RVs, am I right? She toured Canada in a convoy of them, stopping in every town that she went through to preach her message.

She was almost too loopy.

Some QAnon influencers were accusing her of being a government operative whose job was to discredit the movement. Her response was to threaten her accusers with summary execution. This didn't sound like a government operative. Or maybe it did? This was all so confusing.

My plane was finally boarding. I joined a line of seriously massive men who made the gentleman I'd been sitting next to at the restaurant look puny. I was gobsmacked. I appeared to be on a plane bound for Jonathan Swift's Brobdingnag, the land of giants. Unfortunately, we were flying there on Lilliputian Air. The plane was crazy small. There were two tiny seats on each side of the aisle but the airline had clearly done no research on their potential customer base.

My vast fellow passengers were literally unable to fit into the seats. Their bodies spilt over the stick-thin armrests. I grabbed a window seat and prayed to a god I didn't believe in that one of these monsters wouldn't sit next to me. This was becoming a common theme on my flights. Maybe I needed to find a religion that had some sort of commercial flight deity?

I got lucky. A reasonably sized woman sat in the adjoining seat. She was carrying an adorable puppy in a special mesh container. I instantly become a soppy child when meeting any dog.

I started to oooh and ahhhh so hard that I realised I was in danger of frightening her off and vacating the seat for one of the human trees. I did my best to control myself, but occasionally I would sneak a peek at the puppy with a big stupid smile on my face.

Animals are just so much better than humans.

I'm pretty sure that dogs don't harbour conspiracy theories. Dogs are relaxed, positive, loving entities. Dogs would not go for that type of thing, unless they lived with a cat. Cats would definitely be into conspiracy theories. Cats are that type of character. They think that they're smarter than everybody else. They are borderline sociopathic. They sleep all day. Cats are basically stoners and love to fuck with dogs.

'Hey, Dog,' said Cat.

'Hello, Cat. How are you?' answered Dog.

'Shut up and listen, you dumb fuck. There's going to be someone outside the door in a minute. They are coming here to kill you. The human has had enough of taking you for a walk. He has sold you to a laboratory. Do you know what a laboratory is?' Cat looked at Dog.

'No . . . what is it?' asked Dog.

'It's a place where they take bad dogs for Bill Gates to do terrible things to them for kicks. You're going there today.' Cat looked mock-concerned.

'What? Why? What have I done?' Dog was frantic with worry.

'You've been a bad dog, a very bad dog.' Cat was loving this.

'What can I do? I don't want to go,' Dog whimpered.

'Your only chance is to fight. Stand up for yourself. George Soros is coming to the door to take you away. Oh – here he is now.'

And that, I think, was how our postman came to lose two fingers. We have to go and collect our mail from the post office now.

Somehow, the plane took off and we were finally Newfoundland bound. I took another look at my fellow passengers. Almost every one of the giants was dressed head to foot in clothing festooned with either the maple leaf or the word CANADA.

The worst thing that could ever happen to a Canadian was to be mistaken for an American. Nobody was taking any chances.

The usual safety announcements crackled over the tinny PA . . . well, not totally as usual. The last bit, telling us that cannabis consumption was not allowed on board, was a new one for me. I wonder whether this was some kind of safety issue. Just imagine if the giants started to get the munchies and went on a poutine rampage. It would be mayhem and none of us would be safe from their insatiable appetites. The puppy and I looked at each other nervously.

The flight was two-and-a-half hours long and we landed just after midnight in St John's. There had been little opportunity to move on the plane and I was desperate for the bathroom, or the St John as I hoped they might call it.

I was slightly confused by the time until I remembered that Newfoundland had its own time zone. It was a half an hour ahead of Atlantic Canada and an hour and a half ahead of Montreal. Newfoundland had been a separate dominion when time zones were established. This had clearly been a way of letting the rest of the world know that Newfoundlanders were not wholly Canadian.

Since their union with Canada in 1949 there had been the occasional attempt to move the province to Atlantic time. This, however, had been firmly rejected by the populace, of whom a vast majority still considered themselves to be Newfoundlanders first, Canadians second.

One of the accidental benefits of this slightly bolshy time zone was that Newfoundland was the first place in North

America to greet the new millennium. This forced news crews from all over the continent to broadcast from Newfoundland and thrust this unique island into the global spotlight. It was a genius PR move.

I was considerably faster on my feet than the giants and so I was the first person to reach the facilities. A man was lying unconscious on a urinal. He was drunker than anybody I had ever seen before, and I'd been to Dublin. An empty bottle of vodka at his feet confirmed the source of his current incapacity, were the smell not evidence enough. If I had lit a match in that place the whole airport would have gone up. It was an impressive state of inebriation. I wondered whether I needed to do anything and, if so, what? Thankfully, as I deliberated, two airport officials, who had clearly been summoned by somebody else, turned up on scene.

I did my business and exited the bathroom. Large signs were everywhere welcoming me home. I was not home; I had 'come from away' – the popular expression used by Newfoundlanders for visitors, which I loved. Back in the UK, there is a band I adore called Wet Leg. It's not the greatest name for a band as it conjures up all sorts of curious imagery. It turned out, however, that the two women in the band are from the Isle of Wight. Wet Legs is the term that islanders use to describe mainlanders.

It's not just islands. Americans, often the focus of a multitude of names when travelling themselves, have a plethora of terms for visitors to their home states:

1. New Yorkers call visitors from the Midwest, who tend to be overly trusting and naive, 'Dorothys', as in 'You're not in Kansas any more.'

2. In Florida, the elderly who flock to the sun to escape the harsh northern winters are referred to as 'Q-Tips' as they tended to have white hair and wear white tennis shoes.

3. In Arizona, Californians are known as 'Granolas' from the land of fruits, nuts and flakes.

4. Visitors to the Rocky Mountain states are known as 'Flatlanders'.

5. American visitors to Canada are known as 'assholes'. Actually, I might have made that one up.

I was stopped for a random bag check. The official smiled at me. This was so unsettling. Officials never smiled in the UK.

'Good evening, sir! Welcome to Newfoundland. What is your reason for visiting us, sir?' asked the smiling official. It was as though I was time travelling.

'I'm here to travel to the edge of the flat earth,' I said.

The official didn't bat an eyelid.

'Aha, Fogo Island. I haven't actually been myself but I'm told it's spectacularly beautiful.' He smiled like a Christian camp counsellor. 'Enjoy your stay in Newfoundland.' He waved me on.

There really had to be something in the water that made Canadians so nice.

My old friend Pete was waiting for me outside. We had known each other since we'd met on a ski trip in the French Alps when we were sixteen. Pete and I had enjoyed many adventures together. We'd lived together in London. Then he'd followed me to Prague, where he ended up meeting his wife, Michelle, a Newfoundlander. They married, had four daughters and moved back to a little place called Clarke's Beach, about an hour out of St John's.

I went on to make a television series with Pete, whom I called Tiger. We made *Dom Joly's Happy Hour* in which we went around the world getting drunk, or 'investigating cultural attitudes towards alcohol', as the Sky lawyers insisted we describe it.

I hadn't seen Pete since before the pandemic. Newfoundland had pretty much sealed itself off from the outside world. This trip was going to be a splendid opportunity to catch up. I was going to stay with him for a couple of days before we set off for Fogo Island.

We were out of St John's fairly quickly and straight onto the Trans-Canada Highway. This rather extraordinary road starts in St John's and ends on the other side of Canada in Victoria, British Columbia. It crosses all ten Canadian provinces and, should you decide to drive the whole thing, is 4,645 miles long. That is quite the drive. I had to admit to being sorely tempted. Pete and I used to love a big road trip. But we needed to concentrate on the matter at hand.

It was pretty much a white-out. The road was frozen and the snow beat solidly and horizontally against the windshield as we sped towards his house. In the UK, this would have been game over. There was no way you would go anywhere on a night like this. In Newfoundland, however, this was daily life. He barely concentrated on the road ahead as he fiddled with the car stereo, keen to play me new tunes that he'd discovered since we'd last hung out.

After an hour or so we turned off the highway and were soon driving through Clarke's Beach. We parked up outside Pete's house, a large wooden building with views across the bay. This had been Michelle's childhood home. Pete had now been in

Newfoundland for over twenty years. He was almost a local. When he'd first moved to the island, he'd become something of a celebrity as, at the time, everybody was leaving. It was almost unheard of for somebody to choose to move there.

Once inside the house we had a couple of drinks by the fire, but I could barely keep my eyes open. It was time for bed. As I buried myself under the covers, I got an email. It was from my friend Chris, of *The Downhill Hiking Club* fame – my book about walking across Lebanon. He knew why I was in Newfoundland and had sent me something he had found on Facebook, on a flat-earther forum. It was not to do with Newfoundland, but Australia.

Have you ever been to Australia?

Australia is not real. It's a hoax, made for us to believe that Britain moved their criminals over to someplace. In reality, all these criminals were loaded off the ships into the waters, drowning before they could see land again. It's a cover-up for one of the greatest mass murders in history, made by one of the most prominent empires.

Australia does not exist. All things you call 'proof' are actually well fabricated lies and documents made by the leading governments of the world. Your Australian friends? They're all actors and computer-generated personas, part of the plot to trick the world.

If you think you've been to Australia, you're terribly wrong. The plane pilots are all in on this, and have in all actuality, only flown you to islands close nearby – or in some cases, parts of South America, where they have cleared space and hired actors to act out as real Australians.

Australia is one of the biggest hoaxes ever created, and you have all been tricked. Join the movement today, and make it known you have been deceived.

First, Finland . . . now Australia. I just didn't know what to believe any more.

I awoke late and sauntered down to the kitchen. Pete was making a coffee and about to go off to work. The concept of work and Pete together was an unusual one. He had always been a bit of an 'artistic' type, flirting with art and writing, and doing his level best to avoid anything that looked like a nine-to-five job.

But things had changed. This was Pete 2.0 and he was now the proud owner of a distillery. It seemed that the TV show we did together had really had an effect on him. When we made the show, we'd visited a lot of distilleries and they were always pretty boring. We would nod and pretend that we were interested, patiently waiting for the pay-off. The opportunity to sample the goods.

Now, Pete ran the Newfoundland Distillery Company and was something of a business celebrity in Newfoundland. He even had his own cocktail book about to be published. I was utterly gobsmacked, but so happy for him. Pete is one of the loveliest people in the world and oozes charm. This new career was perfect for him, as long as he didn't get too high on his own supply.

What could be better than to find out that one of your best friends now owned a distillery with a bar attached? Pete asked me whether I'd like to come to work with him. He didn't need to ask twice.

The commute was not a taxing one. The drive from home to distillery took about three minutes. Pete admitted that this did mean, should things get out of hand at work and he found himself 'over-sampling', then he could just walk home. Truly, this lucky bastard was living the dream.

His establishment was a series of long wooden buildings, right on the shore. He gave me a quick tour of the distillery itself, which was like any other, before we entered the bar that was attached to it. It was wonderful. A large, open room filled with non-matching tables and chairs, a cosy wood burner and, at the end, picture windows looking out over the sea. A clear lens on an endlessly changing still life.

Apparently, Pete had 'work to do'. He disappeared into the office, leaving me with the dangerous words 'Help yourself.' Sadly, I couldn't help myself. I did exactly what he suggested. I sampled his Seaweed Gin, his Maple Rum, his Chaga Rum, his Gunpowder Rum . . . everything became a bit of blur after a while, but it would be safe to say I had a smashing morning. I had, it seemed, organised a piss-up in a brewery with ease.

I met Pete's partner in the distillery, a gruff, silent type who asked me what I was doing in Newfoundland. He didn't ask it in a confrontational manner. He just looked a tad surprised that I'd bothered.

'I'm writing a book on conspiracies,' I said.

'Aha, so you're here about the Bell Island Boom?' he said, confidently.

'The what?' I replied.

'The Bell Island Boom,' he replied, pointing out to sea through the massive windows. 'It's just around that corner at the top of the bay.'

'And what was it?' I asked.

'Well, exactly . . . that's the point . . . nobody knows.' He looked out to sea mysteriously.

On Sunday 2 April 1978, a massive explosion occurred on Bell Island, the largest island in Conception Bay, where both Pete's house and distillery were located. In between 1895 and 1966, the island was a place of international economic significance as it had one of the largest iron ore mines in the world. During the Second World War, the Nazis attacked the island twice as the ore was incredibly important to the Allied war industry.

With the cessation of mining in 1966, most people left. So, there was hardly anybody living on the island when the explosion occurred in 1978. The blast was heard up to a hundred miles away. It was so powerful that it was even picked up by the Vela satellites that the USA used to detect nuclear tests by foreign powers.

Of course, conspiracy theories abounded. Some claimed it was a secret test by the American government. Others thought it was some sort of electromagnetic pulse weapon. Many blamed UFOs, especially after the son of the family whose farm was at the epicentre of the blast stated that he had been on his bicycle at the time of the explosion and had seen two luminous spheres flying by.

Eventually, the consensus seemed to settle on it being a 'superbolt'. This is a very rare type of lightning that emits an incredible force. Nobody could be sure, however, and speculation was still rife as to what had caused the Bell Island Boom.

This was great stuff. Weird islands, explosions and Nazis. What was not to like? But I had to stay focused. I was there to travel to the edge of the world. I had to be disciplined.

A couple of hours later, Pete appeared and announced that we were going to lunch.

'Where are we going?' I asked.

'We're going to Dildo, son.' Pete smiled.

I'd forgotten all about Dildo. It was a little town about half an hour from Pete's, situated right opposite the town of Spread Eagle, on the other side of the bay. I had driven through Dildo on my last visit to Newfoundland and had desperately tried to find some souvenir from the place – a fridge magnet, a baseball cap, a T-shirt – but there was nothing. The town was sitting on a childish tourist goldmine and was doing nothing about it. I'd spoken to somebody who I'd been told was the mayor of Dildo. I told him how crazy I felt it was that they were doing nothing. He just looked slightly confused and I started to wonder whether he actually was the mayor.

I'd ended up in a bar at a karaoke night. My film crew started filming as the whole scene was gold dust but this got the locals strangely angry. The mood changed and we were chased out of the bar. We were lucky not to have been beaten up. I hadn't been able to understand what the problem was until we got back to Pete's house and he made some enquiries. Apparently, a lot of the patrons of the bar were on disability benefits. Shots of them drinking and dancing were not something they wanted to be broadcast.

That was back in 2003.

'Just you wait, son. Dildo has changed,' said Pete.

We headed off to Dildo for lunch. The town certainly had changed. Firstly, it was very clear that somebody had heeded my advice as there were now souvenir shops everywhere and lunch was booked at the Dildo Brewing Company. As we entered the establishment, we had to walk through a shop absolutely crammed with everything you could think of with the word 'Dildo' on it.

We sat down at a table by the window with a panoramic view of the bay. Pete pointed to something on the hill opposite.

'Check that out, son,' he said.

I looked. On the heavily wooded hill, overlooking the town, was a large Hollywood-type sign with the word 'DILDO' on it.

Pete started to explain.

In 2019, just before the pandemic, the late-night talk-show host Jimmy Kimmel found out about Dildo and became briefly obsessed with the place. He featured it several times on his show and was made honorary mayor. Kimmel declared that Dildo was now Hollywood's 'honorary sister' and paid for the Hollywood-style sign to be put up on the hill above the bay. This notoriety had put Dildo on the tourist map for a while. The place was still cashing in on the unexpected tourist dollars.

We had fish and chips. The cod was the tastiest that I have ever had. This was hardly surprising as this was the island's main industry. Newfoundland was once known in Scottish Gaelic as *Eilean a' Trosg* (Island of the Cod) and in Irish as *Talamh an Éisc* (Land of the Fish).

After lunch we walked down the seashore and had our photograph taken next to a dodgy-looking wooden statue of a fisherman. He bore a startling resemblance to Captain Bird's Eye. Sadly, it wasn't the patron saint of fish fingers. It was a gentleman who went by the name of Captain Dildo. This place had gone from ignorance to overkill very quickly.

That evening we headed into St John's to have a look around. Our journey to the edge of the world started the next day and I was keen to get our last fix of relative civilisation. Fogo Island was considered to be remote, even by Newfoundlanders. This was worrying.

St John's is a city wrapped around a spectacular natural harbour. We drove up to Signal Hill and gazed down into the 'narrows' – the slim channel that transported vessels out of the wild ocean and into the calm safety of the harbour. Signal Hill was the site of the first transatlantic wireless transmission, hence the name, and it afforded us a panoramic view of both the harbour and the city beneath us.

We drove around the streets of the capital for a while but, if I was being honest, there was not a vast amount to see. Occasionally we would come across a row of multi-coloured wooden houses stretching down towards the harbour that were quite pleasant to look at. Overall, however, St John's came across as a place you wouldn't much pine for once you had left.

We dined in what passed for the funky modern quarter of town in a poncey boutique hotel that you just knew every band that ever visited the place would take refuge in. The food was good, maybe trying a little too hard to be all sophisticated, but it was a fun night. Pete was treated like a VIP as his bottles of liquor lined the shelf behind the barman. Everybody likes somebody who owns a distillery.

Pete told me that he had put the word out and that we might have a possible flat-earther in a place called Gander. It was on our way to Fogo, so this might work. Even more excitingly, although he had not spoken to the guy, his contact said that he might be persuaded to go with us to Fogo.

I now had myself, the proud owner of a distillery and a flat-earther. It looked like we had us the makings of a classic road trip.

The following morning saw us packing Pete's car with supplies. He had included a quite staggering amount of alcohol.

'You don't want to run the risk of running out, son,' said Pete, with a very concerned expression on his face.

'Quite right, son. You can't be too careful,' I replied.

We set off and joined the Trans-Canada Highway at mile marker thirty. We turned right and headed off into the great interior.

St John's is on the Avalon Peninsula that makes up the southeast portion of the island. Despite it being only a very small physical part of Newfoundland, more than 52 per cent of the island's population live there as it protrudes into the rich fishing zones near the Grand Banks. These is a series of underwater plateaus where the mixing of the cold Labrador Current and the warm Gulf Stream serves to lift nutrients to the surface, creating one of the richest fishing grounds in the world.

Overfishing of the area in the late twentieth century caused the collapse of several fish species, leading to the closure of the fishing areas. It brought economic chaos to Newfoundland. Thirty-five thousand fishermen and plant workers became unemployed overnight. A large number of them emigrated, looking for work. This was why the sight of somebody like Pete, who had actually immigrated to the island, had been so startling to locals back then.

We left the Avalon Peninsula, driving across the three-mile-wide isthmus that connected it to the main section of the island. Once across we were on the island proper. Around us was nothing but barren, frozen tundra. As we drove, I played music, and Pete and I reminisced about our misspent youth.

Life was good.

There were signs everywhere warning drivers of moose. I knew little about moose except that they appear to be rather badly designed deer. It's as though they are some sort of demo version. They are misshapen, over-sized and incredibly awkward looking. It was as though somebody had drunkenly crossed a cow, a camel and a mule. Were they a vehicle, there would be an urgent product recall. As it is, they roam free and are, apparently, a massive problem. Newfoundland has the highest density of moose per square kilometre in all of Canada. There are, on average, six hundred moose-related car accidents a year on the island.

It turns out that their curious design does have some sort of logic to it. They are, essentially, a pointy barrel on long sticks. The reason for their very long, thin legs is that they enable them to wade through deep snow, at great speed, with ease. It also makes them very dangerous when hit by a car. The vehicle tends to collide with the legs, sending the tank-like body smashing through the windscreen. According to Pete, people were endlessly inventing anti-moose devices for their vehicles.

Personally, I was rather longing to see a moose as the scenery itself was quite monotonous. Occasionally we'd catch a little glimpse of a fishing inlet but, for the most part, we drove alone, along a seemingly endless highway.

A sign informed us that we were entering the National Park of Terra Nova, the old Latin name for Newfoundland. There didn't appear to be any particular difference in terrain. Pete told me that hunting was not allowed in the National Parks. I wondered whether the animals knew this. If they did, they must have all made a rapid beeline for the place as Newfoundlanders, like most Canadians, love to hunt. I could imagine a couple of moose having a chat in the local bar.

MOOSE ONE: Things are getting crazy out there. You can't walk anywhere without bumping into another moose nowadays.

MOOSE TWO: I know, eh?

MOOSE ONE: I remember the days when I could walk for a day without seeing another moose. Now, I'm lucky if I get ten minutes to myself before I bump into some moosey bonehead who is definitely not from round here, but is all 'hey, how ya doing?' like we've been friends for ever.

MOOSE TWO: I know, eh?

MOOSE ONE: I wouldn't mind too much, but it's hiking up the cost of berries and I don't even get why they're here? Don't get me wrong, Steve, I love this place, but it's hardly special, is it? What the heck brings them here?

MOOSE TWO: I know, eh?

MOOSE ONE: Is that all you ever say, Steve? I'm trying to have a conversation here and you're about as responsive as a mute beaver.

MOOSE TWO: Sorry.

MOOSE ONE: Are you even listening to what I'm saying, Steve? I'm pouring my heart out here and you're just sitting there nodding with that big fricking ugly moose face on you. You actually got any opinions of your own, Steve? You got a working brain anywhere beneath that goddam ugly schnozz?

MOOSE TWO: I got one opinion.

MOOSE ONE: Finally . . . and what might that be, Steve?

MOOSE TWO: It's that I find you increasingly dull, Todd. You're like the bar bore, sitting here yakking on about how you don't like all the incoming moose and how everything was great back in the day when you were the only fricking moose in the place. I'm fricking glad there's new moose aboot, Todd. You wanna know why? Because it means I'm not stuck having to talk to you for the next twenty years. I got options, Todd, and I like having options.

[Steve downs his pint and leaves the bar. Todd sits forlornly by himself nursing a beer. The door opens and another moose walks in.]

MOOSE THREE: Hey, how ya doing?

MOOSE ONE: Go fuck yourself.

The drive to Gander from Clarke's Beach was around three hours. The plan was to get into town, get something to eat, meet our flat-earther and then take it from there. It was only an hour's drive from Gander to the gloriously named Farewell, the place where the ferry left for Fogo. We, like Steve the moose, had options. if Gander was an exciting place and our flat-earther was socially acceptable, we could spend the night. Otherwise, we would move straight on to Fogo.

We cruised into town at about midday. Snow was everywhere. At first glance, it was not a particularly bustling place. We parked up in an outdoor strip mall. I asked Pete why he'd stopped there, as opposed to driving into the town centre. He informed me that this *was* the town centre.

I looked around, a touch deflated.

We found a shawarma bar and sat down for a surprisingly tasty lunch. The shawarma would not have been recognised as such by any self-respecting Middle Easterner, but nevertheless it was a rather delicious wrap of indeterminate origin. As we lunched, Pete messaged the flat-earther, whose name, we now knew, was John. There was no immediate reply. So, we decided to do a spot of sightseeing in town. We asked a couple of locals what we should go and see. They looked utterly bemused by the concept. Eventually, one suggested we go to the airport. I assured them that we had seen airports before. Was there nothing else to do in town? They both shook their heads.

So, we went to the airport.

Gander Airport, it turned out, was actually quite a big deal. In 1935, it was nothing more than a little village when it was selected to be the place for the construction of a major airport. The reason Gander was chosen is that it was very close to the Great Circle Route that the very first transatlantic flights used to fly from London to New York. Flights could not, back then, be done in one hop, and Gander served as a very useful stopover and refuelling centre. During the Second World War it became a vital staging point for fighter planes and bombers on their way to the fight in Europe. I suddenly realised that my dad, who had been trained to fly his Seafire in Canada before being sent off to the Pacific to fight the Japanese on HMS *Implacable*, must have spent some time there. It was at times like these that I longed for him to be still around so that I could pick his brains. What an adventure it must have been for him, fresh out of school and only eighteen years old, to be sent there to train for war.

After the war, Gander became known as 'the crossroads of the world' as every transatlantic flight had to stop and refuel there.

All the world had to pass through this place until, in the mid-sixties, more modern planes started to be able to make the trans-atlantic flight without stopping and Gander slowly became redundant. Maybe a visit to the airport might be of more interest than we imagined.

We drove out of what was loosely termed a town and were soon parking up outside the terminal building. We were slightly underwhelmed upon entry. The place was a bog-standard, modern, local airport terminal, mainly hosting internal flights with the occasional plane flying to the Canadian mainland. We strolled around until we came across an entrance to what seemed like another building. We walked through and were instantly transported back in time. The enormous hall we'd walked into was totally deserted. It felt like we'd stepped onto the set of *Mad Men*. We were suddenly in a forgotten age, an age when air travel was special and glamorous.

The Canadian government of the time, realising that the great and the good from across the globe were all being forced to spend time in this remote destination, saw an opportunity for them to showcase modern Canada to the world. And so, they went for it. The ghost terminal we had inadvertently wandered into was opened in 1959 by Queen Elizabeth II. It had been built in an incredibly avant-garde 1960s Modernist style. Shiny marble floors, gorgeous cutting-edge furniture, vinyl sofas designed by Robin Bush and vast, stunning artworks on the walls. I peered into the ladies' washroom, where a row of pristine Charles Eames chairs waited in vain for somebody to powder their nose.

Because wait in vain is what they did. It was only about five years later that Gander Airport became a white elephant as newly developed jet engines no longer needed to make a stop-over and Gander became redundant. This served to leave the terminal almost unused and like a perfectly preserved time capsule of what the golden age of air travel used to be like. It was peak sixties in aspic. It felt as though at any moment a plane could land and the terminal would fill up with glamorous passengers.

And there used to be plenty of those. People from the town used to go to the airport for entertainment as you never knew who might be there. One local remembered queuing up at the bar only for Frank Sinatra to try to cut in and be sent to the back of the line. Another bumped into Marilyn Monroe in the ladies' loo. The Beatles first set foot in North America there. Every night in Gander Airport was a kind of curious lucky dip of international glitterati.

When transatlantic planes no longer needed to stop over in Gander in the late sixties, the airport got a curious new lease of life by catering for passengers from communist countries who were not allowed to travel through the United States. Fidel Castro once landed and asked some locals to be taken sledging. He was, according to a local woman, Geraldine Maloney, 'like a child when it came to getting on the toboggan and going for a run'.

Many of the communist travellers did not leave Gander. They used the opportunity to defect. Passengers were allowed into a special area to stretch their legs, without the documentation required for longer stopovers at other airports. The passengers could drink a beer or even visit the duty-free shop. Many, however, took the opportunity to approach a Mountie and ask to be admitted to Canada as refugees. Many settled in Gander itself.

This multi-cultural background served Gander well in 2001 when it had another brief moment in the international spotlight. Following the terrorist attacks of 9/11, all American airspace was closed and planes were ordered to land immediately. Thirty-eight planes landed at Gander, with more than seven thousand passengers and crew members stranded. For a tiny town like Gander, whose population numbered only ten thousand, this was a massive event. Passengers sat in their planes on the tarmac for twenty-four hours as local authorities checked that there were no terrorists aboard each flight.

While this was happening, the local inhabitants gathered together and decided to do everything they could to help the 'plane people', as they became known. They demonstrated quite remarkable levels of hospitality, organising food and putting many of them up in their own homes. They even provided entertainment, which included guided tours of the town (can't have taken long), live concerts by local artists and local culinary delicacies like stewed moose. They must have had the time of their lives . . .

This event was made famous by a musical called *Come from Away*. Originally just a local production in Toronto, it went on to become a massive global hit.

Conspiracies abound around 9/11. They tend to be divided into three theories:

1. That the US government had prior knowledge of the event, but let it happen as it would serve as a useful excuse for military intervention. Similar conspiracy theories were bandied about regarding the Japanese attack on Pearl Harbor.

2. That the US government was responsible for the attack, which they then blamed on other people, again giving them an excuse for military intervention.
3. That the attacks were not real. We were watching a hologram, a deep fake; the victims were crisis actors.

Sadly, none of these theories made it into the musical.

For a tiny little town in the middle of nowhere, I had to admit that Gander had quite the history once you dug beneath the snowy wasteland. The big question, however, was whether it would it provide me with my real goal: a square-flat-earther.

7

Glastonbury

A thought is a cosmic order waiting to happen.
Stephen Richards

Before we continue our journey to Fogo, I thought I should
take a moment to lay out here what I already knew about
flat-earth theory.

Back in the UK, I'd actually met a flat-earther, face-to-face,
not that long ago. Following my stay at Camelot Castle I'd
decided to look a little more into conspirituality, the theory that
New Age types were more likely to be conspiracy-minded than
most.

So, I'd driven down to Glastonbury, in Somerset, to investigate. Now, Glastonbury is obviously world famous for the festival on nearby Worthy Farm, but the whole town is a mecca for
all sorts of New Age thinking and alternative lifestyles. I felt
very confident that I would be able to find a flat-earther or two
to chat to.

Also, Glastonbury was both where King Arthur was buried
and one of the destinations that Jesus had visited when he'd
accompanied his uncle on a business trip to England.

This made for some nice symmetry with things that I'd looked
into so far.

Upon arrival, I popped in to see Haggis. Haggis was a juggler who also happened to run the theatre and circus area of the Glastonbury Festival. I'd met him when he'd booked me to open the main tent the previous year with my show *Holiday Snaps*. If anybody knew a flat-earther I could talk to, it was Haggis. As we had a cup of tea, he made some enquiries. Several people suggested the same person for me to talk to. Haggis scribbled down his name and number. I was off.

I left the guy a message and decided to have a wander around town as I waited. I thanked Haggis for his hospitality and information. It was only a five-minute walk from his house into the centre of town and I was soon in the thick of it.

I checked a public noticeboard to see what was available should I be interested. The choice was endless. I could try:

1. Alien body-art lessons.
2. Sound healing.
3. Full moon healing.
4. Heart healing.
5. A samba band concert (followed by a silent vigil for the planet).
6. Shamanic healing.
7. Soul retrieval.
8. Chakra balancing.
9. Priest or priestess training.
10. Goddess temple ceremony.

Truly, all of alternative life was there.

I figured I was probably most interested in soul retrieval. I read up on what this might involve.

During the soul retrieval process, the shaman moves into an altered state of consciousness to travel to realities outside of normal perception, also known as hidden spirit worlds, to retrieve the lost part of the soul.

Once the lost soul is located, the Shaman will acknowledge the former pain and gently negotiate the soul's return to the body. The Shaman then brings the soul back to normal reality and blows the missing soul part back into body through the head or heart.

In some cases, there is reluctance of the soul to return, or the soul may not even know that a separation has occurred. In some cases, the soul does want to return. It is, however, important to note that when the soul returns, it comes back with all the pain it experienced when leaving.

This all sounded pretty traumatic, but I supposed that this was the point.

My phone buzzed. It was Jacob, the flat-earther, and he was happy to meet up and talk. We agreed to meet in a café called the Crown at the bottom of the high street in an hour's time. I was finally going to meet a real-life flat-earther to whom I could ask all the questions that had been plaguing me.

This gave me an hour to kill in Glastonbury. I decided to go shopping. Every other shop was either selling crystals, hippy clothing or New Age ephemera. I popped into one that seemed to specialise in crystals and baggy tie-dye trousers. The smell of incense was almost too much. I kept as low to the floor as I could and started looking about. A small woman standing behind a tall counter popped out and made me jump.

'Salutations,' she said.

'Hey,' I replied.

'What can I help you with today?' she asked.

The truth would be that she could best help me by leaving me alone, but she had a sweet smile and clearly meant no harm.

'Nothing . . . just browsing,' I said, with a forced smile.

'Nobody enters here by chance. You are here for a reason,' smiled the teeny hippy.

'I'm really not. The truth is, I'm meeting somebody in forty minutes and I'm just killing time.' It felt good to be honest.

'We are all just killing time,' said the minikin with a serious look on her face.

'Yes, I suppose we are,' I replied.

'What is your soul stone?' asked the pocket rocket.

'My what? I don't know . . . look, I'm really not here for that.' I started edging towards the door.

'Your soul stone can be a mirror or a guide. It serves as a touchstone. It can give you illumination, solace, energy . . .' The itsy-bitsy lady had moved fast to subtly block my exit strategy.

'It's not really my sort of thing,' I mumbled, trying to manoeuvre around her.

'AMETHYST!' she said very loudly.

'Sorry?' I said.

'Amethyst, that's your power stone, your soul crystal. It's amazing for anxiety. You seem very anxious.' She moved further in front of the door.

The truth was that I was anxious, very anxious. Mainly because I was asphyxiating on the incense in a weird shop whose short-statured owner appeared to be holding me hostage.

'Actually, maybe Tiger's Eye. It releases you from both fear and anxiety. Would you like to feel one?' She moved fast to her left and opened a glass cabinet.

'I'm sorry. I have to go. Soul-retrieval appointment . . . mustn't be late.' She had left a gap and I grabbed the opportunity and was halfway out of the door before I'd finished speaking. I took a deep gulp of fresh air. It felt good.

'SORRY!' I waved at her through the glass and bolted down the high street.

Twenty minutes later and I was sitting in a nook opposite the bar, waiting for Jacob. He had told me that I would recognise him as he would be 'wearing an Afghan hat'. Unfortunately Glastonbury was probably one of the very few places in the UK where this was more hindrance than assistance.

I needn't have worried, however. When Jacob appeared, he was wearing way more than just an Afghan hat. In fact, he looked as I imagined Roger Waters might look, should he have joined the Mujahideen. There was no mistaking Jacob, even in Glastonbury.

He shook my hand and sat down opposite me. I really didn't know what to expect, but I liked him immediately. He had a kind, gentle face. I dived straight in. This was the question I'd been longing to ask somebody for ages.

'So . . . you believe the earth is flat?' I asked.

'Yes. That's right,' he said.

A couple sitting on a table near us both looked up in surprise and stared at us.

'And you're not doing this as a joke or as some form of intellectual contrarianism?' I continued.

'Not at all.' He looked at me directly in the eye.

'Can you talk me through your flat-earth theory? What made you get into it?'

239

'Well, I went to a talk at a festival about it and it made me think about the idea. Actually, I became a flat-earth sceptic at first. To counter an idea, you first need to understand it. So, I really researched the ball-earth theory in detail. Then I bought myself a camera to watch boats supposedly go over the horizon. There are lots of these sorts of films on YouTube but they've all been taken down now.'

He was starting to get into his stride, but I had to stop him.

'Sorry, who took them down?' I asked.

'YouTube, I suppose.'

'But why?' I asked.

'Exactly,' he answered, raising his eyebrows at me.

He carried on talking while I quickly googled 'ships being filmed disappearing over the horizon. Flat earth.' There were loads of clips still available to view.

'I filmed the ship and basically it just goes out of sight but you can still see it . . . it's just the haze and you can only see things so far. I put a camera so that it was just at ground level, at the edge of the sea and we filmed a beach seven miles away, which you shouldn't be able to do.' He was freestyling now.

'What do you think the earth looks like?' I asked.

'There are theories that it's a limitless plane, but actually the key point about flat earth is that it's still. In fact, that's more important than it's flat for me. Nobody can sense any movement.'

'You mean we can't feel the earth flying or rotating through space?' I asked.

'No. There are no instruments to record that,' he replied.

'What about photographs from space?' I asked.

'When you're a flat-earther you question NASA. They're a complete lie,' he replied.

240

'Why would they do that?' I asked.

'It's difficult to know,' he replied.

We sat in silence for a couple of minutes.

'Do you know about the Sea Sparrow guided missile?' he suddenly asked.

'No,' I replied.

'They're on American warships and are used to take out another ship twenty miles away.'

'What's weird about that?' I asked.

'They use a laser to guide the missile. How does a laser bend around the curve?'

I wished I had some scientific knowledge as I had no idea how to refute this.

'I suppose my main thing is that all this has to be such a vast, massive conspiracy. It would be impossible to keep all this secret,' I said.

'There are two things that stop people speaking out. Firstly, the ball earth is a belief system and you need to step out of that system to question it.'

He was speaking very quietly. He was calm, as though explaining something simple to a child.

'I started questioning belief systems when I was shown a documentary refuting the supposed truth about 9/11.' He appeared to have forgotten the second thing that made people speak out, but it didn't seem to matter. 'I question everything now.'

We sat in silence again for a moment, before he started again.

'If you have a ball earth . . . somebody is upside down. So how do they do things like jump? How do birds fly around? How do fish swim?' he asked.

'Isn't that gravity?' I asked.

'Yeah, but flat earth totally disses gravity. We replace gravity with density and buoyancy. If you study Isaac Newton, he had his doubts. Science is just theories, not laws. The only provable law in science is that things get old and fall apart.'

He was going for it now and I wished I had the firepower to hit back. I tried my best.

'If there is no gravity, how come the sea doesn't just fall off the edge?' I asked.

'So, this is where I do tend to believe in the ice wall,' he replied.

We had now gone, in my opinion, full *Truman Show*. The couple sitting next to us were no longer even pretending to talk to each other. They were hanging on Jacob's every word.

'We study flightlines, where commercial airlines fly. They follow the flat earth, not the ball earth. Nobody flies over the Antarctic. I've flown to China. I landed in Denmark and then I got a flight to Beijing, but we didn't fly over the Arctic. Why? That's why a lot of flights fly over the Arab countries, because it's the centre.'

I just nodded frantically. I was losing touch with reality now. I tried to reel it back to what I was there for.

'Do you think there is a link between New Age thinking and conspiracies?' I asked.

'No, certainly not with flat earth as you need to be pretty switched on scientifically to counter it. Maybe, more around refusing vaccines, but not flat earth.'

We sat sipping our coffees for a while. There was one obvious question I had to ask, but it felt a bit cheap.

'Umm . . . do you mind me asking – do you take a lot of mind-expanding drugs?' I asked.

'I certainly did when I was younger.' He smiled.

Another silence that I felt forced to interrupt.

'Final question, do you come across a lot of square-flat-earthers? I ask this because I'm off to Fogo, to one of the corners of the square flat earth.' I smiled encouragingly.

'Ha! No, they are a very small splinter group. They would almost consider me to be a ball earther,' he replied, giggling at the thought.

I really liked Jacob. He seemed to be a kind, thoughtful man. He believed in a flat earth but didn't appear to be too bothered if anybody else did or didn't. He wasn't some zealot constantly haranguing 'ball earthers' like myself about his reality. In fact, he had actually stopped giving talks on flat-earth theory at festivals because people would come along to argue and become very aggressive.

That was not his vibe.

My takeaway from the conversation was that once you had stepped away from believing one generally accepted narrative – for instance 9/11 – starting to question every other mainstream narrative became almost normal.

Jacob called it 'leaving mum and dad'.

I left the café in something of a daze. It was so interesting to meet someone with such a totally divergent worldview to my own, and yet, as it had been with other encounters, it left me with mixed emotions. Part of me did genuinely worry about whether these people were all there. A smaller part of me wondered if there might just be the faint possibility that they could be right and that I was the ignoramus.

This certainly hadn't been my first time in Glastonbury encountering people who had 'left mum and dad'. In fact, the previous year, I'd performed at the festival for the first time.

'You going to Glastonbury?' I've been faced with this question pretty much every year for the last thirty years. My answer has always been always the same.

'God no. I'd rather eat my own excrement.'

I'm just not the camping type. I'm not into big crowds and have never been overly keen on communal crapping. Glastonbury, for me, has always been something I watch and enjoy from afar, with all the delights of home at my fingertips, including the 'off' button.

So, when I was asked to open the Cabaret Tent, I was unsure as to what to do. I was interested in seeing what it was all about and, if I was ever going to go, it would have to be as a performer.

As a charitable organisation, Glastonbury pay way below the usual performing rates but they soften the blow by offering four weekend tickets complete with backstage passes. We held a family meeting and the decision was made. We were going, whether I liked it or not.

We drove down from Cheltenham on the Thursday afternoon, expecting terrible traffic but, as there was a train strike on that day, most people had gone in on the Wednesday and the roads were clear. Once in Glastonbury, we headed to Haggis's house where we were met by a lovely French lady who inundated us with info.

We got our tickets, our car passes and instructions about which gate to drive through. A large map of the site was laid out on the table and she talked us through where everything was. It was all quite disorientating. We were about to enter a temporary city of 300,000 inhabitants and it was going to take us a while to find our bearings.

The French lady then left us with the final advice that we MUST take loo paper in with us. According to those in the know, it was more valuable than a bag of ecstasy tablets.

As we drove onto site, I tried to take in the sheer size of this festival. It was extraordinary. Just the fence that surrounded the entire site was a monumental feat of engineering. Everywhere we looked, festival-goers sporting every form of festival fashion drifted towards the delights of the day from their distant campsites.

Upon arrival we were shown around the Theatre and Circus backstage area. This was to be our base for the next three days. There was a bar, a restaurant, showers and loos.

'This is our safe space that we can retreat to,' said Charlotte, my lovely production manager.

The idea that the circus folk needed a 'safe space' within which to retreat from the weirdness of the festival proper spoke volumes about what we were about to encounter. The performance went well. The tent, with a capacity of two thousand people, was packed and I had the bucket-list-ticking opportunity to finally strut onto stage and shout, 'Hello, Glastonbury.'

With my bit over, I was now free to enjoy the festival without the nagging pre-performance anxiety that had plagued me all morning. We filled up our water, confirmed that we had loo paper and set off into the unknown. My only definite plan was that Porridge Radio were playing on some tiny stage over the weekend. I had to watch them play.

We passed through the Other Stage and ended up on the hill above the Pyramid Stage where Stacey and I sat down to watch Wolf Alice. The kids went off together to explore.

We nodded at our new neighbours. We were sitting next to a gentleman called Dave and his wife, Judy. We got chatting. They told me that they had come up from Dorset where they lived in a bender. I tried unsuccessfully not to giggle. A bender, it turned out, was a tent made out of a flexible frame of willow and covered by a tarpaulin. Dave was a zero–Zen massage practitioner, while Judy was a sound healer. They seemed pleasant enough and we watched Wolf Alice together.

The flags people wave on long poles are an integral part of Glastonbury and I would occasionally spot someone wandering past me struggling to keep this surprisingly heavy piece of kit aloft. Fun as they undoubtedly are, it seemed quite the commitment to decide to take one around with you all day.

They ranged from photos of Boris Johnson kissing the King of Saudi Arabia, to more basic ones saying 'TITS' to a brilliant yellow one proclaiming that 'This is a work event'. My personal favourite was one that had a drawing of a piece of cheese along with the word 'Gouda'. I enjoyed watching Gouda's journey through the crowd during various performances. I was slightly puzzled by just how many Isle of Man flags were flying.

I asked Dave if he knew why. I regretted this immediately.

'Because the people running that island are Archons,' he said, looking around to see if anybody was listening.

'What are Archons?' I asked.

'They are an inter-dimensional race of reptilians, a hybrid race. They are shape-shifters.'

'What?' I was not expecting this.

'They're what you call the Illuminati, the Babylonian Brotherhood. They're the ones that control world events. They fuck everything up to keep us all in constant turmoil.'

246

Dave's countenance had not changed since I met him, but it was if a switch had been turned on. He was a different man. Judy got in on the action.

'Homosexuality was illegal on the island until 1992. They were forced to legalise it but they just pay lip service. The rulers can shape-shift. They can change from human to non-human form at will.'

Dave nodded in agreement with Judy.

'They encourage wars, genocide, animal slaughter as this creates negative energy that they feed off,' said Dave.

'This is the government of the Isle of Man we are talking about?' I was so confused. This had all come out of the blue.

'That's right. Most of the island to be honest. The flags here are a sign of their power.' Dave looked around disapprovingly.

'Do you know about Denver airport?'

'Denver airport? No, What about it?' It was Dave's turn to look surprised.

'Oh nothing – it's just supposed to be where the Illuminati are going to hide from the Rapture.'

'Oh, no, I've never heard of that. But it wouldn't surprise me,' said Dave.

I got the feeling that it would take a lot to surprise Dave.

Halfway through Sam Fender the sheer volume of pints consumed hit me hard and I was forced to face the public facilities. I joined a massive line of people waiting to enter an empty green metal stall and stare into the pit of hell. This was the closest I think I'll ever get to understanding daily life in a refugee camp. People jostled and fought for the doors, some going into these excretion stables, two, sometimes three at a time.

After twenty minutes I pushed a slow, stoned hippy out of the way and forced myself into one that had the words 'Amber Heard shat in my tent' scrawled on the back wall. I grimly did my business while desperately thinking of my happy place, which was home. I came out and lined up again for the sink to wash my hands clean of the horror. A rather sweet-looking twenty-something, clearly mashed out of her head, was trying to fill her water container but seemed entirely unable to grasp the concept of the screw top. After two desperate minutes she looked up at me and whispered 'HELP' in such a sweet manner that I couldn't be angry with her. I unscrewed it for her, handed it back and then watched her pour water down the side, completely missing the hole for about a minute before she tottered off, unsteadily, into the heaving wall of humanity.

Back on the hill, Sam Fender was drawing to a close and three student types in front of me were celebrating by scooping vast spoonfuls of cocaine out of a small leather pouch and ingesting it like it was going out of fashion. They were sitting right next to a young couple with two tiny children, both of whom were sporting ear defenders. The couple looked longingly at the carefree student-types and most probably longed for some chemical assistance themselves.

There were a lot of people with small children and babies, and the theory was that most of them had bought tickets three years ago before it was cancelled. In the intervening years they had procreated and their Glastonbury 2022 experience was a very different one from what they had originally anticipated.

Dave and Judy looked at the students with ill-concealed contempt. I was surprised as I'd started to wonder whether they might be on hallucinogens, as this might go some way towards explaining their curious beliefs.

My wife's phone rang. It was our son and they started chatting. Both Dave and Judy bristled and shifted a little away from her. I apologised and explained that we needed to keep a vague eye on where our kids were. Judy was not impressed.

'You shouldn't let them have phones,' she said.

'Why not?' I asked.

'Because of the 5G,' she said.

'I've only got 3G here,' I said, jokingly.

'It's not a joke. The COVID thing is caused by 5G. There was no COVID in Africa because they are not on 5G networks.' Judy's eyes widened as she talked.

'The virus is transmitted by radio waves. The electro-magnetic fields around the masts mutate our cells and that's what causes the virus,' Dave chipped in with some science.

I was now pretty convinced that both Dave and Judy were quite unusual. They were both very pleasant, however. If you could get them off the David Icke-type theories and didn't make any phone calls, then they were almost normal.

We all stopped talking for the main event – Billie Eilish, the pint-sized Manga Goth Girl. There were rumours flying about that Harry Styles was going to join her on stage. This was a big part of Glastonbury. Rumours regarding secret gigs or appearances by Harry Styles, Eminem, Ringo, the Archons . . . most of which were always bollocks.

It was time to go to bed. I was strangely enjoying the weird conversation with Dave and Judy. It was like a portal into another dimension. I told them that we might see them again. They said that they would be in the exactly the same place the next day. I said we'd probably see them then.

Day two started well. The sun was shining and life was good. We stopped off at the West Holts Stage to watch Brass Against – a brass band version of Rage Against the Machine that, unlike jazz, was actually a lot better than that sounds.

We had Foot-Long Hot Dogs, Singapore Noodles, Poutine and pudding from the Crumble Shack; all of which could be food or the name of bands . . .

We met up with friends, one of whom was carrying a bag containing an industrial amount of magic mushrooms.

'Are you selling these?' I asked.

'No, they're for personal consumption,' he replied with a big, goofy grin and eyes so glazed that it was clear why it had taken him a good twenty seconds to reply.

Pretty much everybody was 'on it' from what I could see. Whatever 'it' was, was unclear but it must have something to do with the unbelievable mellowness of the crowds. I have never been anywhere in the UK where crowds of this size have not had a high percentage of aggressive wankers, lairy arseholes and total twats.

AJ Tracey came on. He is a rapper from west London, Ladbroke Grove, to be precise. I know this because he literally could not stop telling us. He must have informed of us his home location about thirty times. It was almost obsessive. He finished up with video footage of the mean streets of Notting Hill flashing up behind him, just in case we hadn't understood.

Our party split as some went off to check out Metronomy and Glass Animals. I was assigned to keep a place on the Pyramid Hill and so I headed off for our position the day before. Sure enough, there were Dave and Judy. I said hello and they smiled and waved as though we were old friends. I sat down next to them, just as a special speaker was introduced by Emily Eavis, the vegan-looking daughter of Glastonbury founder, dairy farmer and devout Methodist, Michael Eavis.

'Ladies and gentlemen, please welcome to the stage, Greta Thunberg.'

The Swedish Joan of Arc of the environment movement came on and gave us all a doom-laden talking-to that must surely have been the inspiration for Kendrick Lamar's 'Bitch, Don't Kill My Vibe'.

Several of the surrounding drug-takers descended into their own paranoid K-holes as we were told, over and over again, that we were all going to die in a fiery, famished, flooded Armageddon of our own making.

I wondered what Dave and Judy would make of this. They had sat stony-faced through Thunberg's speech. Were they climate-change deniers? I really didn't know which way they would go.

'What did you make of Saint Greta?' I asked.

'She's a useful idiot,' said Judy.

'She's working for China,' said Dave.

'China?' I was confused.

'Sure. What does she want us to do? Stop fossil fuels and replace them with renewables? Am I wrong?' Dave asked.

'You're not,' I said, wondering where this was going.

'So, wind turbines. Where do they come from?' he looked at me expectantly.

I had no idea and shrugged my shoulders.

'China,' said Dave.

'And solar power. Where do all the solar panels come from?' he continued.

'Umm . . . China?' I answered.

Dave nodded solemnly.

'Then you start a proxy war between Russia and the West in the Ukraine. You slap sanctions on Russia. Who is the winner?' Dave looked at me triumphantly.

'China?' This was all I was saying now.

'And who is the loser because the energy prices are going up?'

'China?' I said, like a stuck record.

'No! The West. They want to destroy the West,' said Dave.

'Who do? China?' I wasn't sure if he was talking about them or whether we were back on the shape-shifters.

'Of course,' said Dave and Judy nodded vigorously in agreement.

'And Greta Thunberg is working for China?' I asked again.

'Of course,' he said.

I sat in silence and thought about this for a while as Haim, a band of sisters, took to the stage. They were definitely prepared for global warming as they were all sporting matching black bikinis.

I leaned over to Dave, just before they started playing.

'Sorry – just to be clear, you think global warming is real, or a hoax?' I asked.

'A hoax. Total nonsense. Humans are carbon-based. If you start getting less carbon you get less humans . . . and less trees.'

Haim kicked into their first number and further discussion was impossible.

This was probably for the best.

There was a very weird moment halfway through their set when, as part of some 'strong women sticking it to men' bit, the singer pretended to take a phone call from some surfer called Brad, who she then told to fuck off because she was onstage at Glastonbury.

Unfortunately, the phone ring they used for this bit was the Nokia tune made famous by my very own *Trigger Happy TV* Big Mobile character. It was totally surreal. People all round started to shout 'HELLO . . . WHAT? NO, I'M AT GLASTONBURY!' And then spotted me and had their minds blown. I started to wonder whether I had partaken in a mushroom or ten and had forgotten that I had agreed to do a 'bit' with Haim. It was all very confusing.

Dave and Judy noticed this happening and seemed bemused. At the end of Haim's set, Judy leaned over.

'Why was everybody looking at you?' she asked.

'It's complicated,' I answered.

'Go on,' said Judy.

'I was on a TV show called *Trigger Happy TV* and I used to shout into a big mobile phone, and that was my ringtone and so people thought we might be doing a bit,' I replied.

'A bit of what?' asked Judy.

'A "bit". It's a comedy term for material, a sketch,' I replied.

'And did you?' she asked.

'No . . .' I replied.

I felt that my quixotic relationship with Dave and Judy had probably run its course.

I now faced a dilemma. I bloody love the Waterboys, but they were headlining the Acoustic Stage at the same time as Paul McCartney was taking to the Pyramid. In the end, despite the utter brilliance of Mike Scott and his gang, I opted for Macca as it was definitely one of those once-in-a-lifetime moments, plus there was another rumour circulating that he was going to appear alongside a hologram of John Lennon in the style of the new ABBA show.

The crowd was vast . . . insanely so. I couldn't move and there were people as far as the eye could see. And then, suddenly, he was onstage, the world's most impressive-looking eighty-year-old, launching into 'Can't Buy Me Love'. Everybody went apeshit. Obviously, it couldn't last.

Macca is a bit like Robin Williams in that, although he's an utter genius, he has a tendency, if not properly supervised, to descend into slightly naff, almost child-like material which, in his case, culminated in the monstrosity that is 'We All Stand Together' with the Frog Chorus. Fortunately for us, he did not go that low, but there was a long period in which he noodled away at songs that nobody was much interested in.

But it all came together in the end. He introduced a special guest from 'the East Coast of America' and everybody thought it was Ringo, but it was Dave Grohl. Dave Grohl told us all a rather long story about the series of delayed flights that he had to take to get here before launching into a couple of songs with Macca.

Then . . . another surprise guest . . . 'It's Harry Styles,' screamed my daughter. It was not. It was Bruce Springsteen. The crowd went batshit crazy and started screaming 'Bruuuuuce', which, to the untrained ear, as with 'Joe Rooooot' at the cricket, sounded like we were booing him. Macca and Bruce were unfazed and launched into 'Glory Days' and everything was all right in the world.

Finally, with Grohl and Bruce off the stage and after another amazed explanation from Macca about how both of them had flown over 'in planes' from America to be here, we got to the main course.

Macca launched into 'Let It Be', 'Live and Let Die' and then what felt like a thirty-minute sing-along-with-Gramps version of 'Hey Jude', which really should be the UK national anthem.

After a quick trip to the oxygen tent, he came back on to do a song in which he virtual duetted on 'I've Got a Feeling' with film of John Lennon from the Savile Row rooftop concert before sending us off into the Somerset night with 'Helter Skelter', 'Golden Slumbers' and 'The End'.

We staggered back towards the Circus and Cabaret area, almost speechless. All around us, night-time Glastonbury was waking up. It was like walking through some surreal neon-lit movie set. High above us, go-go girls danced in flaming cages, carnival barkers urged to us to watch escapologists, tripping punters dancing in slow motion wandered in front of a screen that turned their movements into light forms.

A man to our right, carrying a Daunt Books tote bag, stood staring at a tree in utter wonder. It was as though Moses had just descended from the mountain and handed him the stone tablets. Occasionally he would look around in astonishment as to why nobody else could see what he could see, lost in his own private Glastonbury.

I couldn't help wondering what strange night awaited Dave and Judy.

On the final day, we re-joined our mushroom friend who, being of purposefully eclectic tastes, had decided to watch Herbie Hancock. Just before Herbie came on, somebody introduced a special speaker. Surely China Greta wasn't going for round two? She wasn't. The speaker was an elderly hippy woman from Newfoundland. She was part of the local Methodist church to which the Eavises belonged.

Although I was devoutly anti-religious, one thing she said stuck with me. She said that the secret to Glastonbury was to capture the special feeling that existed at the festival and to take it out with us and spread it to the rest the world. It was true – there really was something special about this place and some-body needed to bottle it.

Herbie Hancock came on and I lasted about ten minutes before getting the strong feeling that I was trapped in some infernal jazz elevator. We went for a wander around to look at the sights. Somebody started shouting at me rather loudly but I wasn't in the mood for drunken antics. I put my head down and walked on before realising that it was Dave and Judy. We simply had to stop bumping into each other like this. They were off to see Declan McKenna and so we went with them. The kids dived into the front of the crowd while I lay on the ground next to Dave and Judy, who, mercifully, stayed silent. I baked in the sun, staring up at the flags and soaking it all in.

This was my most chilled Glastonbury moment. I was seri-ously in the zone.

Then Stacey announced that she had lost her bag with her phone, money, tickets and credit cards inside it. This was a nightmare. There was zero chance of finding it.

We said our goodbyes to Dave and Judy and retraced our steps. We spotted an information booth. We asked where we would go on the vague chance somebody might have handed the bag in?

'What kind of bag is it?' asked the sweet woman at the booth.

'A small leather handbag,' replied my wife.

'This one?' asked the woman.

It was Stacey's bag. Everything was still in it. Somebody had just handed it in. You had to bloody love Glastonbury, conspiracy kooks and all.

I remembered what the Methodist lady from Newfoundland had said. The world needed more of the Glastonbury spirit.

I'd totally forgotten all about the Newfoundland lady. I should have grabbed her at the time and got some advice on my upcoming trip to the island. I was fairly sure she would have known every flat-earther on the island. It was Fogo time and I really needed to bag me that rarest of prey, a square-flat-earther.

8

Fogo Island

I don't like museums. They tend to be custodians of mistruths.
John

Back in Gander, as we waited for Pete's flat-earther connection to make contact, I filled him in on my encounter with Jacob in Glastonbury. I wanted to let him know what we might expect. Pete was stupefied but intrigued. I felt pretty confident that, whatever John turned out to be, I was equipped to deal with the situation.

In a sense, it was all quite fitting. Just as Fogo Island was thought of as remote by Newfoundlanders, we were going to meet a guy that was considered wacky by flat-earthers.

As if on cue, Pete's phone beeped. It was John, our renegade flat-earther. He was in town and wanted to meet. He suggested a diner called Mystic Dining Room, which seemed rather appropriate. We drove back into town and parked up just outside the place. It was just off what was, rather laughably, called the Town Square – the desolate strip mall we'd been in earlier.

We walked into the diner. It was empty except for a bored-looking waitress who was sitting, scrolling through her phone. She didn't look up when we entered. Then I noticed him. He was sitting in the far corner just staring at us intently. We approached gingerly.

'John?' I asked.

'I might be? Who wants to know?' he answered.

I wondered how many people he might be expecting in this god-forsaken place, but opted to play along.

'I'm Dom, this is Pete. You messaged us and suggested we meet here?'

'Let me see some ID,' John snapped, curtly.

The waitress looked up briefly before returning to the transient delights of her phone. We fumbled around for ID. Pete produced his driving licence while I showed him a credit card. John studied them for a good two minutes before chucking them onto the table.

'Take a seat, gentlemen.'

He kicked a chair away from the table in a curiously theatrical manner. We both sat down and I took a good look at who we had in front of us. John was about sixty years old and looked like a man who had undergone a rough journey in life. He was tall and skinny. He was wearing mixed camo gear and a baseball cap that was way too small for his oversized head. It bore a logo that read:

WOMEN WANT ME. FISH FEAR ME.

He was like a skinnier version of the giants I'd shared a plane to the island with. What made him different, however, were his eyes. They had a hard intelligence to them. This guy was clearly not stupid. They fixed you with a hypnotic gaze. They were quite arresting. It was as though they didn't belong to him as they were so jarringly in juxtaposition to the rest of his weathered body. It was as though somebody had stuck a couple of priceless rubies on a tramp.

He had quite the authoritative air and I took an almost instant dislike to him. I looked at Pete to see if he was getting the same vibe. It was clear that he was.

'So, tell me the story. What's the deal with you guys?' John barked.

We began to tell John about our back story and why I was there. He was not a good listener. He was constantly interrupting.

'So, you're both Brits? Wish I'd known that before I agreed to meet. That would have changed things a lot,' he said.

'In a negative way?' I asked.

'Let's just say I'm not a massive Anglophile.'

'May I ask why?' I stammered.

'Because you're mostly arrogant assholes,' he said as he nodded at the waitress, indicating that he wanted a refill.

'You guys are paying, right?' he looked daggers at me.

'Sure . . . yes, obviously. Have whatever you want.' I sounded like a total loser. This was certainly very different from my coffee with Jacob.

'What do you want to know?' he asked.

'Well, I gather you believe in the flat earth and I'm writing a book about conspiracies and so I thought it might be interesting to visit Fogo Island as it's supposedly one of the four corners of the flat earth—' I was about to continue but he interrupted.

'Supposedly? OK, so you're a debunker, a fucking globetard?' his eyes flashed angrily.

Pete, who was not one for confrontation, spoke up.

'Dom is a comedian, very well-known in the UK and he is writing a book, but it's more a travel book, and we're just interested in the subject but don't really know too much about it either way.'

Pete did his goofy smile thing that nearly always disarmed anybody we spoke to.

'That is not unapparent,' said John.

'Did you say "globetard"? I love that. I've only ever been called a ball earther before.' I smiled, trying to put some fun in the room.

'That surprises me,' said John, downing his coffee in one.

'So, are you a Gander local?' I asked, trying to lighten the mood.

'No, but who I am and where I'm from is not your concern.'

John was pretty much the opposite of lovely Jacob back in Glastonbury. It felt like I'd left the acceptable media-friendly mainstream of flat earthism. I was now hanging out with the radical underground.

'OK . . . could I ask what your thoughts are regarding a flat earth and Fogo's place within it?'

I hated myself for being so meek but I already knew that, however unpleasant this guy was, he was box office in conspiracy-road-trip terms.

'I've never been to Fogo,' said John, a little calmer than before.

'Oh. Is there any reason you haven't been before? It's only an hour or so drive to the ferry,' I asked.

'I'm not from here.' John looked like he was sick of both Gander and my questions.

'OK. Are you up for coming with us then?'

'If you're paying, I'm coming,' replied John.

'Great. Sorry, can I just check, you do think that Fogo Island is at the edge of the flat earth?'

'Yeah, of course. It's one of the four corners.'

I waited for him to continue, but that was it. I wondered whether we should check his credentials further somehow before embarking on a road trip with him. What if he was an axe murderer, or on the run from the law? I looked over at Pete and could see that he was harbouring similar thoughts. The problem was that there was not some sort of central reference authority where you could check the legitimacy of a flat-earther.

'When are you leaving?' asked John.

'Umm, in an hour or so. We've got a couple of things to do in town and then we're off. We will catch the last ferry, which I think is at seven p.m.' I looked over at Pete, who got my drift and he nodded.

'Why don't we meet you outside here in an hour and a half?' said Pete.

'Sure. I ain't going nowhere,' John said.

Pete and I headed outside and got into the car. There was silence for a moment.

'Thoughts?' I asked.

'He might very well kill us on the way there,' said Pete, giggling.

'My thoughts exactly,' I said.

'So, shall we just fuck off and leave him?' he asked.

'It's tempting but I kind of want to see how this pans out,' I replied.

'What, and see if he murders us?' laughed Pete.

'Kind of . . .' I laughed and so did Pete.

It looked like we were taking John with us to the edge of the world. It would only be three days. What could go wrong?

Pete and I drove over to a Walmart and marched up and down

the endless aisles looking at things we didn't need. We ended up in front of a large display of hunting knives. We looked at each other and we both instinctively knew what the other was thinking. Should we get one as emergency insurance, just in case John went full serial killer? In the end we opted not to.

We returned to the car defenceless except for a small metal fridge magnet of Gander.

We messaged John. He was standing outside the diner when we pulled up. He didn't have any luggage with him. He got into the back of the car.

'You got everything you need?' I asked him.

'Yup,' he said.

'No . . . luggage?' I asked.

'Nope,' he said.

We drove out of town and got onto the road towards Farewell. John sat in the back saying nothing. Pete and I tried to carry on as normal but it was a bit awkward. I tried to break the ice.

'Shall we put some music on? What do you like, John?'

'Rush. Put some Rush on,' he said in a tone that did not encourage dissent.

I loathed Rush. Almost everybody I didn't like liked Rush.

Rush was a Canadian prog-rock three-piece that appeared to have been going since the beginning of time. Their lyrics were all sci-fi, fantasy and cod philosophy. Their fans always claimed that they were the most accomplished musicians in the world. It came as no surprise to me that a flat-earther would love Rush.

'Umm, sure . . . Why not?' I said.

I flicked through my phone until I found some Rush. The only song I really knew was 'Tom Sawyer'. I pressed play and it came on.

It was as awful as I'd remembered. Comical spaceship-style

synth sounds competed with showy drum fills and an annoyingly whiny vocal. Pete and I drove on in silence, eyes fixed on the road ahead. Eventually I glanced in the mirror; John was doing full air-guitar and his eyes were glazed over in ecstasy.

This was going to be a long trip.

The road to Farewell was not exciting but it did get rather lovely as we approached the coast and the road started to run along the side of Farewell Harbour. Every house we passed appeared to have a brightly painted wooden cabin on stilts sitting above the water. These were, according to Pete, where fishermen could gut and store their fish and were very typical of the area. As we approached the ferry, I tried to engage John in some conversation.

'So, John. When did you first start to believe in a flat earth?' I asked casually.

'I always knew,' he replied.

'What, since you were a kid?' I replied.

'Absolutely. It never made sense to me. I remember my parents calling me in from the garden to come watch the moon landing on TV. I knew it was horseshit.'

'How old were you then?' I asked.

'I was ten.'

'And what made you think it was horseshit?' I pressed.

'Because it was just so clearly faked. It made me despise my parents. They were like guppy fish lapping it up.' He laughed.

'But you do believe the moon exists, right? I mean we can see it, and it's round.'

'Sure. It exists but it's not a ball, you can see it's flat. How do you know it's a ball? Because somebody told you?' He laughed again.

'But it's definitely round, you can see that at least,' I persisted.

'Yeah, it looks that way to you maybe.'

'But you think the earth is flat and square?' I was truly fascinated. It was like talking to another species.

'Yes.'

We drove on in relative silence. I didn't want to turn Rush off
but I was hoping my phone would do the right thing and change
the next track to something more palatable. It didn't. I noticed a
message from a friend. He knew what we were doing and had sent
me an article he had found in an Italian newspaper from 2021.

It was about a couple of flat-earthers who, during lockdown,
had decided to break the curfew and set off in a boat to find the
ice wall that they believed surrounded the earth. They believed
that the nearest part of the ice wall to Italy was south of Sicily,
near an island called Lampedusa. They were not natural naviga-
tors and ended up on the island of Ustica, which was 200 miles
north of their destination. They were immediately quarantined
by the authorities on the island but they then escaped and set
sail for the ice wall again. Eventually they were caught and sent
home.

We got to Farewell Harbour and joined a long line of grit-
encrusted pick-up trucks. We watched the ferry come slowly
into view. It was a pretty small vessel and I worried that there
would not be enough room for us all. The ferry docked and we
started to trundle on board. It was bigger than it looked as all
the vehicles in the queue got on.

It reminded me a little of the ferry that I'd taken to the Isle of
Wight. There were no frills. This was no pleasure cruise. This
was a floating bus. There was no bar and nothing to eat so we
sat on uncomfortable plastic seats and waited. We were very

clearly the only non-islanders onboard. We were Wet Legs. I wondered what the local vernacular was.

Pete and I tried to watch a football game but the buffering was so bad that we eventually gave up. John sat two seats away from us, staring out of the window. He was like a statue. He didn't move an inch. There was something about him that slightly creeped me out.

We sailed past the Change Islands, a couple of remote islands with a population of 184. Fogo was a bustling metropolis in comparison, boasting a population of just over 2,000.

We docked in Fogo and joined the long stream of pick-up trucks driving across the dark island towards the north shore, where most of what passed for action was. Pete had booked an Airbnb in the village of Fogo, which I assumed was the main place on the island. After twenty minutes' drive, we rolled into the town. It was dark and there was absolutely nobody about. It was almost a ghost town save for the occasional glimmer of light behind thick curtains in slatted wooden houses. We found a store that was open. We went in and looked around. There was a surprising amount of produce. John bought himself two large bottles of whisky, which was not a great sign, but we didn't say anything.

We drove around the harbour and onto a little promontory where the Airbnb was. It took us a little while to find as there were no door numbers but we eventually decided on one. The front door was open and we entered. A front door being left open was a pretty common thing in Canada. It could sometimes cause confusion.

I'd once been offered the use of a friend's cottage on Christian Island, a remote, beautiful place on Georgian Bay, Lake Huron. She gave us the address and told us to just make ourselves at home. So, we drove up from Toronto, took the little ferry to the island and drove across to where the cottage was. It was in Big Sand Bay, which boasted a stunning beach and sparkling blue water. It was a little bit of heaven.

There were about five rows of cottages. Ours was in the third road leading down to the beach. We turned off into it. There were eight cottages and we were four back from the beach. We parked up in the little driveway and had a look around our home for the next three days. It was great. It was cosy and quite minimalist, but perfect for a three-day beach break. We bagged our rooms, unpacked and headed off to the beach.

We spent two blissful days there. On the morning of the third day, we were sitting on the front porch, relaxing, when a car pulled up behind ours. A family got out. To say they looked confused would be an understatement.

'Hey, how's it going?' asked the father.

'It's going great, thank you,' I replied.

'That's good . . .' he replied.

'You need any help? Are you lost?' I asked, as though I was some long-time resident.

'Umm . . . no. This is our cottage.' He looked almost apologetic.

'What? Your cottage? No, this is Jennifer's.' How dumb was this guy?

'No, Jennifer's is next door. This is our cottage . . .' His wife nodded as though to confirm.

There was a long, terrible silence as I took this news in. The door had been unlocked. We'd just wandered in. I must have miscounted. I was mortified.

'Oh. My. God. I'm so sorry. How embarrassing. I can't apologise enough,' I stammered.

The dad now looked embarrassed. He was Canadian. He hated this.

'Oh, no problem. Listen, how long are you supposed to be here for?' he asked.

'We leave tomorrow,' I said.

'Well then, we'll move into Jen's until you guys leave,' he said and his wife nodded like this was totally normal.

'Absolutely not. Are you crazy? I'm so sorry. We'll vacate now,' I said.

'Absolutely no way. We will move into Jen's. It's no trouble,' said the dad, turning to get back into his car.

Eventually I had to almost force them to enter their own cottage while we moved, sheepishly, to Jen's place. Canadians really were a different breed from the rest of the world.

Back in Fogo, I got Pete to check the paperwork and to make sure that we were in the right place. I wasn't sure that Fogo islanders would be quite so accommodating to unexpected intruders. We unpacked before meeting back downstairs. John, who had no unpacking to do, was sitting at the kitchen island and already a third of the way through a bottle of whisky.

Pete wanted to visit the Fogo Island Inn. This was a mega-luxurious hotel, perched on stilts atop rugged rocks that had rather put Fogo Island on the map since it opened in 2013. It was the brainchild of a woman called Zita Cobb. She was born on Fogo before moving to Toronto and making a fortune in fibre optics. She then moved back to Fogo and founded Shorefast, a non-profit foundation designed to encourage economic and cultural resilience on the island by promoting it as an eco-tourist destination.

The hotel, designed by Todd Saunders, a world-famous architect who was born in Gander, had won accolades all over the world. It was constantly booked solid, despite being eye-wateringly expensive. It had been way too expensive for Pete and me to have considered staying there and non-residents were not encouraged. Pete, however, had an in at the inn. They stocked his Seaweed Gin and the chef was supposedly a big fan. Pete had thought ahead, and brought him a couple of bottles of his new rum. He hoped that this might get us into the inn.

The inn was in a place called Joe Batt's Arm, about a fifteen-minute drive from where we were. We decided to take a punt. We asked John whether he wanted to come with us. He poured himself another large whisky and informed us that he was fine where he was. We were both rather relieved. Flat-earth investigation day was tomorrow so, tonight, we could hopefully have some fun.

We hopped into the car and drove off. We both looked at each other and laughed.

'He's not all there,' said Pete.

'You think?' I replied, sarcastically.

'It's not exactly comfortable with him around,' said Pete.

'Totally agree, but at least we have the night off.'

I put some music on – 'Stoned at the Nail Salon' by Lorde. We drove in contented silence through the black night towards a sole distant light on the far shore that we assumed must be the hotel.

Upon arrival, we turned off the road and bumped down a track until we parked right underneath the building. It was quite the construction. It loomed above us. We walked around it, slipping and sliding on rocks and moss. The rear, where we'd parked, was dark and functional but, once you got to the ocean side, it was extraordinary. Giant picture windows afforded guests

a panoramic view of the wild shore and bathed us in a soft arti-
ficial light. The contrast between the serene *hygge* of the interior
and the raw sound of the waves smashing on the rocks behind
us was brutal. It was as though these waves had hurled a giant
ocean liner onto land but left it intact and fully functioning.

It wouldn't have been the first time. The *Titanic* had sunk off
these very shores, 300 miles or so south-east of the island. The
giant icebergs that you could see floating past Pete's house were
testament to the dangers of navigation in these dark waters.

Looking out across the screaming sea that night, I shivered
quietly at the thought of the poor souls who had found themselves floating in it on that terrible night in 1912. I thought of
Mary Brown, the woman from Denver, with the lovely house
in the Golden Triangle. What emotions must she have dealt
with?

We completed our circle, pushed open the door and found
ourselves in what looked a little like the boot room of an English
country house. Passing through another door, we were suddenly
in the cathedral heart of the building. It was about as *hygge* as it was
possible to get. Cool, organic open spaces, log fires, furs casually
draped over everything and a gloriously low-lit, fully stocked bar.

But first, we had to get past reception who were eyeing us
suspiciously.

Pete put on his best confident British voice and asked if the
chef was around. The receptionist looked hesitant, but somebody was despatched to find him. When he appeared, Pete
introduced himself and handed him the bottles of Newfoundland's finest. It was as though we had tripped a magic
switch. We were whisked to the bar and plied with cocktails as
the chef talked spirits with Pete.

A couple sitting by the fire were clearly eavesdropping. After a couple of minutes, the man jumped up and demanded to know if this was the guy responsible for that amazing gin. Pete confirmed that he was. The man introduced himself as being the owner of Toronto's finest cheese boutique. He had been brought in for the weekend, along with a massive suitcase of cheese, to cook a cheese-based culinary adventure for the guests. Would we like to sample the menu? He didn't need to ask twice. Pete and I were soon surrounded by plates of delicious food and fine wines. Sometimes, just sometimes, conspiracy tourism was rather a pleasant affair. Like a Boris Johnson marriage, however, it couldn't last long.

I looked at some of the guests eating in the high-ceilinged dining room next to us. It was like the set of a curious season of *The White Lotus*. Everybody wearing effortlessly expensive, unbranded clothes. All tucking into a seven-course cheese-based menu while downing 300-dollar bottles of wine like they were going out of fashion. We felt like drowning refugees who'd been rescued at sea by some absurdly luxurious ocean liner. We were isolated from the grim realities of the world outside. God Save the HMS *0.001%* and all who sailed on her.

Supper over, the cheesemeister invited us upstairs to the private cinema where we and the pampered guests were shown a documentary that he had made about Québécois cheesemaking. All in all, it was a very curious evening and I worried that, having consumed my bodyweight in cheese, nightmares awaited me. The cheesemeister told me that this was just a myth, but I wasn't convinced.

Maybe it was because of where we were, but I felt a storm brewing.

We bid farewell to our new friends at about midnight. Invitations were extended for us to join a shed party the following day. This was a Fogo tradition in which people created pop-up pubs, known as sheds, to which everybody was invited. We made no promises. Tomorrow was a work day. Tomorrow, we were going to the very edge of the earth.

We drove home carefully, congratulating ourselves on what had been, even for us, a monumentally successful blag. We parked up outside our Airbnb on the little concrete parkway. It was pitch black and I longed for the morning light to unwrap our surroundings.

We opened the front door and walked in.

It was carnage.

The kitchen was a mess, the supplies we had brought with us were strewn around the room, some half-opened, some poured on the floor. An empty bottle of whisky lay on the kitchen island along with what looked like the dregs of the beer we had brought. Somebody had tried to cook something as the hob was still burning but the pan that had been placed on it was on the floor along with about seven rashers of very burned bacon.

We went on through into the sitting room. John was lying face down on a wine-stained white faux-fur rug. He was not wearing any trousers or pants and his T-shirt was doing a shocking job at covering everything else. His hairy arse was on full display, along with about three hideously unsightly pimples. Pete and I looked at each other in horror.

'Shall we leave him here?' I asked.

'We can't,' said Pete.

I had just done a refresher hostile environment awareness course back in the UK in preparation for a proposed trip to Ukraine. I learned to deal with grenade attacks, carjacking, gunshot wounds, kidnap survival. Nothing had prepared me for this.

'We should put him in the recovery position, at least, so he doesn't do a Hendrix and choke on his own vomit,' I said.

Looking around, it was doubtful that he had any vomit left. He had spewed in about four different locations. I knelt down and tried, with Pete's assistance, to put him into the recovery position. As I touched him, he awoke. His eyes flashed open and darted around the room. He lashed out and his fist caught me square in the mouth. I went flying back and landed in a pile of his vomit. Pete tried to calm him down.

'John, it's Pete and Dom. We're trying to help you. Why don't we just get you sitting up?'

'GO FUGGGG YOURSELVES,' screamed John, getting up on his knees unsteadily.

He looked around the room groggily. He looked at us. He looked down at his exposed penis. I could see the cogs in his brain whirring, adding two and two and making five.

'John, we've just come back and found you like this. I think you drank too much,' I said, trying to keep my voice friendly and non-rapey.

'YOU FUGGIN' FAGS!' he screamed.

'No, John, we've just got back,' said Pete.

John was now, somehow, on his feet and lurching towards us with his fists swinging.

'YOU FUGGIN' GAY BRIT BASTARDS,' he screamed as he swung at Pete.

Pete managed to duck out of the way and the momentum of the swing sent John reeling across the room. He ended up smashing into an armchair and toppling over hard.

One thing was now for certain: we were not getting our deposit back.

The fall seemed to take all of the fight out of John and he lay there, on the ground, groaning. Eventually, Pete and I managed to pick him up and lead him slowly to his bedroom which, fortunately for us, was on the ground floor.

Having placed him carefully on the bed, we gently closed the door and went and sat in the trashed kitchen. We didn't say anything for the longest of time. Then Pete looked up.

'Well, that was unexpected.'

We both laughed, but quietly, as we were terrified of a sudden return to the fray from John. We did a very quick tidy up, avoiding the piles of vomit, before retiring to our rooms. I was relieved to see that they had locks on them.

To say that I did not sleep well would be an understatement. I had absolutely no idea how the following day was going to pan out. It was difficult enough to try to plan a trip to the edge of the world without the added wild card of a drunken, homicidal lunatic as a cabin mate. These were the unexpected perils of conspiracy touristing.

I got up early, about seven-thirty, and flung open my curtains. It was my first actual look at Fogo. We were in a rocky, snow-flecked bay. Dotted around the shoreline was a multitude of slightly dilapidated, two-storey wooden buildings. The sea was rough. It frothed and boiled in seemingly angry frustration at being trapped by the surrounding land. Everything in sight was essentially a differing shade of grey. It looked like I imagined the Falkland Islands might look, were I, for some peculiar reason, to wake up there.

It was windy, very windy, so I layered up before going downstairs. The house was dead silent and I hoped that I might be the first up. I stepped over a congealing pile of vomit and went into the kitchen. I was out of luck. John was sitting at the island with a cup of coffee. He looked like death warmed up.

'Good morning,' I said.

'Hey,' he said, looking up at me like an apologetic puppy.

'Quite the night,' I said.

'I'm really sorry, man. I don't remember too much, but what I can ain't too pretty.'

'Yeah . . . you were . . . quite drunk.' I nodded.

'It's a problem,' he said meekly.

This was a new John. One I hadn't seen before and who was much nicer than the previous version.

'Shit happens,' I said.

'I'm serious. I'm really sorry. I'll clean it all up. I just need to get my head together.'

John downed his coffee and poured himself another from the glass filter coffee jug that North Americans were so inexplicably attached to. He was hunched over and seemed half his normal size.

There was the sound of a door opening upstairs. Pete was up. We listened to the sound of his footsteps on the tight wooden steps. He walked into the kitchen.

'Good morning, everybody. How's your head, John?' Pete was rarely fazed by things.

'Not good. I'm so sorry about last night.' John was clearly hideously embarrassed.

'Looks like you had a proper session. You're probably in need of some fresh air,' said Pete, smiling.

'Well, as it so happens, we're going to walk to the edge of the world today. That should help shake it off,' I said.

Both Pete and I were trying our best to be super jovial but there was still an air of tension in the kitchen. John, having finished his coffee, got a cloth and made some not-entirely-successful attempts at clearing up his vomit. Half an hour later and we were all outside and clambering into the car. It was definitely a relief to be out of the house and on the move. John was slumped in the back and did not look well. I was tempted to put some Rush on at full volume to punish him but decided that this would be more of a punishment for us than him.

I had decided on a rough itinerary. Our first destination was going to be the Museum of the Flat Earth. I'd discovered the place when I'd been researching Fogo. It was in the middle of nowhere, which was appropriate. It was also pretty much the only flat-earth-related thing on the island, which I thought was odd.

I thought it would be a great place to start our journey into the unknown. I informed John of the plan.

'I don't like museums. They tend to be custodians of mistruths.'

I was strangely relieved that there still appeared to be some fight left in John. We followed the map point I had on my phone and, after about ten minutes, we came to the gloriously named community of Seldom Come By.

We parked up outside a small supermarket and got out. The supermarket was next to a small single-storey building with a yellow ramp leading up to it. I recognised it from photos online. The photos I'd seen, however, showed it to have a sign saying 'Museum of the Flat Earth' above the door. The sign was gone and the building looked even more abandoned than most of the others on the island.

'This is it?' asked John.

'I think so,' I replied.

'It doesn't look great,' he said.

'No shit,' I replied.

We went into the supermarket and spoke to the cashier. She told us that, yes, that had been the Museum of the Flat Earth but that it had closed down and that the woman running it had left the island.

'She was an artist or something. The whole thing was a bit crazy,' said the cashier, who seemed excited to have customers.

'Crazy how?' asked John curtly.

'I dunno, she had all these things about the earth being flat and she'd dress up as this other person and I really didn't understand what it was all aboot.' The woman smiled at John.

'The earth is flat,' said John, who appeared to be rapidly recovering.

'If you say so, hun.' The cashier smiled ever so sweetly and even John stalled for a second.

'Thank you,' I said, ushering John out before things got heated again.

We made our way over to the little building intending to have a look through the window. The door, however, was ajar. I pushed it and it opened fully. I stepped inside, followed by John. Pete stayed outside, saying that he was a little worried that this was technically breaking and entering.

'It's definitely entering, but no breaking,' I said.

'Up to you, son,' smiled Pete.

'There are no cops on this island,' said John, who appeared much more interested in a closed museum than an open one.

John and I entered the place. On the right was a large sign on the floor that read:

Flat Earth Coffee Company

It had a yellow and white logo of a sailing ship about to fall off the edge of the world. I pointed it out to John, who nodded.

'Is this what you think happens, just a sheer drop? Or are you an ice-wall guy?' I asked.

'It's complicated,' he said, moving into the next room.

There were still some words printed on the wall over what had clearly been some sort of display:

The displays here tell the story of Bartholomew Seeker's life and his flat earth experiences on Fogo Island, Newfoundland and in Fredericton, New Brunswick.

The Flat Earth Society of Canada began in Fredericton, NB in 1970. Bartholomew was an active member before and after his move to Fogo Island. The artefacts here pertain to Bartholomew, and to the history and evolution of the Flat Earth Society of Canada.

It was maddening. What were the chances that I had finally made it to the only flat-earth museum in the world only for it to be closed?

'I think I read about this guy,' said John.

'Which guy?' I asked.

'Seeker. He moved here. I think I've read some of his stuff.'

'Is he still alive? We could go visit him?' I asked.

'I have no idea,' said John.

It took us about three minutes to look around the rest of the place. Whatever the exhibits were, there had clearly not been many of them. Most of the place appeared to have been a small café.

I googled Bartholomew Seeker. There was only one thing online about him and that was on a Facebook post from the Museum of the Flat Earth itself:

Bartholomew Seeker was born in Halifax in 1919. He studied at the normal school in Edmonton at the University of Alberta from 1937 to 1940 to become a teacher. Although he had an interest in alternative geographies and maps of the world most of his life, he became interested in the Flat Earth Society of Canada while teaching in Fredericton in the 1960s. He took a teaching position on Fogo Island, the location of one of the corners of the Flat Earth in 1971. There, his more important and lesser-known mission was to act as a guardian of the corner.

These are artefacts or objects belonging to Bartholomew Seeker. The first two are photographs of Seeker in his home on Fogo Island, the third artefact is Bartholomew's member-ship certificate to the Flat Earth Society of Canada.

These are just a couple of several miscellaneous snapshots that were found amongst Bartholomew's belongings although all information gathered about Bartholomew indicates he was mostly a recluse during his time in Fogo (other than going to the school to teach). It is assumed that these were taken when his friend, Flat Earth Society President Leo Ferrari from Fredericton, came to visit.

This was the certificate given to Bartholomew after his initiation into the Flat Earth Society of Canada, on April 1, 1971.

Along with the post were two photographs of a man, one of him standing outside what looked suspiciously like the Museum of the Flat Earth, although most houses in Fogo looked similar. There was also a certificate which read:

The Flat Earth Society
By the Authority of the Board of Governors
And with the Approval of the Senate

Bartholomew Seeker
Being of Sound Mind and Moral Character
Having fulfilled all the Society's Requirements
And having sworn Solemnly to Combat
The Globularist Heresy and all its Dupes and Hirelings
Has this day been admitted to Full Membership in

The Flat Earth Society
With all the Rights and Privileges that attach thereto

The certificate was signed and stamped by a couple of people. It all looked legit, but there was something a bit fishy about the whole thing.

I tried to google more about the museum but didn't get very far. Eventually I came across the name Kay Burns and an article about her flat-earth exhibition in Calgary. From the article, I learned that Burns was the artist who had run the museum until it folded.

The article was trying not to give too much away, but it discussed the mysterious disappearance of both Seeker in 1978 and a woman called Iris Taylor in 2018. Taylor, it seemed, despite Burns denying it, was her alter ego. She would greet visitors to the museum as the supposed new president of the Flat

Earth Society of Canada. This must have been what the cashier at the supermarket had been on about. I was now pretty sure that Seeker was also fictional.

This was all getting seriously confusing. I read a quote from Burns: 'A lot of what it's about is to play with the idea of what the function of a museum is. It's situated in a museum but also questions the premise of museums.'

Weirdly, this echoed the earlier thoughts of John about them being the 'custodians of mistruths'. But now he was claiming to have read some of the fictional Seeker's work, which he couldn't have done. Nothing in the world of flat earth was as it seemed.

This was blowing my mind.

I googled Leo Ferrari. He did appear to have actually existed and was the founder of the Canadian Flat Earth Society. I found a couple of photographs of him. He looked like one of the Freak Brothers. If you had told me that he played bass for Rush, I would have believed you.

Ferrari had been a professor of philosophy at St Thomas University and an internationally recognised authority on St Augustine of Hippo; a renowned theologian and supposedly one of the most significant Christian thinkers in history. This all sounded totally made up as well but, as far as I could tell, it was true.

Ferrari had a playful side and he set up the Flat Earth Society of Canada. Nobody could seem to agree whether he genuinely believed in the theory, whether he was using it as a way of teaching people about critical thinking, or whether it was a curious blend of the two.

Whatever, it seemed to confirm my belief that modern flat-earth theory had originally been born out of intellectual mischief.

It seemed to me that, by promoting such a ludicrous theory, they were trying to force people into doing some 'critical thinking' – a phrase that itself had become something of a cliché – in order to refute it. They were trying to get people to challenge authority. It was what Jacob, back in Glastonbury, had called 'leaving mum and dad'.

The post 9/11 advent of QAnon-style conspiracy stuff, with its anti-science, anti-expert mantras, was definitely heretical and certainly challenging authority. It was just lacking the thinking bit.

We were in the TikTok Konspiracy era. Every theory had been boiled down to almost nothingness and spouted out in bite-sized morsels of shock entertainment. It was depressing.

By now we were back in the car.

'How was it?' asked Pete.

'Better than I expected,' announced John.

'You've changed your tune,' I said.

'It was clearly a serious attempt to document the science, that's obviously why they closed it down,' said John.

'Who is they?' I asked, greatly enjoying this.

'The government, the people in charge. If you get too close to the truth, then they shut you down.' John looked serious.

I tried not to laugh. My brain hurt. This was falling down rabbit holes within rabbit holes.

'Right . . . who's up for a visit to the corner of the world?' I asked.

'Let's do it, son,' said Pete.

John did not reply. He was deep in thought in the back of the car.

Our destination was Brimstone Head, one of the four corners of the flat earth and the very reason for the strange journey that we had embarked on. The highest point on the island, it was a massive rock on the north-western shore that loomed over the town of Fogo like some defunct volcano. It was actually walkable from our Airbnb but I'd decided that it would build up the tension more if we visited the Museum of the Flat Earth first.

Tension was certainly building in the back of the car. It seemed that our visit to the museum had reignited John's grumpy side again. He was restless and muttering a lot to himself. I kept nervously checking him in the rear-view mirror. We were driving through the middle of nowhere. Should he suddenly decide to murder us both, we would not be found for years. I sped up slightly, eager to get to somewhere, anywhere with a couple of people about, no mean feat on this remote rock.

We drove down into Fogo with Brimstone Head dominating the horizon and dwarfing the sleepy little town beneath it. As we navigated our way towards it, I spotted a souvenir store at the side of the road. On a whim we stopped.

'What are we doing?' asked John.

'I'm going to look in this shop,' I said.

'Why?' he asked.

'Why not?' I replied.

'I thought we were climbing Brimstone,' he said, petulantly.

'We are, but there's not exactly a massive rush. I want to see if they have any flat-earth souvenirs.' I realised that I was rather enjoying annoying John.

Pete and I got out of the car and entered the store while John stayed in the back seat. It was what North Americans called a 'mom and pop' store, which was generally a euphemism for a place that looked like a hoarder's sitting room.

It was not far off. A bell rang when the door opened and an

elderly woman behind the counter looked totally shocked to see a customer. This was pretty much the default setting for any encounter with anybody on Fogo. I assumed that summer must bring more visitors but locals did appear to be unusually startled by the presence of outlanders.

'Hello,' I said.

'Hey there,' said the old lady.

'I was wondering if you had any flat-earth stuff?' I asked.

'You what now?' The old lady appeared totally baffled by the term.

'Flat-earth stuff . . . fridge magnets, stickers, T-shirts, anything really?' I smiled.

'Where are you from then?' asked the old lady.

'I'm from the UK, from England,' I replied.

'Are you now?' she asked, looking suspicious.

'I am,' I said.

There was an uncomfortable silence.

'So . . . do you have any?' I asked.

'Any what?' she said, looking baffled.

'Flat-earth stuff. Anything I could buy.' I smiled, trying unsuccessfully to look charming.

'No,' she said.

'Oh, why not?' I asked.

She looked totally baffled by what I was asking her. It was as though I was speaking a foreign language, which, in a sense, I was. I babbled on to muffle the silence.

'I had this same thing in Dildo. I was there twenty years ago and they had nothing, not a sausage, so to speak, but now it's Dildo frenzy. There's nothing you can't buy without Dildo plastered all over it.'

As I said this, I realised that I was saying the word Dildo a lot and that the old lady's face winced every time I did. Pete nudged me in the ribs.

'Anyhow, we've got to go. Lovely meeting you,' said Pete, making for the door.

The old lady just stared at us in total incomprehension as we exited.

I wasn't wrong, though. Fogo could clean up by milking the flat-earth connection. They could do boat tours to the ice wall, open a flat-earth pancake house, go crazy on the merch.

> I went to the edge of the flat earth
> and all I got was this lousy T-shirt.

They were missing a trick. I wondered if it was, possibly, a Zita Cobb problem? She had definitely done great things for her island but, as we travelled about, it did start to feel a little like the early days of a personality cult, a closed shop. I felt that the ludicrousness of flat-earthism didn't really fit into the Disneyfication of Fogo's fishing history.

Maybe if all else failed, I would move to Fogo and set up a T-shirt shop. I had some great ideas. Leo Ferrari used to call himself a Planoterrestrialist. There was great black and white photo of him holding a sign saying, 'I am a Planoterrestrialist.' That was T-shirt number one. He would also call a non-believer a 'Globularist' – that was T-shirt number two. We also had 'Ball-Earther', 'Globetard' and 'Conspiritualist'. This was a merch gold mine. I'd also chuck in a random wild card, 'Ne Travaillez Jamais!' which was my favourite bit of Situationist graffiti, something that I felt Kay Burns would have approved of.

We walked back to the car and got in. John was staring out of the window and did not acknowledge our return. We set off again and, five minutes later, were nearly at the foot of Brimstone Head. We parked in the car park, next to a wooden hut. Below us was surely one of the world's most remote RV sites. Every plot faced the abyss, looking out towards the edge of the world. Visitors had finally come to the end of their lifetimes of pointless journeys. They parked up, got out, and fell off the edge of the earth, never to be seen again.

We walked through the site and approached the base of Brimstone Head. It was freezing cold and the wind swirled around us, seemingly pushing us back from the abyss. But we were not to be halted. We were on a mission. Somebody had built a set of stairs all the way up the rock. There used to be a sign there saying:

WARNING
YOU ARE NEARING THE
EDGE OF THE FLAT EARTH.
ONE FALSE STEP COULD BE
YOUR LAST. NUMBER OF
PEOPLE LOST TO DATE '0'.

Sadly, the sign, which I presumed was more of the work of Kay Burns, was long gone. I turned to look at John, who was not the nimblest of folk. I could hear his heavy breathing. He was making quite a meal of the five-minute walk along fairly flat ground. I was not massively optimistic about his progress up the steps.

We started climbing. The steps were icy and slippery, and I gripped hard on to the thoughtfully placed handrail. As we climbed, I remembered taking on the tortuous steps of Jezzine, the first day of my walk across Lebanon, in *The Downhill Hiking Club*. I remembered thinking that maybe we had bitten off more than we could chew. And we had, but we soldiered on. I was certainly not going to get this close to the edge of the earth only to turn back.

Higher and higher we climbed. Occasionally, the steps would just disappear and we would have to clamber over slippery rocks before re-joining the next section of assisted climbing. Halfway up, we stopped to wait for John, who was clearly struggling. I took the opportunity to take in the view. Below us lay the town of Fogo over the isthmus. Everything came in and out of focus as the wind and snow flurries danced around us. Not for the first time, I thought of the Falkland Islands. Of the SAS forces on Mount Longdon facing both the enemy and the bitter South Atlantic climate. In comparison we had a twenty-minute climb of some steps accompanied by a mildly psychotic flat-earther.

We had it easy. I told myself to get a grip.

John reached us. He was breathing really heavily and seemed to be finding it tricky to focus. He held the handrail in a vice-like grip and looked around us.

'Are we here?' he asked.

It was so obvious that we were not 'here' that I laughed. He looked daggers at me and I stifled the laugh.

'No, no we are not here, but not long now. Look, you can see the place.' I pointed up ahead to what seemed to be a viewing platform, maybe 300 feet ahead above us.

'The air is thinner up here. I can't breathe. It must be because we're close,' he said.

'We're only about fifty metres above sea-level, John. I think we're just unfit,' I said.

'No, we are close to the edge. It's happening.'

I had no idea what it was that was happening but there was no use in discussing it. We continued on. The wind nicked our faces like a thousand tiny razor blades. It was deeply unpleasant, but the end was in sight. Just like climbers on Everest, destinations that appeared to be mere seconds away took a stupid amount of time to reach.

Eventually, we made it. We found ourselves on the steps up to the viewing platform. We were about to look over the edge of the world.

There was a map and a sign on the fence surrounding the platform. The sign announced that we were at the top of Brimstone Head, Fogo, NL. The map showed the four corners of the world and the distances between them. Papua New Guinea, Hydra and Fogo made an elongated triangle shape. The fourth corner, the Bermuda Triangle, appeared to be more of a waypoint and made no geographical sense whatsoever.

Then I remembered that none of this made any geographical sense. I wondered whether Leo Ferrari had chucked in the Triangle after a particularly heavy smoking session. Possibly the thinking behind it was that because all these planes and ships were supposedly disappearing in the Triangle, then they must have fallen off the edge of the earth?

We had a quick chat as to who would be the first to step onto the platform. Pete and I felt that it should be John as this was presumably going to be a significant moment in his life.

He thanked us, climbed the steps and walked to the fence at the edge. He stood staring out to sea, seemingly transfixed. Pete and I gave him a minute and then climbed up to join him. For a second or so we all stared out to sea in silence. I realised that we had been so immersed in all this that there was a tiny part of me expecting to see the drop, or the ice wall. Of course, there was nothing of the sort. We looked out over an angry sea. Rather disappointingly, to our left was more land; a series of little islands.

'If this is the corner of the world then what about those?' I asked pointing at the islands.

John looked at me as though I was stupid. He turned to his right and pointed out to sea.

'You have to go north. That's where it is.' He was in the zone.

'Can we see it from here?' I asked.

'No,' he answered.

'Oh,' I said, genuinely disappointed.

'What's the point of this then?' I asked.

'It's for tourists,' he replied.

'I'm a tourist.'

'Exactly,' he said.

'Did you not want to come up here then?' I asked.

'Sure, I did. We're so close, you can feel the change in energy.' He looked all mysterious.

'But we can't see anything?' I asked.

'No . . . we have to get into a boat to do that.'

'A boat?' asked Pete, who looked very uncomfortable with that idea.

'Sure, it's the only way we can get to the actual corner,' said John.

'How come you've only just mentioned this?' I asked.

'You didn't ask,' he said.

We all separated and spent some solo time staring out to sea, each deep in our own thoughts. I was pretty sure what Pete's thoughts were, and that they mirrored mine: terrible anxiety at the idea of getting on a boat with John. After a couple of minutes, we regrouped and prepared to go back down.

'Umm, if we go on a boat . . . what will we see?' asked Pete.

'Everything,' said John.

'Aha, right,' said Pete.

We started to climb back down. The wind had picked up and the sea boiled below us like a savage cauldron. The idea of being in a small ship on it was not appealing. I'd found a passage online from Bartholomew Seeker's journals, supposedly kept in the Iris Taylor archives. It was rather appropriate.

Each day when the weather is good, I go out in my boat as far as I can to look for that edge, that corner, knowing that the ocean currents continually veer me back away from the corner as it does with all those unsuspecting fishermen who come too close. It is only possible to find in a small boat; if looking from within a large vessel one will miss the corner completely as big ships are simply forced along the perimeter with a deceptive mirage hiding the boundary. Only from the corner, can you actually see the edge, only at the corner is the edge really a risk. Seabirds and other creatures are able to find many access points to the edge and to the underworld, but to the best of my knowledge humans can only find the edge through the corners. So, I continue to look while venturing out in my small punt and I mark my bearings and distances in the notebook I keep handy in my boat so that I can systematically eliminate where it isn't.

The key takeaway from this was 'when the weather is good'. The weather was far from good and we were leaving the following day. I hoped that John would forget about the boat thing. John would not forget about the boat thing. Having not mentioned it at all, he was now a man possessed. Once back in the car, we turned on the heating and tried to defrost ourselves. While we did this, he babbled on with his ideas about what we should do.

'We go to the harbour and talk to boat owners. They'll be desperate for the cash and they will know where to go. They all must know. If you've been fishing around here, you have to know. Let's go to the harbour. I'll find somebody.'

It was good to see John so enthused.

I was pretty sure that no boat would go out in this weather and so I was happy to play along, especially if it would help to calm him down. The last thing we wanted was a repeat of the previous night.

We drove down to the harbour. Thankfully, there weren't many boats about, but we drove around a bit until we saw a man who looked like he owned one. John and I got out to talk to him while Pete wisely stayed in the car.

He had just got done fiddling with stuff on his small boat and was getting into his beaten-up old pick-up truck.

'Hey bud, you got a minute?' asked John.

'Got shoo shoo to be fornartur better way,' said the man.

This was the best I could make of what he said. The blend of the fierce wind and his eighteenth-century Irish accent made communication difficult. I assumed John would understand. I was wrong.

'Sorry, bud, we . . . want . . . to talk . . . to you . . . about . . . renting your boat,' said John, a little slower, as though talking to a simple child.

'What you marnar? Pleash fur for for if you mmashee niblet,' answered the man in what appeared to be a non-encouraging manner.

'We want to go to the corner. Can you take us to the corner? We'll pay for your time.' John nodded at me as though he had this in hand.

He didn't.

'Mann, o'potato burning! For peshe no toke spoke are ye now?'

The man laughed and got into his truck. As he turned the engine on, he wound down the window.

'Felitia pebody cracky cronk, if you mashto goblet belief free ladoo.' He chuckled and drove away, shaking his head.

John looked dispirited. I was secretly relieved. We had given it our very best shot but, sometimes, getting to the corner of the flat earth was just not possible. John got back into the car. He was deflated again. I told Pete what had happened and he did his best to look disappointed. We had dodged a bullet.

We drove to a place called Tilting where, unsurprisingly, most of the buildings were tilting. We found a coffee shop and went in for a sandwich and a coffee. The owners were surprisingly charming and we sat for an hour or so. John was glued to his phone while Pete and I tried, unsuccessfully, to eavesdrop on a nearby table where three local women were in full gossip. Sadly, for us, it was as unintelligible as the man with the boat.

To be fair, we were warned. There was a sign, in actual Gaelic, at the entrance to town, that said 'Failté go Tilting', which meant 'Welcome to Tilting'. I spotted a plaque on the wall of the café that explained things a little further:

Tilting

Originally founded by the French in the 17th century as a
base for their transatlantic fishery, Tilting became a station
for the English and Irish migratory fishery sometime after
1713. Permanent settlement followed in the 1720s, and by
the 1770s it had become a predominantly Irish community,
shortly evolving into an exclusively Irish preserve. The
cultural milieu in which those early Irish thrived is
evidenced today, both in the material culture and vibrant
oral traditions for which Tilting is so well-known.

'Vibrant oral traditions'. You could say that again.

We pottered around Tilting for a while but there was little to
see. It felt very much as though we had come to the end of our
visit and were just killing time until we could depart. These
moments in a journey were always the dangerous ones. Boredom
would set in as would the options available to alleviate them. We
went back to the Airbnb. John was still glued to his phone. This
suited us. Pete and I checked the ferry times for the following
day. We didn't say anything, but we were both over John and
couldn't wait to drop him off somewhere. Half an hour later,
when we were trying to work out where to go that evening,
John bounded into the kitchen.

'I've got one,' he said.

'Got what?' I asked.

'A boat. Weather is much better tomorrow and I've found a
guy who will take us out at eight a.m.' He was beaming.

'Right . . . And how much is that?' I asked.

'He said he'll do it for two hundred dollars. He'll take us out
for two hours.' John was seriously excited.

Pete and I looked at each other wearily. I really didn't want to go, but the idea of taking a flat-earther in a boat to the edge of the earth was pretty intoxicating. I nodded and John went back to his phone to seal the deal.

Alea jacta est.

There was not a massive choice of places to go for a drink on the island. I assumed that there would be more in the summertime, when there was a mild influx of tourists. At this time of year, however, with the harsh Canadian winter fast approaching, I guessed that people just got drunk at home and cut out the middle man.

After searching online we found a place on the other side of the bay and set off to locate it using our satnav. We spent a fruitless fifteen minutes driving slowly up and down little lanes. There was absolutely nothing at the spot where it was marked on the map. Eventually we gave up and drove into the middle of the island where we had previously spotted a building that looked like it was a bar and welcomed visitors. It was closed and didn't open for another half an hour. We sat in the car in frustrated silence.

I reckoned that it would only be a couple of weeks living on the island before I contemplated my first murder.

Forty minutes later, a woman appeared and opened up. Inside was a tiny bar and five fruit machines facing the wall with accompanying stools. It was distinctly lacking in atmosphere but it was open. We ordered three beers. The woman told us that the internet was down so we had to pay cash. At least, I was pretty sure that's what she told us. She also could have told us that she had just called three men to come and kill us and feed our bodies to the seals.

We had no cash, but there was a store in Fogo called BJ's that would do cashback if we bought something. I left Pete and John in the bar and drove the twenty minutes to BJ's, bought a stick of gum and got some cash, before driving all the way back. I made sure that I got enough to cover the boat trip the following day. I was pretty sure the guy would not take cards . . .

When I re-entered, the bar was busier. Not busy, but busier. Two locals sat forlornly in front of the slot machines feeding coins into them and hitting the buttons in an almost robotic trance. Pete and John were sitting at a table in silence. I handed over the cash and we started drinking. The beer choice was terrible, Coors Light or Molson, both of which were disgusting. After a couple of bottles, however, we began to feel the buzz and we relaxed somewhat.

'You been screeched in, Dom?' asked John.

'Oh no,' said Pete, raising his eyebrows.

I knew what it was. I had been threatened with it in Dildo the first time I'd visited the island. It was a traditional welcoming ceremony that supposedly transformed an outsider into an honorary Newfoundlander. The word 'screech' was used to describe any terrible, strong alcohol such as moonshine. Some canny company had named their rum after it, and so you saw it everywhere. The ceremony itself involved a shot of screech, some random lines of poetry and then kissing a cod on the lips.

John started to get very excited.

'We've got to get you screeched in. Hey, we need to screech this guy in!'

He stood up and tried to get the two people playing the slot machines interested. They weren't.

'Come on, let's do this,' he said and ordered some rum at the bar.

The bar lady had no rum but said she had some at home and that she also had a fish. I waved my hands at her indicating that this was really not necessary, but John was on a mission.

The bar lady disappeared. It turned out that she only lived two houses away. She returned with a bottle of Screech, some shot glasses and, unbelievably, a massive frozen cod. The two locals at the slot machines, sensing the opportunity for some free rum, were now way more interested.

Everybody got a shot of rum and I was asked where I was from. I announced that I was from England and there was much tutting of disapproval from the locals.

'Do you want to be a Newfoundlander?' asked John quite aggressively.

I nodded unconvincingly and John urged us to drink the rum, but a local stepped in.

'He ought nest proclaim the tirye feel,' he said unintelligibly. Everybody nodded.

Pete told me that there were certain words I had to say. He mumbled them and I repeated them as best I could.

'Indeed, I am, me old cock! And long may your big jib draw!' I was dying on the inside.

I was sure that Pete had made me say something that would get me savagely beaten but everybody seemed content and the rum was downed. John then proceeded to recite some nonsensical stuff before the bar lady approached me bearing the cod. It was offered up to me and I found myself kissing its cold, clammy lips. Everybody drank another shot of rum before the two locals returned to their slot machines and the bar lady took the cod off to an undisclosed location.

That was it. I was screeched in. It was all a bit peculiar and pretty harmless, until the bar lady gave me the bill for the rum. I bit my cod-stained lip and paid the exorbitant mark-up. The only interesting part of the ceremony was that it could only be performed by a Newfoundlander.

'So, you are a Newfie,' I said to John.

'I am many things,' he said, trying unsuccessfully to sound enigmatic.

'You certainly are,' I mumbled.

The bar was pretty depressing, and we would have gone on somewhere else if we could, but there was nowhere. We were both pretty worried about John's alcohol intake and so we called it a night quite early. I had a feeling that the following morning was going to be quite the strange one.

Once back at the Airbnb, John was keen to crack on with his whisky but we told him that if he did, then he would have to make his own way back to the mainland the following day. He was clearly pissed off at this but he agreed and the second bottle of whisky was put into Pete's room for security.

I lay in bed that night thinking about our upcoming boat trip. For ages, while touring my live show, I had made a joke about getting hold of a boat on Fogo and taking a flat-earther with me towards the edge of the world. If I took this boat trip, I used to joke, we would get an answer, one way or another. If I was right, there was no edge. If I was wrong, and we did end up falling off the edge of the world, at least I'd killed a flat-earther. It was a win–win.

Faced with the actual reality of the situation, however, it really didn't feel like any sort of victory.

Morning came fast and we were all up at seven with no vomit or violence during the night, which was a result. John had possibly had too many coffees for my liking but I was almost demob happy. All things going to plan, we would be going our separate ways soon.

We bundled into the car and followed John's directions. We were meeting the guy at his house and he would then take us to the boat. Ten minutes later, we pulled up outside a fairly modern-looking house. We weren't talking concrete minimalism or anything, but the wood seemed a little less weather-beaten than most. John messaged him and the front door opened and out strode a gentleman who would have definitely got down to the last three in any open audition for the role of crusty seadog.

He wore a thick white jumper, green waterproof waders and sturdy boots. His face was like a library, every battered feature telling a story. All he needed was a captain's hat at a rakish angle to finish the look. Instead, he sported a tuque, the Canadian term for a woollen hat.

He jumped into his car and we set off following him until we got to a little jetty where, next to one of the omnipresent tilting fish shacks, was moored a boat. I wasn't exactly sure what I was expecting. I think I was hoping for a full-on, proper fishing boat and dreading it being a people-smuggler-style rubber dinghy. It was somewhere in between. We got out of our respective vehicles.

The sun was shining wanly. The wind, so fierce the day before, was negligible. The water looked as flat as John's earth.

It was a good day to fall off the edge of the earth.

John shook the guy's hand.

'Hey, good to meet you,' he said.

'Yup,' said the man.

'This is Pete and Dom. As I mentioned, they are also coming.'

'Yup,' said the man again.

He was clearly another strong, silent type.

'Right, so shall we get going?' asked John.

'I'll have the money first,' said the man I had immediately named as Captain Morose.

I handed over 200 dollars and he carefully counted them out. Once he was satisfied, he chucked us each a life jacket.

'Two hours. Not a moment longer,' he said.

'That will be long enough to get to the corner?' asked John.

Captain M stopped and stared at John for an unsettling amount of time without saying a thing.

'We'll do our best,' he said, a hint of a smile appearing at the corner of his mouth.

'Do you know how to get there?' I asked, hoping to stoke the situation further.

'That depends,' he said as he hopped onto the boat.

'Depends on what?' asked John.

'Depends if you believe in it strongly enough.' Captain M smiled.

He was having a joke and obviously assumed that we were joking as well. This did not sit well with John who, we had come to learn fast, was quite an earnest fellow.

'This is not a joke. We are paying you to take us to the corner.' John's cheeks were red.

'You're paying me to take you out to sea for two hours. You tell me where you want to go in that time and I'll do my best to get you there.' Captain M's tone was stern.

He reminded me of Captain Lee on the reality series *Below Deck*. Captain Lee would have given John both barrels and kicked him off the side, so he had actually got off quite easy.

The good news was that, so far, he didn't appear to be totally unintelligible. He was more old Canadian as opposed to Irish. He turned and helped all three of us on board. There was a small wheelhouse that would offer some degree of shelter from the elements if things got rough. Once again, I found myself praying very hard to a god that I did not believe in that this would not be needed.

'We should be all right weather-wise today. Storm coming in tomorrow though,' he mumbled to himself as though in some canned tuna advert.

And then we were off. We pulled away from the shore and out into the middle of the bay before turning to face out to sea. Captain M pushed the throttle down and we chugged into the great wide open. I looked at Pete and John. Pete was his usual relaxed self, but John was in a curious state of near ecstasy. He couldn't keep still and was hopping from one side of the boat to the other, staring out to sea like a child awaiting presents on Christmas Day.

As we left the bay and got into the ocean proper, the boat rocked a little more but not to an uncomfortable level. John moved to the bow and put his hand above his eyes in order to scan the horizon. I joined him. We really hadn't discussed what he was expecting to see out here and I needed to be prepared for all eventualities, including him going psycho killer.

'So, John, seriously, what are you looking for? What are you expecting?'

'If we head north from where we were standing yesterday, we should reach it in under an hour. It's supposed to be very close.' He looked ahead expectantly again.

'And what are we looking for? An ice wall? A drop? A corner?' This was nuts, but it was what it was.

'My best guess is we see a two-sided drop but there will be some kind of force field, so I'm not sure how close we will actually get.'

'I'm sorry to ask this, John, but you genuinely believe this. You do know how crazy this sounds? You actually think we are going to see the edge of the world?'

I was trying to sound calm and polite.

'You've just paid two hundred dollars to give us the chance. Who's the crazy one?' said John, fixing me with his blue-steel stare.

He had a point. This was all loop the loopy. But I knew why I was doing this. It was like when people asked me whether I wasn't embarrassed to crawl across a zebra crossing in front of traffic, while dressed as a snail, as I had done in my previous life as a TV prankster. No, I wasn't embarrassed because I knew why I was doing it. I knew it was being filmed. I knew that it was going to be really funny in the context of the finished show. If there were no cameras, however, and I was just crawling around the streets of London in a snail suit, then I probably would be embarrassed. Having said that, if I was really doing that, then I'd most likely have totally lost my mind and had a shattering nervous breakdown, so would be beyond the concept of embarrassment.

Whatever happened, I was along for the ride. I tried a different tack.

'What would it take for you to be persuaded that this was all nonsense and that the world was as mainstream science explains it?' I asked.

'What would it take you to stop unthinkingly believing what you've been brought up to believe and to question your supposed reality a bit more?' John countered.

There was no use. He genuinely believed that the earth was flat and I firmly believed in 'mum and dad'. It was as though we'd been hurled together in some form of blended multiverse.

The boat ploughed on through the Atlantic. Pete was chatting to Captain M. John manned the bow, still scanning the horizon for the end of the world. I sat in the chilly sun trying to savour the glorious madness of life.

About forty-five minutes out Captain M popped out of the wheelhouse and came over to me.

'Have we gone far enough?' he asked.

'I have no idea. You'll have to ask him. We're just here for the ride.' I smiled.

'You're not one of them then?' He smiled.

'If we drop off the edge in the next ten minutes or so, I'm prepared to apologise and admit that I'm wrong.'

We both laughed. Captain M made his way to the bow. Pete and I followed a few steps behind.

'What do you want to do, sir? We have about ten minutes left before we need to turn around.'

'Have we gone due north since Brimstone Head?' asked John, turning his head continually from us towards the seemingly endless horizon.

'Yes, we have. I can show you if you like.'

'Have you been this far out before?' asked John, ignoring his offer.

Captain M laughed. 'You could say so, yes. Many, many times.'

'And you've never seen it?' John looked suspicious.

'If by it, you mean the edge of the world, then no, because that's totally nuts.'

Captain M looked almost sad, like a disappointed father checking out his middle-aged, emo son.

'Then it must be a force field or some sort of loop thing keeping things from the edge.'

John was not really talking to us. He was in a (flat and square) world of his own.

'So, I'm turning back?'

Captain M spoke softly but was looking at Pete and me for direction. We nodded and he headed back to the wheelhouse gently shaking his head and chuckling. John looked crestfallen. I realised that, in his mind, he had genuinely been expecting to see the edge of a flat earth that morning. But instead of possibly reassessing his views, he was now fully engaged in damage limitation.

'It was stupid to think we could see it.' He shook his head.

I wondered whether this might be a good time to show him the extract from Bartholomew Seeker's journals, the bit about the 'deceptive mirage'. I decided against it. Besides, he'd probably already read it . . .

'This proves nothing one way or another,' continued John.

I had to say that I agreed with him. This whole trip was insane, but it had been highly entertaining. I wanted to argue more with John but I couldn't. He looked so upset, it felt mean.

Besides, if there was one thing I had learned in the last year, it had been that arguing with conspiracy theorists was essentially pointless, because it was a belief system. It was the 'Finland didn't exist' thing all over again. You couldn't prove a negative. You couldn't argue with alternative facts. You couldn't trump faith.

We bid farewell to Captain M at the dock. In the car, you could have cut the tension with a knife. I prayed fervently to my now-familiar non-existent deity that John did not have one. We drove across the island and arrived just in time to join the end of an already moving queue of cars getting onto the ferry.

Pretty soon we were out and up in the minimalist passenger lounge watching Fogo slip slowly away behind us.

I looked around at our fellow passengers. Aside from travelling Canadian giants, off on another trip to god-knows-where, there were also a couple of groups that really stood out. They were clearly leaving after a stay at the Fogo Island Inn and looked very uncomfortable with this enforced interaction with the rest of the world. One man tried to make himself a little nest in an effort to keep the horrids away. He carefully placed a large, tasteful paper bag with the Fogo Island Inn's logo on it on the table, This was so that nobody would be under any misapprehension of his status. Then he placed a small, beautifully packaged box of sushi on the table in front of him. He put on a pair of enormous and very expensive headphones and fired up his spanking new, shiny Apple laptop. Now, surrounded by the expensively familiar, he appeared to relax a little. Occasionally he would look up and get a fleeting reminder that he was not in his happy place. He was not with his own kind. He was adrift in 99.99 per cent land and it was scary.

Once back on Newfoundland proper, we drove towards Gander. We had not asked John where he wanted to be dropped off. We were secretly nervous that he would want a lift all the way to St John's. Pete and I had a diversionary plan agreed, should this happen. I broached the subject.

'So where are we dropping you off, John, same place that we picked you up?' I tried to eye smile in the rear-view mirror.

'I'm not sure yet,' he said, rather worryingly.

'Well, anywhere before or in Gander is fine by us,' I said.

'As I said I'm not sure yet. I'm waiting for calls. You guys just keep going, I'll let you know.'

He looked back down at his phone. Pete and I glanced at each other nervously.

'Sorry, John, but Pete and I have plans in Gander. We have more stuff to look into, so we'll have to part company there.' I flashed him another nice eye in the mirror.

'Oh, what are you guys doing? I could help maybe?'

'No, thanks very much. You've been so great, but we've got some family business to do.'

I was riffing now. Pete looked nervously over at me.

'You got family in Gander? Poor fucks. Whereabouts?' John would not let this lie.

'Not me. Pete had some, so we are going to pop in, say hello, since we are here.'

'No way. Whereabouts, Pete?' John leaned forward.

'Umm, just outside town. It's a tiny place, almost on their own.' Pete was livid with me. I could sense it.

'What are their names?' John was suddenly Mr Bloody Social. He was impossible to read.

'I thought you weren't from Gander?' I tried to side track.

'I'm not,' he said.

'Where are you from then?' I asked.

'Everywhere and nowhere.' John was back to being Mr Enigmatic.

'Anyhow, we'll drop you in the town square and say our goodbyes. It's been fun,' I said.

John got the message and went quiet. I felt guilty and tried to make things up to him by putting more Rush on for the last fifteen minutes of our drive into Gander. This really annoyed Pete. The United Nations couldn't have sorted this out, but then again, they never really sorted anything out.

We parked up in exactly the same place that we'd picked John up from. It felt like a lifetime ago. We got out to say our goodbyes. I was still astonished at his complete lack of luggage. I thanked the lord that we hadn't planned a longer trip. If we had, one of us wouldn't have made it off Fogo.

We gave each other awkward hugs. It was clear that none of us were hug-people so quite why we were putting ourselves through this was unclear. Whatever, this would soon be over and we would be free.

'Bye then, John,' said Pete.

'Yup, it's been . . . interesting,' I said.

'So, you got what you needed for your book?' he asked.

'I think so,' I answered.

'What happened this morning didn't prove jack shit. You know that, right?'

I laughed in a non-committal fashion.

'I mean, I know you're going to write this all up to make the globetards happy and that's your prerogative. But you're wrong. You're one hundred per cent wrong.'

I nodded. I just couldn't be arsed any more.

'I probably am, John. We're going to have to agree to disagree.'

'But you have no proof.'

I shook John's hand and opened the car door to indicate that this was it. Pete had already jumped into the driver's seat.

'Bye, John. Best of luck.' I shut the door and Pete gunned the engine.

John stood and watched as we drove away. Alone in a curious town. We drove out of Gander as fast as we could. When we felt as though we were far enough away, we stopped at Newfoundland's very own fast-food chain, Mary Brown's, famous for their chicken and taters. We were starving, but also still strangely anxious about John.

We sat in a corner munching on our Big Marys, nervously looking at the door in case a tall flat-earther should suddenly burst in, find us there and start shooting up the place with an AR-15. I worried that a moose might come flying through the plate glass window. I worried that a UFO might suddenly hover above us and beam us up for some serious anal probing.

Goddammit, this paranoia was contagious.

It was not easy being a Conspiracy Tourist.

Epilogue

For those who believe, no proof is necessary.
For those who don't believe, no proof is possible.
Stuart Chase

When I got back from Fogo, I was pretty wiped out. Constantly thinking about conspiracy theories was suffocating, and a touch depressing. I just couldn't stop wondering why so many people seemed genuinely committed to outrageous, outlandish and, often, frankly impossible theories. What drove people to these extremes?

As it so happened, I followed a mutton farmer on Twitter called Swaledale Mutton. Said mutton farmer was named Dr Graham Bottley, and he also happened to have a PhD in viral immunology. Dr Bottley spent a lot of his time online, challenging people who posted what he believed to be inaccurate comments about the COVID pandemic and vaccines.

He actually had two Twitter accounts, one that described himself as an immunologist and the other as a mutton farmer. As he tended to reply to conspiracy theorists with whatever account he happened to be on, it often led to some entertaining discussions. Anti-vax types, having their half-thought-through posts challenged with some scientific facts by Dr Bottley, would invariably come back with 'OMG, I'm getting lessons in science from a sheep farmer?' or 'Well, well, looks like we have reached peak sheeple.' Then, Dr Bottley would start to take them apart. It was always enjoyable, if not a little depressing, to watch.

I messaged him and we had a Zoom chat. He talked to me from his farmhouse in the Yorkshire Dales. He was younger than I expected and very friendly. Along with breeding mutton he now also trained research scientists in flow cytometry.

This is a technique used a lot in epidemiology to detect and measure physical and chemical characteristics of a population of cells or particles as they flow past single or multiple lasers while suspended in a buffered salt-based solution . . . but you already knew that.

Basically, Dr Bottley was a boffin with a zealous streak.

I told him I wondered why he wasted so much of his time dealing with these people. He chuckled. He hadn't set out to do it but the sheer amount of misinformation he came across online angered him. Whenever he'd attempted to argue with people from his immunologist page, people tended to either block him or just move on. But when he intervened as the mutton farmer, people would not give up, would become patronising and overplay their already limited hand. He just felt that showing up these people in long, rational threads really helped to debunk their claims and expose their lack of serious knowledge.

As Dr Bottley spent more time than most interacting with conspiracy types, I wondered whether he had a theory as to what drove people down these rabbit holes.

'You should have a chat with Brent Lee,' he suggested.

So, I did.

Brent was a full-on 'big time' conspiracy theorist from 2003 to 2018 who was now in what he described as 'recovery'.

I organised a Zoom call and we were soon set up for a chat. I didn't really know what to expect. When the camera flickered on it revealed a tall, lanky-looking dude with long hair and a beard, sporting a beanie hat. He looked like the sort of guy you'd buy some weed off at the back of a dive bar. He was gentle with a surprisingly soft voice that had a mild Bristol burr.

Brent's conspiracy journey started in 2003 when he was surfing the internet and came across a file called 'The Truth'. Having downloaded it 'on dial-up' he watched some stuff that piqued his interest about JFK, lizards and the New World Order. But it was when he watched a couple of documentaries about 9/11 that he really became hooked. The reason, he told me, was because there, right in front of him, was suddenly what he considered to be actual evidence of controlled demolition of the Twin Towers and the infamous Building Seven. It was all a government plot. A false flag operation. A lie.

At the time Brent was a singer in a band and had a keen interest in geopolitics. His stepdad was in the military and his experiences had made Brent very anti-war from an early age. He was a political person anyway, and when he stumbled upon the 9/11 conspiracy theories, things all started to make sense. This was all a dastardly plot to give the West an excuse to invade Iraq and Afghanistan.

He began to be sucked into the movement. He started to hang out online, mainly in the David Icke Forum, meeting more and more like-minded people. But it wasn't just online. Brent's band started to perform at conspiracy functions. His partner was also a conspiracy theorist. This was slowly consuming his life.

Brent tried to explain his thought process back then.

It was a fact that the world was corrupt, that the media lied, politicians lied, corporations and banks fleeced everyone. Ordinary people felt powerless to do anything about it all. Believing in conspiracy theories, believing in some overarching, global agenda that was behind everything, not only made it all seem less random but gave them something to fight against. If you believed in a global conspiracy, a New World Order, then you could suddenly put names, faces, reasons to what previously had felt like a cruel and impersonal world. The very fact that he knew something, that he had this secret knowledge, gave him a feeling of hope, of power, some sense of control over his life.

Brent continued. Back in the early 2000s there had been way less toxicity and far more empathy among conspiracists. But he'd noticed a marked change in the movement around 2012. Everything started to shift. The movement had become very different, way nastier, way more personal, way more illiberal. He also slowly started to notice the arrival of right-wing incel types and angry MAGA types.

This was interesting, because back in the early 2000s, conspiracists, according to Brent, were pretty apolitical. To them, left and right wing were the same, two wings on the same bird. You had Blair in the UK and Bush in the US and they were equally bad. Brent identified as a progressive. They were 'truthers' not conspiracists. The most political it got back then was with movements like 'Occupy Wall Street'.

The shift, according to Brent, really came when people like Steve Bannon showed up on the scene. He, Brent said, had totally politicised the conspiracy movement. Bannon had talked about 'radicalising the gamers'; Donald Trump was regularly showing up on *InfoWars*. This was laying the groundwork for the future extreme theories like Pizzagate and confused movements like QAnon.

What finally made Brent start to seriously question his tribe, the conspiracist movement, was their reaction to events such as the Sandy Hook school shootings, the Aurora cinema shooting and the Pulse nightclub shooting. These all happened around the same period of time and Brent noticed an entirely new narrative being spun: that these shootings were hoaxes and that the victims were crisis actors.

This was a massive shift from Brent's David Icke-inspired beliefs in events like 9/11 and 7/7 being some form of ritual, false flag operations in which the catastrophes were real, but engineered for political gain.

From 2012 onwards, Brent sensed that the conspiracy movement was becoming more and more ludicrous. There was the sudden re-emergence of flat-earthers. Alex Jones claiming that TV stations made you sign a form renouncing God before you appeared on their shows. And, of course, the sickening claims that school shootings were hoaxes and that the victims were all crisis actors.

Brent felt that this was all chipping away at the serious work that he and his colleagues had been doing. He became convinced that they were 'PsyOps', psychological operations masterminded by the Illuminati to make conspiracies appear totally loony and discredit the whole movement.

Then came the three events that finally propelled Brent out of his rabbit hole.

These were: the Brexit referendum result, Trump being elected president and Jeremy Corbyn becoming leader of the

Labour Party. If the Illuminati and the New World Order really were in charge of everything, then in Brent's mind, none of these three events would have been allowed to happen. He was utterly bewildered. It just didn't make sense.

Brent needed to reassess his views. He went offline for three years. When he returned, he had a new mission, to use his experience to help other people shake off their delusional beliefs. He started a podcast and a YouTube channel in which he now tried to help other people who were stuck in similar mindsets as he used to be.

I really liked Brent. Until our chat, I'd not really joined the dots and appreciated just how much the conspiracy theorist movement had shifted in the last twenty or so years.

On my travels in this book, I'd been taking a relatively light-hearted look at this strange world. I hadn't really delved too deeply into the reasons for why these beliefs had become so prevalent. And, make no mistake, these were beliefs, not just theories, to these people; they made up an entire belief system and the believers were as fundamentalist as any religious group. It was an insidious ideology that had infected people like Thomas back in my square in Cheltenham, or the anonymous sticker guy, or the man who believed that earthquakes were in the control of the US government.

Easy as it was to do, to just make fun of them or ridicule them served only to push the believers deeper into their rabbit holes. The truth was that the world could be a terrifying place. Horrible things happened, awful people existed, terrible injustices occurred. But it was my view that these were not part of some secret, global conspiracy; they were more the result of greed and incompetency and base human nature.

I always come back to that quote by Zbigniew Brzezinski, President Jimmy Carter's national security advisor. 'History is much more the product of chaos than of conspiracy.'

This makes perfect sense to me. But not to a conspiracy theorist. To them, Brzezinski (and I) was part of the New World Order. We were probably shape-shifting lizards.

All of this, my travels, my book, had been simply to distract everybody from the real truth.

For the record, I believe Finland does exist. Denver International Airport is a bit weird. There are hundreds of credible reports of UFO sightings. I think JFK was a clear-cut case of suicide (joke). The US government behaved incredibly badly at Waco. Alex Jones is an appalling human being. The inhabitants of Camelot Castle are not people I'd choose to socialise with. Modern flat-earth theory started off as a sort of absurdist prank; it, like many conspiracies, has been hijacked into something way more sinister. We are now in the age of TikTok Konspiracies. It is increasingly the preserve of the alt-right, the grifters and the gullible. The real sheeple, if you like.

My head hurt.

It was time for a break.

I quite fancied Australia . . . but I didn't want to fly all that way only to find out it wasn't there.